Contemporary *L*

Series Editor
Eunice N. Sahle
University of North Carolina at Chapel Hill
USA

Contemporary African Political Economy (CAPE) publishes social science research that examines the intersection of political, social, and economic processes in contemporary Africa. The series is distinguished especially by its focus on the spatial, gendered, and cultural dimensions of these processes, as well as its emphasis on promoting empirically situated research. As consultancy-driven work has emerged in the last two decades as the dominant model of knowledge production about African politics and economy, CAPE offers an alternate intellectual space for scholarship that challenges theoretical and empirical orthodoxies and locates political and economic processes within their structural, historical, global, and local contexts. As an interdisciplinary series, CAPE broadens the field of traditional political economy by welcoming contributions from the fields of Anthropology, Development Studies, Geography, Health, Law, Political Science, Sociology and Women's and Gender Studies. The Series Editor and Advisory Board particularly invite submissions focusing on the following thematic areas: urban processes; democracy and citizenship; agrarian structures, food security, and global commodity chains; health, education, and development; environment and climate change; social movements; immigration and African diaspora formations; natural resources, extractive industries, and global economy; media and socio-political processes; development and globalization; and conflict, displacement, and refugees.

Advisory Board
Bertha O. Koda, University of Dar es Salaam, Tanzania
Brij Maharaj, University of KwaZulu-Natal, South Africa
Thandika Mkandawire, London School of Economics and Political Science, UK
James Murombedzi, Council for the Development of Social Research in Africa, Senegal
John Pickles, the University of North Carolina at Chapel Hill, USA
Wisdom J. Tettey, University of British Columbia, Canada

More information about this series at
http://www.springer.com/series/14915

Mark Langan

Neo-Colonialism and the Poverty of 'Development' in Africa

palgrave
macmillan

Mark Langan
Newcastle University
Newcastle upon Tyne, UK

Contemporary African Political Economy
ISBN 978-3-319-86430-3   ISBN 978-3-319-58571-0   (eBook)
https://doi.org/10.1007/978-3-319-58571-0

Cover image: © PeskyMonkey/gettyimages

Printed on acid-free paper

This Palgrave Macmillan imprint is published by Springer Nature
The registered company is Springer International Publishing AG
The registered company address is: Gewerbestrasse 11, 6330 Cham, Switzerland

For Drs. Michelle and Charles Langan (Mum and Dad) for your love and support

ACKNOWLEDGEMENTS

Special thanks to Sophia Price for your encouragement and advice. Thank you also to Leon Cameron, Chris McMinn, Chet Bundia, Andrew Futter and Jon Moran for your friendship and support which helped me to complete this work. I thank and acknowledge Taylor and Francis for giving permission for use of some of my earlier work on Turkey's entry into Africa in the second half of Chap. 3. The article is due for publication later this year: M. Langan (2017) 'Virtuous Power Turkey in Sub-Saharan Africa: The Neo-Ottoman Challenge to the European Union', *Third World Quarterly*. An early view edition of the article can be found on www.taylorandfrancis.com.

CONTENTS

Acronyms

AASM	Associated African States and Madagascar
ACEP	African Centre for Energy Policy
AFD	Agence Francaise de Developpement
AIF	Africa Investment Facility
AKP	Justice and Development Party (Turkish)
AOPIG	African Oil Policy Initiative Group
BRICS	Brazil, Russia, India, China and South Africa
CAP	Common Agricultural Policy
CDC	Commonwealth Development Corporation
CFA	Cooperative Framework Agreements
CIF	Chinese Investment Fund
CNMC	China Nonferrous Mining Co. Group
COVEs	Corporate Village Enterprises
DDA	Doha Development Agenda
DFID	Department for International Development
DFIs	Development Finance Institutions
DRC	Democratic Republic of the Congo
ECGD	Export Credit Guarantee Department
ECOWAS	Economic Community of West African States
EDF	European Development Fund
EIB	European Investment Bank
EITI	Extractive Industries Transparency Initiative
EPADP	Economic Partnership Agreement Development Programme
EPAs	Economic Partnership Agreements
EPZ	Export Processing Zone
EU	European Union

EU-AITF	EU-Africa Infrastructure Trust Fund
FCO	Foreign and Commonwealth Office
FDI	Foreign Direct Investment
FOCAC	Forum on Chinese and African Cooperation
FTAs	Free Trade Agreements
GIGs	Ghana Institute of Governance and Security
GNPC	Ghanaian National Petroleum Company
GOGIG	Ghana Oil and Gas for Inclusive Gas
GPC	Ghana Petroleum Commission
GSP	Generalised System of Preferences
HIPC	Highly Indebted Poor Country
HLP	High Level Partnership
ICAI	Independent Commission for Aid Impact
ICT	Information and Communication Technologies
ODA	Overseas Development Assistance
ODI	Overseas Development Institute
IMF	International Monetary Fund
IPRs	Intellectual Property Rights
IR	International Relations
MDBS	Multi-Donor Budget Support
MDGS	Millennium Development Goals
MFEZ	Multi-Facility Economic Zone
MSD	Mines Safety Department
NANTS	National Association of Nigerian Traders
NEPAD	New Economic Partnership for African Development
NIEO	New International Economic Order
NRGI	Natural Resource Governance Institute (NRGI)
NTBs	Non-Tariff Barriers
OAU	Organisation of African Unity
OECD	Organisation for Economic Co-operation and Development
OWG	Open Working Group
PAF	Performance Assessment Framework
PANiDMR	Pan African Network for the Defense of Migrants' Rights
PF	Patriotic Front
POME	Palm Oil Mill Effluent
PRC	People's Republic of China
PSA	Production Sharing Agreement
PSD	Private Sector Development
PSIs	President's Special Initiatives
PSP	Private Sector Participation
ROC	Republic of China
RSPO	Roundtable on Sustainable Palm Oil

SADC	Southern African Development Community
SAPs	Structural Adjustment Programmes
SCTIP	International Technical Policy Cooperation Department (French)
SDGs	Sustainable Development Goals
SIAs	Sustainability Impact Assessments
SMEs	Small and Medium Enterprises
STABEX	System for the Stabilisation of Export Earnings
SYSMIN	System for the Stabilisation of Mineral Earnings
TIKA	Turkish Co-operation and Co-ordination Agency
UK	United Kingdom
UKTI	UK Department for Trade and Industry
UN	United Nations
USA	United States of America
WAOM	West African Observatory on Migrations

LIST OF TABLES

CHAPTER 1

Neo-Colonialism and Nkrumah: Recovering a Critical Concept

INTRODUCTION

Walter Rodney (1972: xi) remarked in *How Europe Underdeveloped Africa* that the 'phenomenon of neo-colonialism cries out for extensive investigation in order to formulate the strategy and tactics of African emancipation and development'. Unfortunately, in 2017, 60 years after Ghanaian independence (the first African state to liberate itself from formal Empire), the phenomenon of neo-colonialism still cries out for extensive investigation.

Neo-colonialism—a situation of infringed national sovereignty and intrusive influence by external elements—is now often regarded as an outmoded concept in International Relations (IR), and in Development Studies. Many scholars are decidedly squeamish when the term is invoked.[1] Additionally, many are squeamish about discussions of 'Africa' as a whole—rather than about individual African states. Of course, there is analytical danger when speaking bluntly of either 'neo-colonialism' or 'Africa'. Equally, however, there is analytical danger when trends affecting a collection of states are ignored. Brown (2012: 1891), invoking Harrison, states that 'there are at least three senses in which speaking of "Africa" as a whole might be justified... as a collective international actor; as a collection of states with (in the 'broadest of sweeps') a shared history; and as a discursive presence, used by both Africans and outsiders, in international politics and policy'. Moreover, from the pan-Africanist perspective of Nkrumah, speaking of Africa as a whole is not merely an analytical necessity, but a vital discursive move aimed at consciousness building and unity.

© The Author(s) 2018
M. Langan, *Neo-Colonialism and the Poverty of 'Development' in Africa*, Contemporary African Political Economy,
https://doi.org/10.1007/978-3-319-58571-0_1

This book examines whether the concept does help us to analyse certain problems associated with current 'development' interventions by foreign actors in Africa. Engaging Kwame Nkrumah who fully developed the concept in his treatise *Neo-colonialism: The Last Stage of Imperialism* (1965), the book argues that Nkrumah's insights remain valid in many respects.[2] Several passages of Nkrumah's (1963, 1965) work appear as pertinent today to an understanding of interventions in Africa as they were in the 1960s. That is not to say that Nkrumah's work is beyond critique. His relative failure to contend with ideational aspects of external influence over African states is something which, for instance, requires redress in any modern application of the concept of neo-colonialism. From a critical constructivist standpoint concerned with the analysis of language and power, it is necessary to assess the interplay between material forces and ideas as it relates to donor/corporate power in Africa (Fairclough 2009; Van Djik 2009).[3] Namely, it is important to examine 'development' discourse and how interventions in the internal affairs of African countries by foreign elements is legitimised as a moral endeavour for 'progress'. Many interventions are in fact undertaken on the basis of a donor (and at times, corporate) language of altruism, despite the fact that the tangible consequences of such action more often than not exacerbate conditions of ill-being and poverty.

This chapter examines Nkrumah's contribution to critical understandings of North–South relations and his focus upon the difficulties facing nominally sovereign African countries in attaining industrialisation and development. It highlights the neo-Marxist contours of Nkrumah's work before addressing his relative omission of ideational factors in the analysis of external influences. It also highlights the work of Fanon (1961) among other writers who expressed similar views on the neo-colonial situation in alignment with Nkrumah. The chapter then explores parallels between Nkrumah's contributions (and these wider works on neo-colonialism) and the *dependency school* that gained intellectual traction in the 1960s and 1970s. It makes clear that there were overlaps in thought between the concept of neo-colonialism and the dependency school. This is not surprising given their mutual neo-Marxist heritage. The concept of neo-colonialism is seen as distinct, however, in that it places heavier emphasis on political agency, as opposed to the apparent economic determinism of many dependency theorists.

The chapter then acknowledges the contemporary influence of the neo-patrimonialism school as perhaps the most popular lens for examining Africa's relations with donors today. It demonstrates how neo-patrimonialism has gained both academic and policy credibility in explaining the apparent failure of African 'development' when compared to former colonial states in other regions, particularly those of East Asia. The chapter explains that the neo-patrimonialism literature is in some ways the obverse of the literature on neo-colonialism, and it is certainly more popular in today's academic circles. It argues, however, that the conclusions of the neo-patrimonialism literature are flawed, and fail to fully grasp how external forces bring about certain aspects of apparent 'neo-patrimonial' rule. The neo-patrimonialism school, moreover, is seen to make essentialist assumptions that sometimes denigrate African culture and African personhood. Nevertheless, Jean-Francois Bayart (within the neo-patrimonial literature) is deemed to hold certain weight in an understanding of African elite relations with external parties. Bayart's (2010) concept of extraversion—when stripped of essentialism—is seen as a useful device for making sense of certain social relations between African elites and their benefactors within the neo-colonial situation. The chapter then concludes by reiterating the need to engage the concept of neo-colonialism in a modern understanding of African 'development'.

Following on from this chapter, the book then explores the concept of neo-colonialism in terms of contemporary African relations with external 'development' actors. Specifically, the ensuing chapters examine neo-colonialism in terms of corporate activities (Chap. 2); Western aid programmes (Chap. 3); 'new' development aid actors (Chap. 4); Africa-EU free trade agreements (Chap. 5); security and development (Chap. 6); the United Nations (UN) Sustainable Development Goals (SDGs) (Chap. 7); and strategies for emancipatory forms of African agency (Chap. 8). In so doing, the book seeks to practically demonstrate the on-going utility of the concept of neo-colonialism in contemporary studies of Africa's situation in the globalised economy, and within donor aid architectures.

Neo-Colonialism: The Continuing Relevance of Kwame Nkrumah

Kwame Nkrumah stands as a potent figurehead in African history, having led Ghana to independence in 1957—the first African colony to emerge as a 'sovereign' state from formal Empire. Nevertheless, his intellectual contribution to the analysis of North–South relations via the lens of neo-colonialism has lost currency in modern academic circles. As mentioned, many scholars are decidedly squeamish about discussions of the concept in academic conferences, and in leading journals. For many, it is associated with vulgar forms of Marxism, deemed unfashionable in the post-Cold War era. For some, it is seen to deny any form of meaningful African agency, reducing Africans to mere 'victims' in the global arena. For others, it is negatively associated with modern tyrants such as Robert Mugabe who have invoked the concept in their political discourse. And for many, it is seen as a brash polemical device that unduly blames 'the West' for the continuing mal-governance of certain African elites.

Nevertheless, a modern reading of Nkrumah's (1965) *Neo-colonialism: The Last Stage of Imperialism,* and his earlier work *Africa Must Unite* (1963), is surprisingly relevant in terms of an analysis of certain aspects of development interventions in Africa by external elements, both corporate and donor. Whether assessing current donor budget support to African treasuries, the activities of the European Investment Bank, the impact of free trade arrangements, or the role of mining companies—Nkrumah's analysis appears both relevant and emancipatory. His work, although controversial, deserves much closer scrutiny. It is therefore important to highlight the contours of Nkrumah's thought, as well as that of scholars who expressed similar concerns about Africa's external relations, notably Fanon (1961). Nkrumah himself defined neo-colonialism as the continuation of external control over African territories by newer and more subtle methods than that exercised under formal Empire. He viewed conditions of neo-colonialism as those in which African countries (which had attained *legal* independence) were penetrated by external influences to such a degree that they were not genuinely self-governing. Moreover, states under the sway of neo-colonialism could not attain meaningful economic or social development for their peoples, since policy was directed more towards the material interests of foreign elements than towards the needs of the local citizenry. African elites who took part in relations of neo-colonialism would govern on behalf of foreign benefactors and would in effect 'betray' the economic interests of their own people. This radical perspective is eloquently stated by Nkrumah in several passages of *Neo-colonialism: The Last Stage of Imperialism.* In his main definition of the concept, he highlighted the economic influence of external forces and how this in turn diminished the political freedoms of African countries:

> The essence of neo-colonialism is that the state which is subject to it is, in theory, independent and has all the outward trappings of international sovereignty. In reality its economic system and thus its political policy is directed by outside. (Nkrumah 1965: ix)

African countries then might enjoy legal or juridical sovereignty in the international system after acceptance of their formal declarations of independence. However, they would not enjoy the fruits of a popular, empirical sovereignty, in terms of the ability to realise and to enact self-determination based upon the social and economic needs of the local citizenry (c.f. Ndlouv-Gatsheni 2013: 72).[4]

In this vein, Nkrumah notably underscored the co-optive role of foreign governments as aid donors, as well as the role of foreign corporations investing capital into African economies. Aid payments made by foreign governments (for Nkrumah's purposes—European countries and the USA) were not seen as altruistic endeavours aimed at the wellbeing of African societies. Rather, donors' aid-giving was viewed as a means of ensuring the compliance of certain African elites and in lubricating forms of corporate economic penetration detrimental to African populations.[5] Aid in this sense was not a 'gift' but rather a short-term payment that would denude African empirical sovereignty:

> Control over government policy in the neo-colonial state may be secured by payments towards the costs of running the state, by the provision of civil servants in positions where they can dictate policy, and by monetary control over foreign exchange through the imposition of a banking system controlled by the imperialist power. (1965: ix)

Moreover, aid monies would soon be recouped by the donor, according to Nkrumah, in terms of the economic gains that they secured under conditions of neo-colonialism:

> "Aid" therefore to a neo-colonial state is merely a revolving credit, paid by the neo-colonial master, passing through the neo-colonial state and returning to the neo-colonial master in the form of increased profits. (1965: xv)

Thus, for Nkrumah, aid monies would help to reinstall foreign control over African territories, even after formal Empire had been dissolved:

[the] hesitancy [of African states to cut ties to former colonisers] is fostered by the sugared water of aid; which is the stop-gap between avid hunger and the hoped-for greater nourishment that never comes. As a result, we find that imperialism, having quickly adapted its outlook to the loss of direct political control, has retained and extended its economic grip. (1965: 33)

In addition to foreign aid, Nkrumah highlighted—and condemned—foreign corporate involvement in Africa where enterprises sought to exploit local labour power and natural resources without appropriately contributing to government revenues, jobs, or industrialisation. Notably, he pointed to the role of certain foreign companies in supporting corrupt African governments, and in financing alternative political elites when those already in power were deemed insufficiently pliable. This situation was seen to perpetuate colonial patterns of trade and commodity exchange between newly 'sovereign' African states and the West: '[our raw materials and produce] goes to feed the industries and factories of Europe and America, to the impoverishment of the countries of origin' (1965: 1).

Crucially, Nkrumah also highlighted the decisions and *agency* of African politicians themselves, particularly those who succumbed to neo-colonial influences from external corporations and donors. He saw that co-opted elites would have little interest in fostering industrialisation and genuine development, but would instead direct their efforts to the maintenance of the external linkages which kept them in power. African leaders—in the neo-colonial situation—would do less to serve the interests of their own citizenries than to assist foreign patrons in a bid to maintain their financial and political support:

The rulers of the neo-colonial states derive their authority to govern... from the support which they obtain from their neo-colonialist masters. They have therefore little interest in developing education, strengthening the bargaining power of their workers employed by expatriate firms, or indeed of taking any step which would challenge the colonial pattern of commerce... [which] is the object of neo-colonialism to preserve. (1965: 1)

Nkrumah's analysis clearly invoked a two-way *relationship* between the external and the internal forces at play in the perpetuation of neo-colonial systems. He did not merely focus on the role of foreign corporations and donors in a top-down process of power imposition. He instead fully *recognised the agency of certain African elites* and their political preference to engage the external as a means of maintaining convenient power structures.[6]

Interestingly, Nkrumah also took pains to indicate that the movement against neo-colonialism should not seek to isolate African economies from the global economy. He explicitly stated that investment from Western powers, in particular, could be welcomed if it was directed to appropriate sites of industrialisation, and if it was regulated by an African government that exercised empirical sovereignty in the pursuit of value-addition and (thus) greater economic parity between North and South (in what we would today describe as a developmental state).[7] He did not endorse autarky, reject industrialisation or condemn international trade. Rather, he sought to ensure that economic forces could be harnessed in such a manner as to equally benefit Africans as it did their foreign 'partners'. In order to do this, moreover, he emphasised the need for pan-African co-operation. Rather than pursue limited development in a 'Balkanised' continent, he called for the creation of economies of scale through pan-African integration. A federal government of an eventual United States of Africa was seen as a necessity to realise the full economic potential of the continent and its resource abundance. This would also guard against neo-colonial pressures, since a unified federal government could negotiate as an equal with donors and foreign corporations. No longer would external elements be able to utilise 'divide and rule' strategies in the maintenance of neo-colonial elites to the detriment of pan-Africanist leaders (such as himself) who sought to genuinely build developmental structures across the continent.

NEO-COLONIALISM AND AFRICAN SOCIALISM: FANON AND OTHER KEY CONTRIBUTORS

This radical stance adopted by Nkrumah clearly owes an intellectual debt to Marxism. The title of his treatise in fact explicitly echoes the work of Vladimir Lenin (2010 [1917]) on 'imperialism as the highest stage of capitalism'. However, Nkrumah's focus on pan-Africanism owes a separate intellectual debt to African liberation leaders such as Marcus Garvey (1923). This duality—between (neo)Marxism, on the one hand, and African liberation ideology, on the other—is found within the wider literature on neo-colonialism. Those who aligned with Nkrumah's analysis equally saw the struggle for genuine African liberation as a movement *against* foreign manipulation, and *for* African unity. Moreover, these authors often advanced African socialism, a form of socialist theory which called for Afrocentric approaches to economic development. Specifically, this encouraged the embrace of traditional 'African values', and resistance against foreign interference in African sovereign affairs. Perhaps most notably, Frantz Fanon (1961) articulately expressed this African socialist perspective. Fanon concurred with Nkrumah that former colonial powers would seek to retain economic, and hence political, influence over their erstwhile territories in Africa. Writing in the aftermath of the Congo Crisis and the murder of President Patrice Lumumba, Fanon (1961) stressed that ex-colonial powers would have little sympathy towards African states that sought to exercise genuine autonomy:

> you may see colonialism withdrawing its capital and its technicians and setting up around the young state the apparatus of economic pressure. The apotheosis of independence is transformed into the curse of independence, and the colonial power through its immense resources of coercion condemns the young nation to regression. In plain words, the colonial power says '*Since you want independence, take it and starve*'. (1961: 76)

African leaders that sought to exercise genuine economic and political autonomy would thus be forced to impose austerity regimes upon their peoples in the short term, as the ex-colonial power worked to debilitate African polities in their infancy:

> the nationalist leaders have no other choice but to turn to their people and ask for them a gigantic effort. A regime of austerity is imposed on these starving men… an autarkic regime is set up and each state, with the miserable resources it has in hand, tries to find an answer to the nation's great hunger and poverty. We see the mobilization of a people which toils to exhaustion in front of a suspicious and bloated Europe (ibid.)

Importantly, in terms of *neo-colonialism*, Fanon also argued that certain African elites would pursue the path-of-least-resistance and collaborate with (ex)colonial centres. These leaders would maintain asymmetric aid and trade networks with the metropole, even at the expense of genuine sovereignty. In fact, Fanon saw the emergence of neo-colonialism as a phenomenon which would affect countries throughout the Third World even after formal declarations of independence had been achieved:

> other countries of the Third World refuse to undergo this ordeal [austerity regimes] and agree to get over it by accepting the conditions of the former guardian power... The former dominated country becomes an economically dependent country. The ex-colonial power, which has kept intact and sometimes even reinforced its colonialist trade channels agrees to provision the budget of the independent national by small injections (ibid.)

Fanon foresaw that these political—and economic—compromises would keep African countries in a position of subordination and ill-being as compared to the wealth of Europe and the USA.

While Fanon's work is arguably less detailed than Nkrumah on the practical workings of neo-colonialism, nevertheless, his writings do more to highlight the psychological—and ideational—aspects of external influence. Fanon explained clearly how African citizenries—and their leaderships—often imagined themselves as belonging to an inferior civilization. Having been subjected to the racialized world views of their erstwhile European 'masters', African peoples had lost sight of their own cultural worth. As a result, certain Africans perceived Europeans as 'superior' on an ontological level. This ideational barrier to genuine African liberty had material consequences, according to Fanon. Namely, it helped to make possible the capitulations of certain African elites to the political and economic pressures of neo-colonialism. Having been educated in Paris or Oxford, collaborationist African leaders saw European (and more broadly Western) culture as evidence of a superior civilizational model. Hence, they were more willing to align themselves to external forces. Accordingly, Fanon emphasised that African peoples must tackle the ideational root of their subordination by consciously rejecting narratives and mental images of European cultural superiority:

> Let us waste no time in sterile litanies and nauseating mimicry. Leave this Europe where they are never done talking of Man, yet murder men everywhere they find them, at the corner of every one of their own streets, in all the corners of the globe. For centuries they have stifled almost the whole of humanity in the name of a so-called spiritual existence. Look at them today swaying between atomic and spiritual disintegration. (1961: 251)

For Fanon, therefore, neo-colonialism might be avoided—or overcome—through processes of ideational liberation. This would inoculate elites, in particular, from collaboration with external elements who sought to maintain African polities in economic and political subordination.

Furthermore, a number of other prominent critics of African relations with erstwhile colonial powers allied themselves to an analytical focus on neo-colonialism. Julius Nyerere and Sekou Touré (then Presidents of Tanzania and Guinea, respectively) concurred with their fellow African socialist, Nkrumah, that foreign powers would continue to seek economic—and thus political—control over African countries. Nyerere—as late as 1978, towards the end of his presidency—argued that neo-colonialism had not yet been thwarted: 'sooner or later, and for as long as necessary, Africa will fight against neo-colonialism as it had fought against colonialism. And eventually it will win' (1978: 11–12).[8] Touré, meanwhile, emphasised the need for a cultural awakening in Africa—echoing Fanon on the evils of colonialism upon African self-confidence. He additionally pointed to the role of foreign corporations in denuding African sovereignty even after *de jure* independence had been obtained:

> The direct colonial exploitation of former days is being succeeded by international monopolies, and this has a tendency to remain permanent. Paradoxically, it is the underdeveloped nations, exporting raw materials and crude products, which contribute an important share of the costs and social improvements from which workers in the fully developed countries benefit. (1962: 148)

Touré (1962) emphasised, moreover, that European powers might embroil African countries in trade and aid arrangements that would retard genuine development. In particular, he noted the then European Economic Community's (EEC) attempts to form 'Association' arrangements entailing free trade between European members and African 'Associates'.[9] Trade liberalisation on the part of newly independent African states, for Touré, would perpetuate economic asymmetries in the form of colonial patterns of exchange. He explained that African countries' 'unconditional integration into a multinational market negates the possibility of industrial development in advance; it could only be the association of the rider and the horse' (1962: 149). Nkrumah (1965: 19) echoed these concerns, warning about the 'collective neo-colonialism of the European Common Market' with regards to its emerging trade and aid 'Association' with Africa. In the words of Segal (1964: 87) writing during the early years of EEC-Africa Association:

> President Nkrumah's objections to associated status are both economic and ideological. According to him, associated states will perpetuate neo-colonialism and provide a fundamental obstacle to the achievement of African political and economic unity, which is the sole means whereby African states can overcome their lack of development.

Interestingly, certain Western writers including Jack Woddis, a prominent British Communist, contributed to the development of the concept of neo-colonialism. In a succinct monograph, *Introduction to Neo-Colonialism*, Woddis critiqued the economic penetration of African countries and subsequent foreign pressures on empirical sovereignty. In this, he saw a deliberate alliance of Western corporate and political elites in the diminution of African countries' policy autonomy:

> At the centre of all the activities of neo-colonialism lies its economic policies. These are directed to assisting the profit-making functions of the big monopolies, to providing the Western powers with the necessary economic powers in the new states so as to be able to wield political influence over the governments there. (1967: 86)

In a critique of comparative advantage theories promoted by Western advocates of free trade between African states and Europe/USA, he also emphasised how African leaders were (wrongly) encouraged not to pursue industrialisation:

> The [African] peoples are constantly told that they need "Western know-how", that they "cannot do without foreign capital", that they should not nationalise foreign enterprises, and that they should base themselves on agriculture and tourism rather than industry, which is something dismissed as mere "prestige building". (1967: 84)

In this context of unequal patterns of trade and commodity exchange, Woddis (1967: 89) underscored that Western 'development' interventions were designed to maintain the economic status quo:

Western investments, loans, trading policies and "aid" schemes are all directed to the aim of keeping these territories as primary-producing hinterlands of imperialism which import the bulk of their machinery and manufactured goods from the metropolitan countries.

To illustrate this point, Woddis (1967: 101)—with parallels to both Nkrumah and Touré—pointed to EEC Association arrangements with African states under the Yaoundé Conventions (1963–1975). Woddis (1967: 101) noted EEC tariffs of 5.4% on raw cocoa beans from Africa, compared with a tariff of 22% on processed powdered cocoa—as evidence that European powers sought to maintain African states in a subordinate position as providers of raw materials (rather than as industrial competitors).

It is important to note, also, that a number of international conferences also sought to define the concept of neo-colonialism, particularly in the 1960s at the zenith of debates surrounding neo-colonial interventions. The All-African People's Conference, held in Cairo, Egypt in March 1961, notably defined the concept in the following terms:

> the survival of the colonial system in spite of formal recognition of political independence in emerging countries which become the victims of an indirect and subtle form of domination by political economic, social, military or technical means. (cited in Martin 1982: 227)

Similarly to Nkrumah, the Conference viewed that such impositions upon Africa could be overcome through pan-African political mobilisation and consciousness raising. These authors (and conferences) helped to delineate neo-colonialism as political concept. They emphasised the ways in which external control was maintained in Africa even after the formal end of Empire. Imperialism—in the Marxist terminology—continued in a new guise, facilitated by foreign aid and corporate activities.

DEPENDENCY THEORIES AND THE CONCEPT OF NEO-COLONIALISM

It is important to highlight here that dependency theories, which became popular in the 1960s and 1970s in the critique of North-South relations, at times overlapped with the claims of African socialists with regards to the concept of neo-colonialism. Dependency theorists sought to emphasise the global economic structures and international trading dynamics that prevented newly independent countries from attaining full industrialisation and economic progress. In particular, dependency theorists pointed to the technological advantages of Western countries in maintaining their economic hegemony over developing states within the world economy (Tausch 2010). In this context, they criticised the diminishing returns of developing states' over-reliance on the export of raw commodities such as cocoa and timber at the expense of industrialisation. As such, many dependency theorists (if they did not avow full autarky) emphasised the need for import substitution industrialisation (ISI) in the Third World. That is, they underscored the need for developing country governments to diversify their economies away from colonial patterns of production and exchange, and to instead build an industrial base capable of generating skilled jobs and prosperity. These industries would be fed by the rural and agricultural hinterlands—thus backward linkages would be established for the benefit of primary producers too. Notably, however, they underscored that industrialisation would not generate meaningful development if foreign companies (and interests) remained dominant (Dos Santos and Randall 1998: 57). Developing states would have to challenge the technological and financial hegemony of Western countries in order to carve out sufficient economic space for themselves, and to resist dependency.

Moreover, from a neo-Marxist position, the dependency theorists underscored how class alliances would hinder this shift to autonomous industrialisation on the part of the newly emergent nations in Africa, Asia, and Latin America (the last of these being the region in which dependency theories originated). Just as inequalities existed at the global level between developed and underdeveloped states, so too did class inequalities exist *within* developing countries. Many dependency theorists therefore pointed to the potential function of a 'comprador class' within developing countries which would align itself to the economic interests of external capitalist interests. This comprador class would welcome skewed forms of foreign direct investment (FDI), and would support iniquitous trade frameworks, as long as they personally benefited from asymmetric North-South ties. A local bourgeoisie, for instance, involved in import businesses would have an incentive to continue dependency relations between their own nation (in the 'Third World') and a foreign nation in the developed West. Andre Gunder Frank, one of the most prominent dependency theorists, explained that:

> This colonial and class structure establishes very well defined class interests for the dominant sector of the [Third World] bourgeoisie. Using government cabinets and other instruments of the state, the bourgeoisie produces a policy of underdevelopment. (cited in Brewer 2002: 196)

This class analysis was taken further by Cardoso and Faletto who pointed to varieties of distinct class formations in individual developing countries (and these classes' interactions with the metropole) as an explanatory variable for degrees of success vis-à-vis 'development' (cited in Kapoor 2002: 649–649). They admitted that certain forms of 'dependent development' might take place in individual Third World countries. There could be the semblance of economic growth and certain sectors might prosper, albeit as an adjunct of the needs of the metropole states in the West. Structural inequalities would remain at a global level, but certain dividends might accrue to poorer nations in Latin America, Asia and Africa—albeit within constrained, limited forms of (unequal) development (Kapoor 2002: 649).

This admission of the possibility of dependent development signalled (for critics of dependency theory) that the school was losing traction in the 'battle of ideas', particularly as Washington Consensus policies prevailed in the 1980s and early 1990s. Cardoso (1977), meanwhile, began in the late 1970s to voice disquiet with rigid forms of dependency theory that failed to acknowledge progress within certain developing countries. He signalled that a progressive reformism might usefully prevail along social-democratic lines, and harness economic industrialisation for the benefits of poorer peoples even within a capitalist global economy (1977: 20). Dependency theorists' insistence that the economic hegemony of the Western metropole 'doomed' poorer states to a perpetual and unyielding underdevelopment appeared less convincing, particularly in light of the successes of the East Asian Tigers in the late 1970s. Accordingly, dependency theories lost a certain degree of intellectual credibility. Indeed, certain figures such as Cardoso (2009) have somewhat repudiated their own earlier work and acknowledged that the dependency school (while valuable in stimulating the sociological imagination) had at times been guilty of a myopic economic reductionism.

It is important to underscore, however, that the concept of neo-colonialism and the dependency school approach should be seen as distinct entities. The dependency school—while acknowledging the role of the 'comprador' local bourgeoisie—largely focussed upon economic factors in the explanation of continuing North-South inequalities. The role of technology, the unequal exchange value of raw materials versus industrial commodities, and the dominance of Western countries in lucrative tertiary services sectors (such as banking and finance) were largely deemed as the root cause of on-going dependency relations. While there was a partial focus upon internal class configurations and the role of comprador elites, there was relatively little focus upon the *political* interventions of external donor officials and foreign corporate actors in exacerbating unequal relationships. By contrast, the literature on neo-colonialism is explicitly *political* and avoids forms of economic determinism—by focussing resolutely on the interplay between local 'comprador' elites in developing countries *and* elite officials/corporate actors in the Global North. Accordingly, it pays much greater attention to the role of aid and 'development' interventions in maintaining the economic *and political* structures that perpetuate poverty. It does not deny the potential for certain forms of (limited) growth. Rather it questions whether African states (in particular) are able to exercise policy sovereignty, or whether or not their state institutions are 'captured' to such a degree that they do more to serve foreign interests than that of their own citizenries.

The decline of dependency theories as a popular lens within IR and Development Studies, therefore, does not necessary signal the irrelevance of the concept of neo-colonialism. Nkrumah's analysis—as illustrated in subsequent chapters—appears prescient when we assess contemporary 'development' phenomenon such as EU budget support or 'pro-poor' trade negotiations. The dependency school did overlap with the literature on neo-colonialism in terms of highlighting North-South inequalities and the role of comprador elites. Nevertheless, a certain form of economic determinism found within dependency approaches is not replicated within the literature on neo-colonialism. The major alleged 'flaw', therefore, of the dependency school—namely its focus on economic forces—is not found within Nkrumah's own framework. Nkrumah memorably noted that African patriots should 'seek ye first the political kingdom and all things shall be added to it'. Moreover, Nkrumah (as the main theorist of neo-colonialism) welcomed certain forms of North-South trade and FDI—so long as it supported the growth of the productive capacity of African economies. What he objected to—and critiqued—was the subversion of African state sovereignty by external elements since this would retard opportunities for industrialisation and social prosperity for African peoples. His analytical contribution therefore is not open to the same avenues of critique as befell the dependency school from the late 1970s and into the Washington Consensus.

Interestingly, many dependency theorists in the 1970s and 1980s themselves made clear distinctions between their own school and the writings on neo-colonialism. Many dependency scholars disavowed what they deemed the overly 'mechanical' and state-centric perspective of Nkrumah and the concept of neo-colonialism. Shaw (1982), for instance, advanced the need for class analysis within—and between—states in order to better understand the processes which gave rise to underdevelopment in the 'periphery'. In particular, he emphasised the role of transnational networks involving multinational corporations, aid agencies and international bodies in ensuring that dependency relations continued between former colonies and former colonial powers. In this context, he issued a rather stern riposte to Nkrumah and those who focussed upon neo-colonialism as analytical concept:

> In short, African states are not robots that merely react to "external" inputs and instructions... rather... structural linkages exist between social formation and those at the centre... so Kwame Nkrumah's rather mechanistic conceptualisation is in need of revision if contemporary structures are to be recognised. (1982: 241)

It is interesting to note, however, that such criticisms of Nkrumah from dependency theorists tended to ignore the nuances present within his work. Nkrumah did not in fact focus on Westphalian state interactions alone. Rather he did acknowledge the personal—and class—dynamics that prolonged unequal relations between African polities and the 'West'. Moreover, he did recognise transnational forces 'above' the state system. As mentioned, he critiqued the emerging influence of the EEC as a supranational entity able to pursue unequal trade agreements with newly emergent African countries. He also pointed to transnational corporate activities and what he described as the 'brazen onslaught of international capitalists... the empire of financial capital' (1965: 35). Within the African state, moreover, he recognised the need for class alliances between agricultural producers, industrial entrepreneurs, factory workers, and political elites as part of a developmental state strategy. This was certainly the case in terms of his own governance of Ghana where he sought to 'unite' divergent class interests within a single political party (much to the chagrin of his detractors).

Again, what Nkrumah did bring to the fore—and which was often omitted by the dependency theorists—was the explicit power strategies and policy interventions taken by foreign policy officials and external corporate interests in the subversion of African state structures, and the promotion of neo-colonialism. This recognised more fully the *political dimension* of Africa's relations with external forces—in the form of aid interventions, the pursuit of free trade agreements, Western corporations' alliances with local politicians and entrepreneurs, and (which was recognised by certain dependency theorists) the role of 'comprador' elites in aligning themselves to the interests of external elements. Nkrumah did not assume that economic factors such as technological know-how or commodity exchange values were determinant in this sense.[10] Instead he illustrated—and sought to practically tackle—the political strategies which foreign elements undertook to cement their positions of influence over *de jure* independent African states. In this discussion, moreover, he remained optimistic as to the potential for patriotic leaders to thwart neo-colonial ambitions via the construction of pan-African institutions able to pursue genuine development on a continental basis.

Neo-Colonialism as the Obverse of Neo-Patrimonialism?

Nkrumah's optimism regarding the ability of African leaders to resist external influence, and to build pan-African structures, contrasts, however, with the (Afro)pessimism of the neo-patrimonialism literature. This branch of thought is important to highlight owing to its ascendance within current African studies. This school maintains that the 'problem' of African development predominantly lies with the cultural attributes of elites within the region. Namely, that an African political culture has emerged centred upon 'Big Men' leaders who utilise state institutions and economic resources to maintain corrupt client-patron networks. These networks are mainly based upon ethnic affiliation (on a tribal basis) and political legitimacy is derived from the ability of the 'Big Men' to reward the loyalty of acolytes (hence patrimony). This neo-patrimonial situation results in the misallocation of state capacities, and a relationship with the external often characterised by 'extraversion'. This latter concept relates to Bayart's (2010) writings on the strategies of African elites vis-à-vis external aid donors. Bayart maintains that African elites are not victims of foreign manipulations but instead actively court aid donors, often through discursive overture to external actors' priorities—for instance, on free markets and private sector development (PSD).

A number of key authors—including Bayart—help to define the concept of neo-patrimonialism. Clapham, writing during the Washington Consensus, described a hybrid state which mixed patrimonial client-patron networks with quasi-rational Westphalian state structures. He defined this 'neo'-patrimonialism along the following lines:

> A form of organisation in which relationships of a broadly patrimonial type pervade a political and administrative system which is formally constructed on rational-legal lines. Officials hold positions in bureaucratic organisations with powers which are formally defined, but exercise those powers... as a form... of private property. (cited in Erdmann and Engel 2007: 98)

This broad definition remains at the heart of the contemporary literature on neo-patrimonialism. Note, for example, Diane Cammack (2007: 600) in her explanation that Big Men utilise state capacities for their own private gain:

> Decisions about resources are made by "big men" and their cronies, who are linked by "informal" (private and personal, patronage and clientelist) networks that exist outside (before, beyond and despite) the state structure, and who follow a logic of personal and particularist interest rather than national betterment.

Diane Cammack thus attributes 'development' failures not to external donor interventions, but rather to the political culture existent within African polities themselves. In expressive language she states, for instance, that 'the shelves of ministries in most African states sag under the weight of [donor-given] good analysis and policy documents' but that unfortunately neo-patrimonial elites shy away from such wise policy implementation (2007: 607).

This line of argument is furthered by scholars such as Taylor (2004), again within an overarching literature on the neo-patrimonial, hybrid state in Africa. Taylor (2004: 411) argues that scholars must not become fixated on the negative influences of Western donors, but must fully recognise—and tackle—the poor governance choices made by African officials. He states clearly that 'the tendency to solely blame external factors for the continent's predicament is... becoming less and less credible'. In a direct critique of Africanists who maintain that Western powers do violate African sovereignty and thereby jeopardise genuine economic progress, he further states that:

> Power relations between Africa and the developed world can no longer simply be understood as top-down impositions from 'the West'. Rather, African elites are themselves agents in—and arguably major causes of—the continent's demise. (Taylor 2004: 412)

In even starker terms, he characterises African political culture as prone to gift-giving from village level up to government ministries:

> Political power in Africa is less about capable administration and the concomitant provision of broad-based benefits to the populace and more about the giving and granting of favours, in an endless series of dyadic exchanges that go from village level to the highest reaches of the central state. The concept of neopatrimonialism captures this reality. (Taylor 2004: 412)

However, such negative assessments of so-called African 'culture' and elite personalities have now come under some criticism in a number of recent defences of African politics and society. It becomes apparent here that the neo-patrimonialism literature—and discourse—leaves itself open to accusations of 'essentialism'. Namely, that its scholars caricature African governance structures based upon a monolithic image of Africa as the site of predatory rulers, corrupt civil servants, and tribal opportunists. While themselves arguing against simplified portrayals of external bogeymen disrupting African economic and social development, they merely replace such images with simplified portraits of African 'Big Men' leading their countries into the mire of corruption and poverty.

Convincingly, Mkandawire (2015) criticises the neo-patrimonialism literature for being wholly pessimistic about the possibility of any form of meaningful development within Africa. Dwelling upon imaginaries of the African elite personality, neo-patrimonial writings often suggest that the task of development is 'inherently futile in Africa or, at best, likely to take a very long time to accomplish' (2015: 564). Mkandawire (2015: 563) usefully sets out how this paradigm has become dominant within academic, media and official approaches to the question of African development:

Over the years this school of thought has shaped the study of Africa through its influence on key donors, its privileged access to leading journals, and the constitution of tight self-referential networks of Africanist scholarship. It has produced an abundance of literature and its intellectual triumph is that its analyses have become part of the general knowledge of foreign policymakers and journalists reporting on Africa.

Mkandawire's challenge to the neo-patrimonialism literature is timely and warranted. This literature does lean towards ontological essentialism based upon negative assumptions of what characterises Africa and its peoples. From a post-colonial perspective, such literature is in fact permeated by colonial legacies and discourse which represent African territories as the uncivilised antithesis to rational European (Western) society. This colonial era dichotomy is merely replicated in the current day writings on neo-patrimonialism, which wholly fail to recognise 'success stories' in African political circles. For instance, note President Kagame of Rwanda who has tackled domestic corruption and promoted forms of economic development, albeit amidst accusations of human rights violations and the abetting of belligerents in the DRC/Kivu province conflict (AllAfrica 2014; Ankomah 2013).

This is not to argue that the insights offered by scholars within the neo-patrimonialism school ought to be rejected in their entirety. As mentioned, Bayart's (2010: 196–198) writings on the concept of extraversion are useful in terms of making sense of African elite actions within North-South relations. Bayart argues that elites make a deliberate and strategic appeal to external donors and civil society groups as part of internal power strategies (which he defines as 'extraversion'). African leaders seek foreign aid donations in order to lubricate their patronage networks, and to satisfy the needs of domestic constituencies. This exacerbates relations of 'dependency' but ensures the short-to-medium term survival of the African regime in question. Moreover, as part of this analysis, Bayart emphasises the ideational aspect of such North–South engagements. Notably, he highlights how African officials at times mirror the discourse of their foreign benefactors to convince external entities that they are deserving of material support. Bayart notes that this agency on the part of African officials underscores their strategic thinking—playing upon the vanity and grandiosity of foreign aid donors in order to lever in additional resources for the state, and thus for client–patron networks (ibid.).

The concept of extraversion can be usefully allied to a reflexive embrace of the concept of neo-colonialism. Nkrumah himself noted that neo-colonial elites in subverted African polities would actively engage their 'masters' in the metropole. That is, co-opted African leaders would energetically seek preferential trade and aid arrangements which would consolidate their political hegemony within their own national contexts. Although neglecting discussion of the precise ideational elements at play, nevertheless, Nkrumah's analysis is compatible with 'extraversion'. Namely, it is possible (and necessary) to acknowledge the agency of African personnel in exacerbating situations of neo-colonialism by inviting foreign elements to further penetrate the African state in question. This gives rise to discussion of 'imperialism by invitation'. Indeed, the so-called 'comprador class' (to use Dos Santos' expression) may embolden foreign elites to extend their economic—and hence—political clout in Africa. What is not compatible with a reflexive utilisation of 'neo-colonialism', however, are essentialist caricatures that assume that *all* African elites act in a predatory manner. Certain neo-colonial or comprador elites may act in such a manner as to validate some of the claims made by Bayart. Crucially, however, not *all* African elites—or civil society actors—engage in such activities. Thus, the sweeping generalisations omnipresent within the neo-patrimonialism literature are inaccurate (and are in fact somewhat perverse). A meaningful analysis of African development and the negative impact of many foreign aid and trade interventions must avoid crude caricatures—either of 'bogeymen imperialists' or of 'bogeymen Big Men'. Moreover, any consideration of corrupt practices in Africa must recognise how external factors often make such strategic power plays possible in the first instance.[11] The alleged political culture critiqued by the neo-patrimonialism literature is often a symptom of asymmetric North–South ties. Many African elites engaging in nepotistic behaviour would not be able to retain power in the long term if they were not continuously enabled by the material interventions of foreign aid benefactors, and foreign corporations.

NEO-COLONIALISM, SOVEREIGNTY AND THE GOVERNANCE STATE

It is important to recognise, moreover, that an analysis of this internal–external relationship (that is, the relationship between African elites and foreign donor or corporate actors) is an essential component of making sense of African development. Certain recent analyses—albeit from a more critical stance than that adopted by the neo-patrimonial school—have unfortunately blurred the internal and external dynamics at play. Specifically, Harrison (2004) has put forward his conception of the 'governance state'. This perspective views African polities as being so permeated by donor development agendas—for instance, the free market agendas of the World Bank—that the distinction between internal and external interests becomes redundant. As part of this argument, Harrison argues for a more fluid definition and understanding of 'sovereignty' as a zonal space in which actors interact, rather than as a definitive aspect of a self-governing nation-state. According to Harrison (2004: 26), this reconceptualization of sovereignty:

> Moves us away from the limiting concerns of 'external imposition', 'national independence', 'self-determination' and so on, that often insinuate studies of the encounter between African states and external agencies. It means that we do not have to 'solve' the apparent contradiction that the Bank both undermines sovereignty (as a boundary) through conditionality and strengthens it through its lending to states.

Moreover, this alternative understanding of the notion of sovereignty is seen by Harrison as a positive step for African studies in that it:

> Allows us to consider the 'content' of sovereignty—its construction, discourse, the interplay between actors—more fully than would be possible it if were merely concerned with the extent to which an imagined boundary has been defended or violated (ibid.)

Harrison's shift from a Westphalian conception of nation-state sovereignty to a more fluid (or even post-structural and Foucauldian) definition does not, however, move African studies forward. Blurring the distinction between internal African policies and external actors' preferences does not enable a more progressive critique of Africa's relationship with donors in Brussels, London and beyond. Instead, it adds to the academic lexicon while distracting attention from the ways in which African nation-states' ability to exercise genuine self-government is compromised by the strategic interventions of external donors and foreign corporate entities. Moreover, a traditional definition of sovereignty, as invoked within the existing literature on neo-colonialism, does not confine itself to imaginations of territorial boundaries being physically violated (as Harrison suggests above). Sovereignty in the Westphalian understanding is better understood as the ability of nations to govern themselves based upon the material interests and political preferences of their own citizenries (what might also be termed popular and empirical sovereignty, see Kilberg 2014). Westphalian norms of sovereignty are undermined, therefore, when external actors are able to compel, coerce, or co-opt African governance officials to such a degree that decision-making is no longer primarily based upon national interests. Relations of neo-colonialism can be discerned when national sovereignty becomes little more than 'flag-independence' where the state is legally recognised (juridical sovereignty) yet cannot enact self-determination (empirical sovereignty) (Nyerere cited in Mwakikagile 2010: 469; see also Ndlovu-Gatshemi 2012: 45). Namely, when African nations remain sovereign in de jure legal terms, but are incapable of exercising genuine de facto self-governance on the basis of their own national interest (whether that interest pertain to the economy, politics, culture or military security).[12]

Harrison's concept of the governance state, by downplaying the significance of the 'internal-external divide', unfortunately draws critical attention away from analysis of the strategies deployed by foreign actors as they seek to maintain hegemony (within relations of neo-colonialism). Moreover, it closes down our critical capacity to make distinctions between the national interest (in terms of the wellbeing of local citizenries) and the interests of foreign actors (for instance, in terms of increased exports through disadvantageous free trade arrangements). Harrison is accurate when he describes the ways in which World Bank officials, in particular, involve themselves in policy formulation at the domestic level in African political institutions. They are in a sense, therefore, embedded and enmeshed within African state bodies. Nevertheless, it remains vital to clearly make the distinction between the ability of a nation to self-govern on the basis of domestic interests (economic, military and political), and the inability of certain neo-colonial African states to govern on such a basis. Policies that favour premature free trade agreements, for example, may be written into the national development plans of African governance ministries with the aid of World Bank officials. This does not mean, however, that the internal–external distinction becomes invalid or distracting. On the contrary, it becomes imperative in such circumstances to examine—and to critique—the ways in which the genuine self-governing capacity of African states has been undermined in such circumstances. That is, how African states' popular sovereignty has been compromised by external actors. A focus on this internal–external distinction, moreover, can help direct emancipatory political action towards challenging disadvantageous relationships which denude empirical sovereignty and retard genuine 'development'. Stating that external elements become part of the national state structure and that the internal–external distinction is therefore redundant appears a curious way to proceed in terms of an analysis of certain African states' on-going conditions of poverty.

This more 'Westphalian' definition of sovereignty is central to the concept of neo-colonialism. Its adoption does not mean, however, that there is necessarily an ontological fetish with physical borders (as Harrison implies). A useful definition of sovereignty, as explained above, relates more to the ability of the nation to govern itself according to its material and cultural needs. Sovereignty as a political attribute can be enacted within the physical confines of the nation, for instance, in the corridors of power of presidential palaces within African countries. It can also be enacted by African officials in their negotiations across a myriad of geographical locations, for instance in trade talks in Brussels with EU Commissioners. Sovereignty is not necessarily thus about questions of border violations, but about the ability of a nation-state (comprised of its citizens and political leadership) to genuinely exercise policy control over its future direction based upon indigenous needs and expectations. Sovereign policy choices may of course be informed and influenced by external constraints, for example, in terms of international opinion on climate change and emissions, or on respect for human rights. Nevertheless, sovereignty itself is forfeited when foreign powers are able to co-opt or coerce internal political elites to the extent that domestic policies serve external interests rather than the national interest. This implies not mere *consideration* for external interests and interdependence (as on climate change) but domestic political actors' fully fledged *dependence* on meeting external preferences for political survival. Policy is thus dictated by the 'external', even if World Bank officials (for instance) are in fact physically present in the ministries of African states.

Furthermore, this more traditional Westphalian conception of sovereignty does not imply a blindness to supranational or transnational trends (as again might be implied within Harrison's analysis). As stated, Nkrumah in the 1960s fully acknowledged the impact of non-state forces upon the exercise of national sovereignty within individual African countries. For instance, he noted the impact of transnational corporations upon newly independent states such as the Democratic Republic of the Congo (DRC). In a more contemporary context, we might note here too the impact of non-state actors in the form of evangelical religious groups that have recently gained prominence in Africa, with significant impact on local culture (notably, growing homophobia; see Kaoma 2012). These transnational elements may be conceived of as 'external' elements nonetheless. Attention to the internal–external distinction (and to situations of neo-colonialism in which national sovereignty is perverted by external actors) is an important factor within the analysis of development issues in Africa today. By contrast, the post-structural turn to an alternative definition of 'sovereignty' as an abstract notion of fluidity, space, interactions and interdependency not only undermines clarity but threatens to distract attention from external political intrusions which ought to be (normatively speaking) contested by African actors who seek to tackle poverty and ill-being within their own polities.

Moreover, Harrison makes interesting reference to the apparent 'paradox' whereby World Bank interventions may violate sovereignty (in terms of self-governance) but enhance 'sovereignty' (in the sense of the government's practical ability to govern via functioning state ministries). This statement captures issues surrounding donor aid, particularly budget support, whereby monies are allocated to civil service staffing and agency capacities to ensure their more effective functioning. Again, however, sovereignty should not be understood as the capacity of state institutions to enact policy programmes regardless of their ideological content. Africa's colonial administrations in the era of formal Empire received monies from the metropole in London or Paris, but this fact did not make them 'sovereign' actors. A meaningful definition of sovereignty implies the nation-state's ability to choose its own policy preferences based upon a process of national self-determination.

Moreover, this apparent paradox is often less troublesome when examined in closer detail. For example, EU budget support monies are allocated to government treasuries in countries such as Uganda. Civil service staffs are thus salaried with the assistance of the European benefactor. This of course does not imply increased sovereignty on the part of the Ugandan state (Langan 2015: 102–105). Its ministers may be able to attend more overseas conferences with the assistance of EU funding, for instance. And ministries (such as trade) may have greater capacity to enact certain policy agendas, for instance, in terms of custom revenue audits at the border (ibid.). This does not amount, however, to enhanced sovereignty if the policy priorities concerning trade and investment are largely determined by the EU itself. Aid in this scenario is less of a sovereignty-enhancing device than it is a side payment used to maintain neo-colonial relationships, as described by Nkrumah.

CONCLUSION

This chapter has outlined the key features of the concept of neo-colonialism, as put forward by Nkrumah as well as other key figures such as Fanon. Their writings together help to define a situation in which African state sovereignty is denuded to such an extent that policy priorities are directed towards the material needs of external actors (notably, in terms of foreign states in Europe, and the USA). These African socialists, moreover, identify two major forms of neo-colonial penetration—namely, that of foreign governments via aid monies; and foreign corporations via capital investments into African economies. Both of these forms of intervention in Africa are seen (in certain circumstances) to entrench relations of neo-colonialism in which co-opted African elites do more to serve their foreign benefactors than to effectively pursue the material and cultural wellbeing of their own citizenries. African countries in the neo-colonial situation enjoy legal independence and are recognised within the international community as possessing de jure sovereignty. However, they do not exercise de facto sovereignty, understood as the ability to tangibly realise self-determination via policies that meaningfully meet indigenous concerns and local needs.[13]

The chapter has also emphasised that there are certain parallels between the concept of neo-colonialism and dependency theories. In particular, the (partial) focus of certain dependency theorists upon the role of the comprador class aligns well to the thrust of Nkrumah and other African socialists on the concept of neo-colonialism. Nevertheless, the dependency school is understood to have engaged in forms of economic determinism, with emphasis on unequal patterns of exchange, technological gaps between Northern and Southern economies, and the predominance of the West in tertiary sectors such as banking and finance. The concept of neo-colonialism, however, focuses much more fully on the political dimensions that help to perpetuate conditions of poverty and ill-being in certain African contexts. Focussing on the 'political kingdom' as per Nkrumah, the concept of neo-colonialism draws more attention to the power strategies and political objectives of foreign actors (including governments and corporations) as they seek to maintain and to extend influence over African governments.

. The chapter has also juxtaposed the concept of neo-colonialism with alternative lens for examining Africa's 'development' in current academic circles. In particular, the existing literature on neo-patrimonialism is seen to be prone to essentialism, based upon negative imaginaries of African 'culture' and elite personalities. Moreover, the neo-patrimonialism literature claims to move beyond bogey-men images of external actors interrupting African development, while at the same time merely creating new bogey-men in the form of 'Big Men' leaders. The concept of neo-colonialism is deemed much more useful in the analysis of African development since it fully recognises how instances of nepotistic behaviour are brought about and enabled by external factors in the first instance. Writings on neo-colonialism eschew cultural essentialism, while at the same time recognising the agency of certain African officials in perpetuating asymmetric linkages with the metropole. In this context, reflexive applications of the concept of neo-colonialism are seen to sit well with Bayart's (2010) writings on elite extraversion. A reflexive application of 'neo-colonialism' may recognise the role of foreign actors in denuding African sovereignty, and the role of certain African elites in maintaining power networks through deliberate appeal to the priorities of the 'external'. Finally, in relation to Harrison's concept of the governance state, the chapter has argued that a more traditional, Westphalian understanding of sovereignty is preferable to alternative modes which reconstruct sovereignty as 'space'. Harrison's critique of works that focus too heavily on the 'internal-external' dimension is seen to be misplaced. Instead, it is wholly necessary to reflect on African states' relations with external elements (and the role of foreign actors in subverting African sovereignties). The next chapter now examines the role of external corporate actors in denuding self-government in African contexts. This demonstrates how the concept of neo-colonialism, as originally proposed by Nkrumah, remains valid for the critical assessment of African countries' position within the globalised market economy.

NOTES

1. With some notable exceptions including Ndlovu-Gatsheni (2013) and Gruffydd-Jones (2015).
2. Gassama (2008: 338) usefully notes that while the term 'neo-colonialism' dates back to the early 1950s and was not coined by Nkrumah

himself that, nevertheless, he deserves 'substantial credit' for the elaboration of neo-colonialism as analytical concept. His chapter on neo-colonialism in *Africa Must Unite* (1963) combined to *Neo-colonialism: The Last Stage of Imperialism* (1965) establish him as the defining author on the subject.

3. Norman Fairclough (2009) provides a masterful account of discourse analysis and constructivist insights about the power of language in presenting ideological programmes as being 'legitimate' or 'necessary'.

4. Empirical sovereignty implies the exercise of self-determination by the 'people', namely the citizens who comprise the nation-state (hence, also the term 'popular' sovereignty, as often associated with the US constitution and its emphasis on government by and for 'the people'). Juridical sovereignty, on the other hand, denotes the legal recognition of a state's claims to sovereign independence (hence also legal sovereignty, or what Nyerere termed 'flag-independence' if unaccompanied by empirical sovereignty). See Jackson and Rosberg (1982, 1986) for their discussions of juridical (legal) and empirical (substantive) forms of sovereignty.

5. Nkrumah was sceptical about the personal motives of aid donors, viewing neo-colonialism as a deliberate strategy informed by Machiavellian power plays. Whether individual officials within donor agencies act in a spirit of benevolence (or malevolence) in Africa is beyond this analysis (since it pertains more to psychology). The material outcomes of their policy interventions, however, is certainly open to examination—and ought to considered in relation to their moralising 'development' discourse which is used to justify their endeavours.

6. Interestingly, in the earlier text, *Africa Must Unite*, Nkrumah (1963) expresses some sympathy for the impossible predicament in which certain African elites found themselves. Namely, that they had inherited states with weak economic capacities that were reliant on foreign aid for the provision of basic services. And yet elites would have to find the means of achieving empirical sovereignty free from foreign tutelage. This quandary and double-bind is discussed more in chapter 8 in relation to recent interventions from Brown (2012, 13). Nkrumah's views, meanwhile, appear to have hardened towards his fellow African politicians in the sense of the stronger wording found within the 1965 text. By 1966, however, he had been ousted by a coup d'etat supported by the US government, amidst his detractors' condemnation of his authoritarian rule.

7. The developmental state is one which historically utilised mixed-market mechanisms to support industrialisation and value-addition away from colonial patterns of production (dependence on raw material exports). It

involved centralised government and 'insulated' bureaucratic elites able to steer the economy onto higher ground, while dealing with domestic dissent in a process of economic nationalism (Leftwich 1995: 402). In the words of Radice (2008: 1152), the developmental state 'is seen as a distinctive political economy that combines elements of market and plan, linking a mixed economy to a political–Ideological approach that combines authoritarian technocracy with a relatively egalitarian distribution of income and wealth'. Chapter 8 addresses calls for a *democratic* developmental state in Africa today.

8. Nyerere, however, differed from Nkrumah on the strategy for mitigating foreign influence in Africa. As the leading intellectual within the Monrovia Group, Nyerere called for a gradualist approach to African unity, emphasising the role of (sub)regional formations such as today's ECOWAS. Nkrumah, on the other hand, advocated for immediate federal government as part of a Union of African States. The debates between the Casablanca Group, led by Nkrumah, and the Monrovia Group marked an early division among 'sovereign' African nations. As discussed in Chap. 8, Nyerere admitted in 1997 that he had underestimated the dangers of neo-colonialism and that Nkrumah's approach, with hindsight, had essentially been vindicated.

9. This relates to the Yaoundé Conventions signed between the EEC and the Associated African States and Madagascar (AASM) from 1963–1975.

10. It should be noted that there are modern Marxist writings on questions of 'development' which raise interesting questions about the linkages between capitalism and 'imperialism'. Namely, that the expansion of a world market as part of economic globalisation has brought African countries into an ever-closer association with foreign corporations and donors. Harvey notably critiques processes of 'accumulation by dispossession' in the Global South as multinationals compete for access to land and natural resource wealth. Works by Aneivas, Pradella and Bieler also provide some fruitful analysis of the condition of developing countries in the global market economy. With some parallels to the dependency theorists, however, their writings—given their Marxist foundations—do tend to omit full consideration of the ideational elements that propel forward 'development' agendas in Africa. At times, the writings also focus more on what C Wright Mills termed 'grand theory' to the detriment of case study analysis of the material impact of current 'development' agendas on the ground. One notable exception here is Cammack (2004) who provides a detailed evaluation of the World Bank's Poverty Reduction Strategy Programmes (PRSPs) in Africa. These writings would do well to engage more with the work of Nkrumah, as well as to balance historical materialism with a stronger focus on the ideational.

11. It would also be useful to reflect here on corruption in Western government—for instance, the recent allegations of gross nepotism and fraud made against French presidential contender Fillon (Meichtry and Landauro 2017).
12. This is discussed in more detail in Chap. 8 with regards to interventions from Brown (2012, 13) on legal sovereignty.
13. Again, this distinction between de jure and de facto sovereignty is discussed further in Chap. 8.

REFERENCES

Ankomah, B. (2013). Rwanda, a star in fighting corruption: Quietly, there is a revolution going on in Rwanda, in the form of fighting corruption. *New African*, March 2013, 526, 50–53.

AllAfrica. (2014). *Kagame calls on judiciary to uphold zero tolerance to corruption*, 5th September 2015.

Bayart, J. F. (2010). *The state in Africa: The politics of the belly*. London: Polity Press.

Brewer, T. (2002). *Marxist theories of imperialism*. London: Routledge.

Brown, W. (2012). A question of agency: Africa in international politics. *Third World Quarterly, 33*(10), 1889–1908.

Cammack, P. (2004). What the World Bank means by poverty reduction, and why it matters. *New Political Economy, 9*(2), 189–211.

Cammack, D. (2007). The logic of African neopatrimonialism: What role for donors? *Development Policy Review, 25*(5), 599–614.

Cardoso, F. H. (1977). The consumption of dependency theory in the US. *Latin American Research Review, 12*(3), 7–24.

Cardoso, F. H. (2009). New paths: Globalization in historical perspective. *Studies in Comparative International Development, 44*(4), 296–317.

Dos Santos, T., & Randall, L. (1998). The theoretical foundations of the cardoso government: A new stage of the dependency theory debate. *Latin American Perspectives, 25*(1), 53–70.

Erdmann, G., & Engel, U. (2007). Neopatrimonialism reconsidered: Critical review and elaboration of an elusive concept. *Commonwealth and Comparative Politics, 45*(1), 95–119.

Fairclough, N. (2009). Language and globalisation. *Semiotica, 173*(1), 317–342.

Fanon, F. (1961). *The wretched of the earth*. Reprint—London: Penguin Classics, 2001.

Garvey, M. (1923). *The philosophy and opinions of Marcus Garvey: Or, Africa for the Africans*. Reprint as Compilation compiled by A. J. Garvey-Dover: The Majority Press, 1986.

Gassama, I. J. (2008). Africa and the politics of destruction: A critical re-evaluation of neo-colonialism and its consequences. *Oregon Review of International Law, 10*(2), 337–360.

Gruffydd-Jones, B. (2015). Le Malentendu: Remembering international relations with Jean-Marie Teno. *Alternatives: Global Local, Political, 40*(2), 133–155.

Harrison, G. (2004). *The world bank and Africa: The construction of governance states*. London: Routledge.

Jackson, R., & Rosberg, C. (1982). Why Africa's weak states persist: The empirical and the juridical in statehood. *World Politics, 35*(1), 1–24.

Jackson, R., & Rosberg, C. (1986). Sovereignty and underdevelopment: Juridical statehood in the African crisis. *Journal of Modern African Studies, 24*(1), 1–31.

Kaoma, K. (2012). Exporting the anti-gay movement. *The American Prospect, 23*(4), 44–50.

Kapoor, I. (2002). Capitalism, culture, agency: Dependency versus post-colonial theory. *Third World Quarterly, 23*(4), 647–664.

Kilberg, A. (2014). We the people: The original meaning of popular sovereignty. *Virginia Law Review, 100*(5), 1061–1109.

Langan, M. (2015). Budget support and Africa-European Union relations: Free market reform and neo-colonialism? *European Journal of International Relations, 21*(11), 101–121.

Leftwich, A. (1995). Bringing politics back in: Towards a model of the developmental state. *Journal of Development Studies, 31*(3), 400–427.

Lenin, V. (2010). *Imperialism: The highest stage of capitalism*. London: Penguin Classics.

Martin, G. (1982). Africa and the ideology of EurAfrica: Neo-colonialism or Pan-Africanism? *Journal of Modern African Studies, 20*(7), 221–238.

Meichtry, S., & Landauro, I. (2017, 7 February). French Presidential candidate fillon apologizes for employing wife. *The Wall Street Journal*.

Mkandawire, T. (2015). Neopatrimonialism and the political economy of economic performance in Africa: Critical reflections. *World Politics, 67*(3), 563–612.

Mwakikagile, G. (2010). *Nyerere and Africa: End of an era*. Pretoria: New Africa Press.

Ndlovu-Gatsheni, S. (2012). Fiftieth anniversary of decolonisation in Africa: A moment of celebration or critical reflection. *Third World Quarterly, 33*(1), 71–89.

Ndlovu-Gatsheni, S. (2013). *Empire, global coloniality and African subjectivity*. New York: Berghahn Books.

Nkrumah, K. (1963). *Africa must unite*. London: Heineman.

Nkrumah, K. (1965). *Neo-colonialism: The last stage of imperialism.* Sixth Printing—New York International Publishers, 1976.

Nyerere, J. (1978). Foreign troops in Africa. *Africa Report, 23*(4), 10–14.

Radice, H. (2008). The developmental state under global neoliberalism. *Third World Quarterly, 29*(6), 1153–1174.

Rodney, W. (1972). *How Europe underdeveloped Africa.* Dar es Salaam: Tanzania Publishing House.

Segal, A. (1964). Africa newly divided? *Journal of Modern African Studies, 2*(1), 73–90.

Shaw, T. M. (1982). Beyond neo-colonialism: Varieties of corporatism in Africa. *Journal of Modern African Studies, 20*(2), 239–261.

Tausch, A. (2010). Globalisation and development: The relevance of classical "Dependency" theory for the world today. *International Social Science Journal, 61*(202), 467–488.

Taylor, I. (2004). Blind spots in analysing Africa's place in world politics. *Global Governance, 10,* 411–417.

Touré, S. (1962). Africa's future and the world. *Foreign Affairs, 41,* 141–151.

Van Djik, A. (2009). Critical discourse studies: A sociocognitive approach. In R. Wodak & M. Meyer (Eds.), *Methods of Critical Discourse Analysis.* Second edition. (pp. 62–86). London: Sage.

Woddis, J. (1967). *An introduction to neo-colonialism.* London: Lawrence and Wishart.

CHAPTER 2

Neo-Colonialism and Foreign Corporations in Africa

INTRODUCTION

Nkrumah's writings on neo-colonialism identified two main sources of foreign co-optation and control. Namely, he focused on the role of multinational companies and foreign donors, such as the USA and Britain. In the case of foreign companies, Nkrumah argued that such entities entered into African territories and accumulated such economic clout that they could sway the political decision-making of host governments. He explained that foreign companies' initial presence within African states could be traced back to processes of (neo)colonial influence, often with the support of foreign states such as the USA (1965: 12–14). Nkrumah stressed that he (and African socialists like him) was not opposed to Africa's participation in global markets. Nor was he opposed to all forms of FDI (1965: 9). However, he did loudly condemn the role of certain foreign companies in entrenching forms of neo-colonial power in their dealings with 'sovereign' African countries.[1]

Accordingly, this chapter examines whether Nkrumah's writings on corporate power and neo-colonialism still bear relevance in the contemporary era of African development. As noted in the first chapter, many scholars are sceptical about the reliability of Nkrumah's analysis. In fact, many are squeamish about the very language of neo-colonialism, arguing that such discourse lends itself to polemic rather than to rational debate, and that it obstructs discussion of the misrule of African elites (see for instance Taylor (2004) on the culpabilities of African politicians). Many

© The Author(s) 2018
M. Langan, *Neo-Colonialism and the Poverty of 'Development' in Africa*, Contemporary African Political Economy,
https://doi.org/10.1007/978-3-319-58571-0_2

33

(neo)liberals, moreover, enthusiastically welcome FDI into Africa's strategic sectors, particularly oil, minerals and agribusiness. They claim that such investments bring new technologies into African countries, provide jobs for otherwise underemployed African citizens, and enhance the productivity of domestic agriculture, central to food security concerns (Moyo 2008). What negative elements exist in dealings between foreign companies and African governments are meanwhile pinpointed on the predatory behaviour of corrupt African politicians. Indeed, many imply that foreign companies are often the 'victim' of foul play and this negatively impacts upon the business investment climate (see for instance Fraser Institute [2017] on mining companies in African contexts).

In this context, the chapter first juxtaposes the warnings of Nkrumah with moralised language surrounding liberal analysis of FDI in strategic African sectors. This explores the ideational legitimation of such endeavours on the grounds of international 'development' and of pro-poor North–South relations. It engages liberal scholars who emphasise the positive potential of foreign investment and who lament the 'resource curse' which African governments apparently bring upon their citizenries. It also engages the language of certain foreign companies, notably in terms of agribusiness interests involved in the New Alliance for Food Security and Nutrition (NAFSN). The second section of the chapter then problematises these positive claims about 'development' in terms of the material impact of corporate interventions for African citizenries. It does this through examination of foreign investment in the oil sector, with particular focus on Ghana owing to its status as Nkrumah's home-nation. The third section of the chapter continues this critique through examination of foreign companies' investment into agribusiness activities. This explores 'land-grabs' associated with the NAFSN and the impact for local populations. The fourth section considers the meaning of the oil and agribusiness case studies for a critical understanding of neo-colonialism in the contemporary era of African relations with foreign corporations. It argues that much of Nkrumah's analysis remains relevant. Moreover, his work remains emancipatory in terms of its call for progressive action to support genuine, empirical forms of African sovereignty. The conclusion summarises these arguments and underscores the need to engage donor forms of influence in Chaps. 3 and 4.

FOREIGN CORPORATIONS FOR 'DEVELOPMENT' IN AFRICA?

Nkrumah did not oppose all forms of FDI into Africa. He emphasised that certain forms of external company involvement—when guided by the African state on a developmental model—could be beneficial for development (1965: 9). He emphasised, however, that newly independent African states should remain sovereign actors, particularly in the cultivation of Africa's natural resource wealth and its land assets. Having fought against old-style imperialism, Nkrumah knew too well the dangers of foreign corporations' potential exploitation of African resources and host communities. He highlighted how mining operations (for gold and other valuable raw materials) had historically worked to the advantage of the colonialists and not to that of African citizens themselves:

> Generally speaking, in spite of the exploration costs, which are written off for tax purposes anyway and many times covered by eventual profits, mining has proved a very profitable venture for foreign capital investment in Africa. Its benefits for the Africans on the other hand, despite all the frothy talk to the contrary, have been negligible. (1965: 13)

Even in the early years of independence in Africa, meanwhile, Nkrumah warned that certain foreign companies were engaging in neo-colonial forms of interactions with African territories. Namely, that they utilised their economic clout to sway the decision-making processes of African elites, to side with alternative elites should their demands not be met, and to mobilise foreign states (through lobbying) to assist the entrenchment of their business interests within Africa. In this context, Nkrumah advised that:

> Colonialism has achieved a new guise. It has become neo-colonialism, and neo-colonialism is fast entrenching itself within the body of Africa today through the consortia and monopoly combinations that are the carpet-baggers of the African revolt against colonialism and the urge for continental unity. (1965: 31)

In the place of such (neo)colonial patterns of trade and investment, Nkrumah advocated for the construction of (what today we term) developmental states in Africa. This, as discussed in more detail in Chap. 8, would be buttressed by a continental Union of African States. Economies of scale conducive to industrialisation and value addition would move African economies away from reliance upon the export of cash crops and minerals to Europe. Certain forms of FDI might be permissible, but only if subordinated and regulated in relation to the needs of developmental planning. In *Africa Must Unite*, he set out this vision of developmental success:

> there is absolutely no doubt that the key to significant industrialization of this continent of ours lies in a union of African states, planning its development centrally and scientifically through a pattern of economic integration. Such central planning can create units of industrialism related to the unit resources, correlating food and raw materials production with the establishment of secondary manufactures and the erection of those vital basic industries which will sustain large-scale capital development. (1963: 170)

Nkrumah's analysis inspired a number of critical authors to investigate this alleged corporate form of neo-colonialism in the first decades of African independence. Woddis (1967: 86) claimed that many foreign corporations extended a form of economic dominance—and rule—over African territories. His analysis underscored the intertwined nature of corporate and foreign donor influence in Africa:

> At the centre of all the activities of neo-colonialism lies its economic policies. These are directed to assisting the profit-making functions of the big monopolies, to providing the Western powers with the necessary economic power in the new States so as to be able to wield political influence over the governments there, and to foster a certain [growth] of capitalism.

Lanning and Mueller (1979) in a comprehensive analysis of mining activities in Africa pointed to the role of certain African elites in allying themselves to the resources of foreign multinationals. With parallels to debates about the comprador class within dependency theory, the authors explained that:

> These elites, accustomed to, and buttressed by, their intermediate role between international capital and national resources, have not been under such political pressure to increase the productivity of the agricultural sector, nor have they chosen to solve the unemployment problem by building up manufacturing industry. Rather they have expanded the government bureaucracy and the armed forces at the expense of productive investment in other sectors of the economy. (Lanning and Mueller 1979: 500)

Their analysis highlighted how exploitative forms of FDI might retard development (and developmental states) in African contexts. Rather than endow the nation with taxation revenues and employment, regressive interventions might provide private 'rents' for co-opted African elites beholden to foreign interests. These neo-colonial African leaders would maintain the status quo for foreign corporations, enriching themselves while neglecting the wider prosperity of the citizenry (on whose taxation they were no longer dependent). This echoed the work of Nkrumah (1965: xiv) who warned that unscrupulous leaders would align themselves to the interests of external business at the expense of long-term development in newly independent African states.

Interestingly, much of the current literature within African studies neglects analysis of the dual role of *both* corporations and African elites in maintaining regressive relations contrary to the achievement of 'development'. Many recent contributions to the 'resource curse' literature, for example, identify African governments as being almost the sole culprit for the ills of certain states, such as the DRC and (to a much lesser degree) Nigeria. Scholars such as Sachs and Warner, Collier, and Atkinson and Hamilton align themselves to the neo-patrimonialism literature, pinpointing the decisions of African leaderships for the misappropriation of resource rents (Hilson and Maconachie 2008: 59–61). This neo-patrimonialism lens is echoed within the official policy sphere in terms of global governance efforts to (apparently) improve the development opportunities of FDI into Africa. For instance, the Extractive Industries Transparency Initiative (EITI) underscores the need for democratic reform of African governments to ensure that predatory elites do not squander natural resource wealth. This EITI emphasis on the behaviour of African leaderships is viewed by critical scholars such as Hilson and Maconachie (ibid.) as an omission that occludes the culpability of foreign actors:

> In explaining why countries in sub-Saharan Africa dependent on mining and oil production are performing so poorly, [EITI] donors have tended to shy away from placing blame on the foreign companies that generally control operations, and from implicating Western parties in general.

Hilson and Maconachie also usefully explain how the academic literature dominant in African studies today shies away from critical analysis of the behaviours of foreign corporations:

> There is now a wealth of scholarly literature… that suggests the paradox of a resource curse in mineral- and oil-rich regions of sub-Saharan Africa is largely due to corruption within host countries. (ibid.)

In addition, they argue that companies value their participation in the EITI programme for the very fact that it downplays their own role in questionable extractive operations (and concomitant 'market externalities') while emphasising the culpability of African governments for any social or environmental consequences of foreign investments.

Many foreign companies themselves, meanwhile, actively utilise a language of 'development' that portrays their interventions into African strategic economic sectors as opportunities for poverty reduction and for social progress. In terms of the EITI scheme, for instance, its participants—including Royal Dutch Shell and Total—emphasise that they are not only committed to tackling corruption issues, but that their presence in Africa positively facilitates economic modernisation and social development:

> Our operations generate revenue through taxes and royalties for governments… These funds can help support a country's economy and contribute to local development. We believe greater transparency in payments to governments… We work openly with governments on matters of taxes and royalties. We are a founder and board member of the Extractive Industries Transparency Initiative (EITI). This initiative requires both governments and companies to disclose revenues received from oil and mineral activities. (Royal Dutch Shell cited in EITI 2017)

This 'development' language is echoed within segments of the current scholarly literature. Many (neo)liberals emphasise that foreign companies investing into agribusiness and other lucrative sectors may bring about modernisation, job creation and tax revenue (Moyo 2008; Barrientos et al. 2011; Gereffi and Lee 2016). This perspective aligns with the Post-Washington Consensus and its recent policy endeavours, such as the UN Sustainable Development Goals (SDGs). The Post-Washington Consensus—supported by major donors and corporations—emphasises that private sector development (PSD) and foreign investment facilitates social prosperity in developing countries. Poorer states must open themselves to the opportunities of FDI and liberalise vis-à-vis imports entering their country from overseas. In a departure from the earlier

Washington Consensus dominant in the 1980s and 1990s, however, developing countries will be given Aid for Trade to ensure that pro-poor forms of development are achieved within a level-playing field. The Post-Washington Consensus will 'make markets work the poor' and put developing countries into the 'driver's seat of reform'. This is in recognition of concerns about the social impact of 'big bang' liberalisation pursued in the 'lost decade' of the Washington Consensus (Stiglitz; Fine). Global governance initiatives such as the EITI and the NAFSN will ostensibly ensure that African countries realise the social potential of free markets in the Post-Washington Consensus.

There are, however, significant grounds on which to contest such positive visions of foreign investment into extractive industries (as governed by the EITI), and African agribusiness (under the NAFSN). In both these spheres, there are serious concerns about the conduct of foreign companies—whether from the West or from newly emerging economies such as China. Accordingly, the next section considers these concerns in the context of oil production. Thereafter, the chapter examines the negative repercussions of certain forms of foreign investment into agriculture as part of the NAFSN, with focus on 'land-grabs'. These sections together help us to consider the current relevance of Nkrumah's warnings about a corporate form of neo-colonialism affecting African development.

AFRICAN OIL AND FOREIGN MULTINATIONALS

The oil sector in Africa is an interesting case for the analysis of FDI and its 'development' merits. Many liberal scholars have welcomed the opportunity for African countries to enact a Norwegian model of petrodollar development. Others, meanwhile, have decried neo-patrimonial rule in countries such as Nigeria and the DRC. Neo-patrimonialism is largely blamed for the 'resource curse'—the apparent paradox that resource-rich African countries fail to achieve economic development. These Afro-pessimists also point to resource abundance as a cause for civil strife and violent conflict within the affected African nations themselves (Taylor 2008; Collier and Hoefller 2005).

However, a critical stance interested in the concept of neo-colonialism can help us to rethink the contours of debate surrounding oil extraction in African economies. Engagement with Nkrumah can help us to consider the relative omission of the role of foreign companies within the current analyses of mal-development that Hilson and Maconachie (2008) identify. The case of recently discovered Ghanaian oil is of particular interest—especially given this country's status as the nation in which Nkrumah rose to power in the throes of the anti-colonial struggle. Ghana in the 1950s and early 1960s was seen as a guiding light within the wider pan-African movement. In the contemporary era, Ghana retains a symbolic status given its apparent democratic credentials in West Africa. It was to Ghana that the newly elected President Obama paid his first African visit. The nation remains at the centre of international debates surrounding the challenge of 'development' in Africa.

The oil industry, meanwhile, has been hailed as a great opportunity for Ghanaians to tackle their reliance on energy imports. It is also seen as an opportunity for the creation of large numbers of skilled jobs, particularly in relation to the offshore Jubilee Fields which fall within Ghanaian waters. In this context, the presence of US and Anglo-Irish oil companies—Kosmos and Tullow (respectively)—with their technological expertise is seen as a positive for the country and its social trajectory. Indeed, many Ghanaians praised God for having delivered them this resource when Kosmos first announced that its exploration in the Ghanaian maritime area had yielded positive results. The then President Kufuor announced that Ghana would 'fly' now that it had discovered oil (McCaskie 2008: 323).

Kosmos—as the leading company in the Ghanaian oil sector—emphasises its on-going commitment to the wellbeing of the Ghanaian people. Its corporate activities will not merely focus upon profit generation but will apparently respect the aspirations of the Ghanaians to better their social and economic standing. A company report from 2014 explains that:

> Some people believe oil and gas companies focus their efforts solely on what happens below the earth's surface. At Kosmos, we've made a choice to operate differently. We recognise that delivering lasting benefits to local communities and developing mutual trust with host governments is just as important as operating competently below the ground… [we aim to be] a force for good in our host countries and create a positive legacy. (Kosmos 2014: 4)

This positive development language is echoed by its Anglo-Irish counterpart, Tullow (2015: 5–6):

As an African-focused oil company, we also recognise the importance of resource-led economic growth in helping to alleviate poverty. The countries where we operate have contributed little to man-made climate change and understandably want to develop their natural resources, as they seek to drive economic development. We need to play our part in trying to ensure that resource revenues help these countries to diversify their economies and to promote sustainable and inclusive economic growth.

In particular, Tullow (2015: 6) makes clear that it is opposed to all forms of bribery, corruption and fraud in its dealings with host governments:

A strong commitment to ethics and compliance has always been part of the way that we do business. Forming an Ethics and Compliance sub-Committee underlines our zero-tolerance approach to bribery, corruption and fraud.

Both of these major foreign investors in Ghanaian oil therefore make clear their commitment to the development of the country and to principles of social justice in their African operations.

An examination of the Ghanaian oil sector soon leads, however, to questions as to whether such FDI is in fact a boon to progressive development or, alternatively, whether the Ghanaian people are being exploited within forms of North–South relations once outlined by Nkrumah. In particular, the Kufuor government—in office during the discovery of oil in 2006—appears to have come to iniquitous arrangements with foreign oil interests. Most notably, the Kufuor government did not come to a Production Sharing Agreement (PSA) with the foreign oil companies as is standard international practice. Instead, it signed what is termed a Hybrid Model Concession which awarded individual oil blocks to specific oil companies for extractive activities. Domestic Ghanaian civil society bodies such as the Ghana Institute of Governance and Security (GIGS) estimate that this failure cost the Ghanaian state approximately $4 billion in the first 4 years of oil production (The Chronicle 2014). Citing the World Bank's figures, GIGS explain that:

Ghana would have earned US$6.428 billion in 4 years and over US$60 billion from the entire production life of the Jubilee fields by adopting pure PSA as against the US$2.75 billion in 4 years, and US$19.2 billion estimated by the World Bank under the current prevailing system. (ibid.)

Interestingly, in terms of the concept of neo-colonialism, there are also apparent claims that Kosmos utilised ties with the innocuously named E.O. Group to secure its oil licence. The E.O. Group, named after its founders Dr. Kwame Barwuah Edusei and George Owusu, apparently played a pivotal role in cementing relations between Kosmos and the Ghanaian government (The Enquirer 2010). Indeed, it is claimed that the E.O. Group successfully negotiated Kosmos' inclusion on an oil licence only 3 days after informing the Ghanaian National Petroleum Company (GNPC) and the Ministry of Energy of its liaison with this US firm. The Enquirer (2010) notes that this 3 days period 'was a record time, as petroleum agreements generally are preceded by due diligence and hard negotiations to maximize benefits for Ghana'. Significantly, one of the founding members of the E.O. Group is said to have had close personal relations with key officials within the Kufuor administration, including the President and the Energy minister. For this liaison role, the E.O. Group apparently received handsome payments from Kosmos as well as shares within the oil block. The Enquirer (2010) notes that:

> The E.O. Group, a company whose 3.5% interest in Ghana's first oil find is estimated to be worth over $200 million, never operated any visible office… whose promoters are about to face trial for various acts, which are said to border on criminality… The Police Criminal Investigation Department (CID) say they have uncovered a web of shocking criminal conduct involving the promoters of the Group and some top government officials connected to former President John Kufuor.

These apparent linkages between Kosmos, the E.O. Group and the Kufuor government in the granting of a lucrative oil deal are supported by Phillips et al. (2016). The authors conducted interviews with key personnel including GNPC staff and found allegations that:

> Kosmos had used openly acknowledged personal connections between the EO Group and President Kufuor to negotiate a petroleum agreement on what GNPC personnel considered to be 'scandalously generous terms'… [the] agreement had been designed to be favourable for international investors, including a significant reduction in both royalties for the government and the participating stake held by GNPC… the specific petroleum agreement offered to Kosmos was on considerably more generous terms than those offered to other international oil companies. (2016: 30)

Kosmos—in this fashion—apparently obtained a multi-million pound oil concession through connections with the E.O. Group and, through it, the government. This recalls certain warnings of Nkrumah about the role of foreign companies to denude the empirical sovereignty of an African nation over its natural resources through lubrication of elite networks.

The case of Kosmos, however, also demonstrates the partial ability of certain African leaders to stall the advance of foreign corporations even within neo-colonial forms of North–South relations. Kufuor's successor—John Atta Mills—successfully impeded the transfer of Kosmos' oil stake to the larger US firm, ExxonMobil. According to Phillips et al. (2016: 31–32), the President was angered by the manner in which ExxonMobil officials apparently presented this transfer as a fait accompli. The President and the wider Ghanaian government, therefore, asserted their right to first refusal on Kosmos' sale of its oil properties. Specifically, the Ghanaian government entertained interest from a Chinese state enterprise that offered to partner with Ghana's own oil corporation (the GNPC) to take over control of production from Kosmos. The ability of the Atta Mill's government to apparently balance US corporate interests with that of Chinese oil corporations meant that Kosmos called off the sale, and ExxonMobil withdrew from the proposed transfer. Kosmos thus maintained its original presence in Ghana, collecting lucrative oil revenues based upon the deal secured with the assistance of the E.O. Group. Nevertheless, an apparent affront to the dignity of President Atta Mills was prevented through appeals to another foreign power, namely China (ibid.). The fundamental power imbalance of foreign corporations gaining riches from African natural resources was not redressed, but the Ghanaian leadership (in this instance) were able to utilise the apparent threat of a Chinese intervention to express displeasure to their US partners.

It should be noted that ExxonMobil and major oil corporations in the USA had long expressed an interest in African oil resources, and had lobbied US government personnel to diversify oil resources into West Africa. ExxonMobil placed an advertisement in the *New York Times* on 1st November 2001 proclaiming 'Africa: A Wealth of Opportunity'. This coincided with the third biennial US–Africa Business Summit 'a meeting of industry and government leaders on American business opportunities in Africa' (Turshen 2002: 1). Furthermore, US oil interests founded the African Oil Policy Initiative Group (AOPIG) in 2002, which lobbied the US Congress on the need to diversify US oil stakes into the 'New Gulf' in West Africa. The AOPIG recommended that the US navy should play a role in securing US interests in the region (McCaskie 2008: 316). The ambitions of large corporations, such as ExxonMobil, to enter the Ghanaian oil sector should thus be contextualised in terms of the broader military and security interests of the USA. The dispute over the selling of Kosmos stakes should also be understood in this wider context of US geopolitical interests. Ghana's decision not to press ahead with the Chinese takeover of Kosmos' oil resources, and to allow this US company to retain its original stake (even after its proposal to sell to ExxonMobil) should be understood in the wider ambit of US–Ghana bilateral ties.

It should also be noted that Chinese interests have successfully been pursued in other instances with regard to Ghanaian oil. In 2012, Ghana's President—John Dramani Mahama—agreed a $3 billion loan from the Chinese Development Bank Corporation, promising to deliver China 13,000 barrels of oil per day. The President also agreed a $850 million deal for the China Petroleum and Chemical Corporation to partner with its Ghanaian counterpart for the construction of a major pipeline (Bloomberg 2012). Interestingly, this Sino-Ghanaian arrangement has met with fierce criticism on the part of Ghana's own citizenry, and even among certain politicians. For example, Kofi Adda—a member of parliament—condemned the fact that oil would be transferred directly over to the Chinese, claiming that this would 'surrender the nation's sovereignty to the Chinese bank'. On a popular Ghanaian social forum, meanwhile, citizens noted that their government had likely been offered side-payments by Chinese oil corporations, and the Chinese government. They doubted the benefit of such arrangements for Ghana's development. One such post commented: 'it is even suspected that our Leaders have dubiously manipulated the system to ensure a special cut for themselves directly or otherwise' (cited in Rupp 2013: 122–123). Another Ghanaian citizen meanwhile stated that:

> Giving out concessions to foreign oil companies is lazy, inefficient use of resources. So the oil will be extracted and sold, like gold and the other abundant minerals, profits will be made by these companies, and we will remain poor in the midst of abundant wealth…. We must act now, else we will continue to wallow in poverty. (ibid.)

Concerns are clearly present within Ghanaian society as a whole. Indeed, this citizen discourse relating to China in Africa reflects existing anxieties (and material problems) as they relate to African development. In certain instances—as in the case of Kosmos oil stocks—the presence of China might be utilised by certain African elites to counterbalance overt forms of power politics displayed by Western corporations such as ExxonMobil. Nevertheless, the emergence of China does not liberate Ghanaian society from the situation of neo-colonialism but instead entrenches it through new regressive linkages to the external.

Furthermore, there are apparent concerns that the Anglo-Irish oil company in Ghana—Tullow—has mobilised home state resources in support of its oil revenues in this West African context. There is concern that the UK's Department for International Development (DFID) has been apparently mobilised as a de facto arm of Tullow's long-term profit-making in Ghana. Notably, DFID (with an apparent view to Tullow's interests) has lent support to groups within Ghana to ensure the government's acquiescence to a new Oil Exploration and Production (E&P) Bill (Lungu 2016a). The E&P bill was passed in August 2016 and prolongs the situation in which oil companies may operate under the 'Hybrid System'—avoiding a more standard PSA. Moreover, the legislation grants the Minister for Energy discretionary power to bypass competitive tendering for new oil resources. In this context, DFID launched what it termed the Ghana Oil and Gas for Inclusive Gas (GOGIG) programme, which has done much to support the long-term viability of foreign corporate extraction. Indeed, as part of such initiatives, DFID allocated £1.9 million to the Ghana Petroleum Commission (GPC) (Lungu 2016b). It also allocated resources to two influential think tanks, the Natural Resource Governance Institute (NRGI) and the African Centre for Energy Policy (ACEP), for what DFID opaquely describes as 'specific advocacy related activities' (DFID 2015). Two of these organisations—ACEP and GPC—openly supported the new E&P bill, while NRGI remained supportive despite issuing certain caveats about the minister's discretionary power on tendering (The Herald 2016).

It should be stressed that these apparent concerns about the influence exerted by foreign oil corporations—directly in terms of their dealings with African governments—or indirectly in terms of their mobilisation of home state governance bodies (such as UK DFID)—are not confined to Ghana. There is widespread concern across Africa that oil corporations are extracting large quantities of natural resources (and profits) without due proceeds returning to local populations for 'development' (Acharya 2013; Cash 2012; Ackah-Baidoo 2012; Vokes 2012; Holterman 2014; Global Witness 2014). Moreover, cases of apparent corruption—as implied by certain commentators in their discussion of the E.O. Group—can be found in other country contexts. Tullow Oil, for instance, was apparently accused of corrupt practices in its dealings with the Ugandan government over that nation's discoveries. Interestingly, this allegation was implied by a corporate rival, Heritage Oil, who had been embroiled in a dispute with both Tullow and the Government of Uganda. Tullow have denied these claims and attribute them to forged documentation (The Telegraph 2013). Nevertheless, in the Ugandan situation, there are widespread concerns that foreign oil companies are operating at the expense of social and environmental standards. There is also concern that the administration of President Yoweri Museveni (while having obtained a PSA arrangement) is gaining largesse from the presence of foreign operators, particularly in terms of election spending in recent years. In addition, his government is seen to have militarised certain oil outlets on the pretext of defending resources. Many fear that this is a means by which the government, alongside foreign companies, can occlude transparency over the use of oil and to remove subsistence farmers from valuable land tracts (Vokes 2012: 309–310). Moreover, the PSA which Museveni has agreed with operators such as Tullow has not been publicly disclosed in terms of specific content. This goes against standard international practice and has raised questions as to the government's rationale for such secrecy (ibid.: 308).

It would seem from such oil scenarios that the warnings of Nkrumah (1965) about neo-colonial relationships between foreign corporations and certain African elites do bear credence in the contemporary era. Rather than omit consideration of the role of foreign companies in entrenching what might be termed 'underdevelopment', a critical engagement with cases such as Ghana and Uganda underscores that companies often *do play* a pivotal role in creating regressive conditions. Whether in terms of the alleged use of liaison outfits such as the E.O. Group, use of lobbying in the case of AOPIG, overtures to home state bodies (such as the US Congress or UK DFID), or the negotiation of lucrative Hybrid System arrangements (or indeed PSAs), oil companies do exert major influence on the outcomes of oil scenarios in Africa. Unfortunately, these scenarios often lead to the diminution of genuine state sovereignty and the perpetuation of poverty for ordinary citizens.

It is important to note, however, that these situations are not unique to the oil extractive industry. As the next section demonstrates, concerns about neo-colonialism are equally apparent in the case of foreign companies' investments into agriculture and land in African contexts.

African Agriculture and Corporate 'Land-Grabbing'

While extractive industries such as oil and mining are often the focus of debates surrounding the 'resource curse' and mal-development, equal attention should be paid to the situation of agribusiness and land. Critical engagements with foreign corporate power in Africa should explore the ways in which companies (such as SABMiller, Diageo, Monsanto, and Unilever) gain access to domestic agricultural systems, particularly in terms of fertile land for intensive agribusiness. In this context, there have been many recent civil society campaigns that have drawn attention to corporate 'land-grabs'. Namely, that foreign companies have negotiated land deals with African governments which lead to the displacement of indigenous communities (Borras et al. 2011; ActionAid 2015). Oftentimes, this is done in the name of 'development' and economic progress—with the implication that the indigenous villagers are backward and unproductive. This is despite the fact that subsistence agriculture in the traditional manner is the backbone of food security (GRAIN et al. 2014). Access to soil—and to local water resources (especially for fishermen)—is essential for the maintenance of food systems that feed the local populace. The entry of foreign agribusiness interests and the takeover of land resources is therefore a highly controversial act, one which threats the food security of local citizens.

In terms of a discussion of the concept of neo-colonialism, the role of foreign corporations within the NAFSN is particularly interesting to examine. Foreign corporations such as SABMiller moved in the aftermath of the World Food Crisis in 2008 to lobby donors for greater access to African agricultural systems (ActionAid 2015). This was promoted in the language of modernity, productivity and food security (Brooks 2016: 770). The World Food Crisis had apparently unveiled the stagnation of traditional African food systems. In the post-crisis phase, therefore, multinational corporations, development donors and African governments would partner together to upscale agribusiness ventures and bolster agricultural productivity. The World Bank, UK DFID, USAID and other Western donors came to enthusiastically back this corporate initiative, concurring with the need to enhance FDI on the basis of food security. An ActionAid report (2015) explains that the wider group of G8 states including the EU, the USA, Canada, Russia and Japan have:

> Committed $4.4 billion to the 10 [African] countries of the New Alliance... the G8 support... is part of a drive to secure larger agricultural markets and sources of supply in Africa for multinational corporations. New Alliance partners such as Monsanto, Diageo, SABMiller, Unilever, Syngenta have major commercial interests in Africa and close connections with Northern governments.

Importantly, the NAFSN discursively moralises foreign corporate involvement in Africa in relation to pro-poor development goals in its official policy statements. These communications—combined to that of the individual donors and participant companies—lay the ideational and discursive framework for the justification of enhanced FDI in Africa's food systems. The NAFSN (2014) website, for instance, declares that the scheme:

> is a shared commitment to achieve sustained inclusive, agriculture-led growth in Africa. Given the overwhelming importance of African agriculture in rural livelihoods and its enormous potential to bring people out of poverty, public investment in food security and agriculture has significantly increased... Agricultural transformation in Africa is a shared interest of the public and private sectors and presents a unique opportunity for a new model of partnership.

Via the language of public–private partnerships, job creation, economic growth, food security and 'development', the deeper involvement of companies such as Monsanto and Unilever in African agriculture is presented as a win–win outcome for all concerned. External companies are not seen merely as profit-driven entities concerned with the bottom-line, but also as altruistic partners concerned with the moral cause of African citizenries' social wellbeing.

Specifically, the NAFSN advocates the construction of agricultural corridors within African nations as part of this legitimising 'development' discourse. ActionAid (2015: 13) explains that these corridors (or staple-crop processing zones) are:

large areas of land that are earmarked for agribusiness. In these zones, companies are incentivised by host governments and supporting donors to establish their operations by a series of tax, regulatory and land incentives, as well as by new infrastructure (roads, railways, ports, irrigation, storage, processing facilities, etc). The projects focus mainly on agriculture, but also include forestry and mining. To ensure big business acquires these large tracts of land, governments are promoting reforms to change land tenure legislation.

The concept of agricultural corridors was apparently the 'brainchild of Yara', a major company involved in the fertiliser sector and actively involved in the foundation of the NAFSN (Pan Africanist Briefs 2014). The land transfers involved in such initiatives can entail massive tracks of fertile soil. Malawi alone has acquiesced to the release of 200,000 ha under the auspices of the NAFSN. The country's National Export Strategy, meanwhile, indicates that up to one million hectares may in fact be allocated to agribusiness and foreign corporations. This accounts for approximately 26% of Malawi's arable land (ActionAid 2015: 1).

Additionally, the implementation of the NAFSN involves the signing of formal Cooperative Framework Agreements (CFAs) between the participating African nations, the donor community and the founding foreign corporations. Ten African countries have currently signed up to the NAFSN and have undertook CFA negotiations—namely Ghana, Ethiopia, Tanzania, Mozambique, Burkina Faso, Senegal, Ivory Coast, Malawi, Benin and Nigeria (ibid.: 12). Raising concerns about a 'new scramble for Africa', each nation has been assigned a donor to lead in the NAFSN roll-out (Frynas and Paulo 2007). For instance, the oversight of the NAFSN in Nigeria has been entrusted to the UK government and DFID (McKeon 2014: 12). Crucially, the CFAs commit the host country to a number of reform measures that entrench earlier liberalisation undertaken in the Washington Consensus of the 1980s and 1990s (as well as liberalisation taken in the early 2000s as part of Post-Washington Consensus) (Oakland Institute 2016). This ensures, for example, that any private property rights associated with land corridors will be safeguarded by the host government. In some cases, there is also emphasis upon respect for Intellectual Property Rights (IPRs). This is particularly controversial in terms of 'seed sovereignty' and the activities of corporate actors such as Monsanto in asserting patents over certain seed configurations (ibid.: 12). The European Parliament (2015: 10) notably published a study questioning the deep reform expected within the CFAs under the NAFSN—with emphasis on these IPR clauses. Meanwhile, the individual companies (such as Syngenta) sign a Letter of Intent as part of the CFA under the NAFSN endeavour. This describes in detail their long-term investment plans for the African nation in question (McKeon 2014: 3–5).

It is these close connections between the participating corporations and the official donor community which are of particular interest for a modern study of the concept of neo-colonialism. Nkrumah indicated that foreign corporations would work in tandem with their home-nation state(s) to penetrate, and secure, African markets and resources. In the case of the UK and its main 'development' arm (DFID), these close connections are very apparent. Kiwanga (2014) notes that Unilever's external affairs director 'was previously at DFID and DFID's director of policy used to work for Unilever'. The World Development Movement (2014: 30) underscores these close connections between corporations and the UK government in even starker terms:

> Unilever board member Paul Walsh (chief executive of Diageo) is an advisor to the Department of Energy and Climate Change and a member of David Cameron's Business Advisory Group. Conservative MP Malcolm Rifkind is also a current board member and former overseas development minister and now Conservative life peer... Former home secretary and trade commissioner Leon Brittan was a board member between 2000 and 2010. Former minister for trade and competitiveness David Simon, now a Labour peer, was an adviser to Unilever and was vice chairman and senior independent director between 2006 and 2009. In addition, staff have moved between the company and government.

The role of the aforementioned company, Yara, moreover, demonstrates the way in which policy formulations derived from corporate headquarters can be successfully integrated into the official 'development' strategy of donor bodies such as UK DFID. There appears to be a blurring of the roles of companies and 'development' donors. Language of win–win cooperation and FDI has so permeated development discourse that this does not apparently raise questions of conflicts of interests. The corporate interest of Yara (and others) in establishing highly contested land

corridors within Africa is deemed fully compatible with poverty alleviation goals of 'development', and with the wellbeing of African peoples
themselves.

There are significant grounds to question whether the corporate
mobilisation of the New Alliance has in fact led to better conditions for
workers and villagers within the participating African countries. As mentioned, there are already major concerns about corporate 'land-grabs'—
that is, the construction of corridors that lead local people being denied
access to their natural resources. There are also widespread allegations
that villagers have been forcibly removed from so-called inactive land
tracts (McMichael 2015: 442). This has involved the use of state security
forces to effectively entrench the rights of foreign corporations and to
infringe the rights of local small-scale farmers. The World Development
Movement (2014: 37) notes that in the case of Ethiopia (a NAFSN
country) that:

> 375,000 hectares of land are being cleared to make way for sugar cane,
> palm oil, cotton and grain plantations... 260,000 people... are being
> evicted from their farmland... leaving them little option but to move to
> designated new villages and work on the plantations for low wages. Those
> people that have resisted have faced beatings, rape... intimidation, arrests
> and imprisonment. In order to force people to move, the military have
> prevented people from cultivating their land and destroyed crops and grain
> stores to cause hunger, then lured them to the new settlements with food
> aid.

Subsistence agriculture is deemed unproductive and, accordingly, the soil
is to be utilised by more 'able' agents—namely the companies involved
in the NAFSN project.

A comprehensive report on 'land grabbing' by GRAIN et al. (2014)
usefully points to the paradox of these activities being justified in via the
discourse of food security. The crops which NAFSN corporations prioritise are export cash crops, rather than foodstuffs for local consumption.
The use of the language of food security to moralise these 'land-grabbing' processes is thus wholly dubious:

> it is clear that these firms are not interested in the kind of agriculture
> that will bring us food sovereignty... One farmers' leader from Synérgie
> Paysanne in Benin sees these land grabs as fundamentally 'exporting

food insecurity' because they are about producing food for export markets, creating food insecurity for the producers. They are about answering some people's needs – for maize or money – by taking food production resources away from others. (GRAIN et al. 2014: 16)

Worryingly, research by Oxfam also indicates that foreign companies are deliberately targeting those nations which perform most poorly in terms of corruption indicators. There is the distinct implication, therefore, that certain of these 'land-grab' deals may not fully adhere to norms about transparency and legitimate revenue accumulation. Despite the development discourse of the NAFSN and its corporate-donor participants, there appears to be a situation in which foreign companies are exploiting the poor governance records of developing African countries. Oxfam (2013: 4) makes clear that:

Oxfam believes that investors actively target countries with weak governance in order to maximise profits and minimise red tape. Weak governance might enable this because it helps investors to sidestep costly and time-consuming rules and regulations, which, for example, might require them to consult with affected communities. Furthermore in countries where people are denied a voice, where business regulations are weak or non-existent, or where corruption is out of control it might be easier for investors to design the rules of the game to suit themselves.

These concerns are supported by Owen et al. (2015: 3) in a report for the London School of Economics. They argue that corporate investors in Zambia have not sought the necessary consent of local chiefs for land acquisitions. Instead, they have bypassed these local authorities by appealing to the Zambian government itself. Conversely, in Ghana, foreign companies have bypassed the national government in Accra and have gone directly to local chiefs to secure land acquisitions. The authors claim that 'bribery by investors has been used to motivate chiefs to neglect the rules [which emphasise the need to respect the wellbeing of local communities] in allocating land' (ibid.).

It is important to emphasise, however, that the NAFSN and the involvement of (Western) corporations such as Monsanto, Diageo, and SABMiller in African agribusiness is not an isolated case. Instead, the concerns raised by the NAFSN point to wider trends in Africa, not always involving traditional Western actors. Notably, there appears to be a rise in investments from Middle Eastern countries, as well as India and China. Middle Eastern nations—and their corporations—are particularly keen to future-proof themselves from water scarcity problems (Robertson and Pinstrup-Andersen 2010: 273). Many argue that land acquisitions may be more about access to water resources in the longer term than about crop production and agribusiness profits (GRAIN 2012). Similar to the involvement of Chinese oil companies in Ghana, the investment of Middle Eastern corporations into Africa again raises the prospect of a wider neo-colonialism. Or in alternative language, it raises the prospect of a competitive 'scramble for Africa' involving many nation states and their constituent corporations. This of course may pose certain short-term benefits for African elites in terms of negotiations and balancing between foreign actors (as occurred in the case of Kosmos oil). Nevertheless, it does little to redress the fundamental inequalities that characterises African countries' engagement with external parties on issues of extraction and land purchase. African sovereignty over raw materials and land resources would appear to be further undermined by a proliferation of 'development' corporate actors and foreign donor bodies, with regressive consequences for ordinary citizens.

CORPORATE ACTIVITIES AS NEO-COLONIALISM IN AFRICA?

The preceding discussion of the oil sector and agribusiness (the NAFSN) raises questions about inequalities in relations between African countries and corporate 'partners'. The oil industry scenario in Ghana demonstrates the way in which governments, such as that of President Kufuor, may agree regressive commercial pacts which are detrimental to the national interest. Kufuor's signing of a Hybrid System arrangement denied Ghana its rightful revenues from oil reserves as compared to a standard PSA. This is corroborated by the World Bank's own figures and drawn upon by civil society protestors who resent the status quo enjoyed by companies such as Kosmos. The apparent intermediary role of the E.O. Group, meanwhile, demonstrates how outfits close to the presidency may exert (undue) influence over such tendering processes. The involvement of DFID, moreover, in terms of the E&P Bill (containing a discretionary clause to exempt the Energy Minister from need to send oil resources out to competitive tender) raises serious alarm about the relationships between foreign corporations and ostensible development donors. The role of the Chinese oil entities, furthermore, raises serious concerns about a proliferation of 'partners' amidst a new scramble for Africa's resources.

The discussion of the NAFSN and the role of agribusiness interests in mobilising Western donor and wider G8 support for entry into African agricultural sectors also raises several important points about inequalities in the global system. The impact of 'land-grabs' secured under CFAs raises alarm about abuse of local villagers deemed insufficiently productive (Oram 2014: 10–11). The alleged use of bribery by certain corporations in their dealings with chiefs and national governments also draws attention to unequal power plays which exist to undermine the sovereign interest of African citizenries in the fair cultivation of their natural resources. Meanwhile, the close connection between personnel situated in the leading corporations and government agencies (such as David Cameron's Business Advisory Group) underscores how corporate and donor interests may become blurred in terms of 'development' interactions with African countries. Furthermore, the entry of Middle Eastern and Asian nations into the 'land-grab' scenarios unfolding in Africa lends itself to another dynamic. Namely, the proliferation of 'development' actors keen to secure their own segment of African resources (often to avoid future water scarcity in their own home countries).

In this context, it is wholly pertinent to ask whether Nkrumah's (1965) concept of neo-colonialism should be reclaimed for contemporary scholarly purposes. While not usually invoked within polite academic conferences and leading journals, the concept does guard against an excessive focus upon the supposed nepotism of African leaders themselves. Nkrumah's analysis—while recognising the potential role of co-opted local elites in maintaining systems of neo-colonialism—sheds critical light upon the actions of foreign corporations and their respective donor agencies (whether UK DFID, USAID, the China Development Bank, and so forth). His warnings about neo-colonialism draw attention to the ways in which foreign corporations seek to maintain colonial patterns of trade and production—namely the export of lucrative raw materials and cash crops from Africa to their home nations. Meanwhile, his analysis also rightly points (albeit not in sufficient depth) to the ideational elements behind this current phase of neo-colonial intervention. Indeed, Nkrumah warned of how development discourses and the language of aid might be utilised to justify (and moralise) new forms of external intervention in Africa despite the detrimental material impact such interventions might have for workers and host communities. This appears a pertinent lesson when examining current phenomenon such as the NAFSN and its impact on subsistence smallholders.

It does seem a peculiar omission, therefore, that Nkrumah's analysis of neo-colonialism remains largely absent from polite scholarly enquiry into Africa's current situation vis-à-vis corporations in sectors such as oil and agribusiness. While Ghanaian citizens themselves align to a critique of neo-colonial intervention in their own discussions about foreign involvement in their oil sector, this discourse remains somewhat taboo within Western academic circles (unless when used to critique Chinese interventions, discussed in Chap. 4). There is in fact a distinct scholarly squeamishness about invocations of Nkrumah, and there is a suspicion that his analysis is a vulgar form of Marxism that is redundant in a post-Cold War setting. The preceding analysis and its 'snapshot' focus on oil and agribusiness points to how the concept may shed light on current controversies in a more fruitful fashion than those accounts which focus preponderantly on the so-called neo-patrimonial regime in African states. Again, this is not to deny that certain African politicians and their civil servants may be implicated in systems of external relations that work to perpetuate conditions of poverty. It is, however, to assert a greater need to engage with the realities of corporate conduct in Africa. It is also to assert a greater need to engage with the realities of donor 'development' agendas, as they pertain to schemes such as the New Alliance and its agribusiness focus.

Furthermore, Nkrumah's focus upon how foreign corporations and governments may work in tandem to subvert empirical sovereignty in African countries opens up necessary conversations about strategies for change. As noted in the first chapter, Nkrumah identified the need for pan-African endeavours to nullify some of the worst effects of neo-colonialism. Rather than depending upon 'global governance' initiatives such as the EITI, for instance, African governments might do better to pursue pan-African solutions to labour rights violations, environmental damage, and resource exhaustion as brought about by certain unscrupulous corporate entities. Rather than engaging in schemes such as the NAFSN, moreover, African governments might do well to establish pan-African development programmes aimed at supporting African agriculture, while supporting the rights of traditional smallholders in rural locales. Nkrumah's work also helps to immunise scholars (and civil society groups) from 'common sense' adherence to the development narratives propounded by donor agencies such as UK DFID and their corporate benefactors. The scepticism which his work invokes with regards to aid monies, for example, lends itself to a critical stance in the examination of the material impact of so-called 'pro-poor' actions in Africa. Nkrumah's work would appear to offer much potential for a reinvigoration of debates surrounding corporate (and donor) power in relations with apparently sovereign African countries.

CONCLUSION

This chapter has examined the concept of neo-colonialism in terms of corporate power within Africa. Nkrumah focused (rightly) on the dual role of foreign companies and donor development partners in entrenching unequal power relationships after the formal end of Empire. He argued that foreign companies could utilise their economic largesse to co-opt certain African elites, to ensure that they sided with their benefactors rather than with the long-term interests of their own citizenries. Moreover, he alluded to the manner in which companies could mobilise foreign governments to assist their business stakes in strategic African sectors. Foreign business enterprise could work to perpetuate neo-colonial forms of North–South relations in which African citizens were denied the fruits of the fair cultivation of their natural resources.

The above focus on the oil sector and on agribusiness demonstrates how Nkrumah's work may find relevance in a Post-Washington Consensus setting. Rather than being condemned to relative obscurity, his analysis deserves much closer scrutiny (and respect) within current academic circles. Citizens in countries such as Ghana when facing the prospect of lost oil revenues through disadvantageous 'Hybrid System' deals with US and Anglo-Irish companies realise the relevance of Nkrumah's critique. As they do also when faced with the prospect of Chinese loans lubricating their government, on the condition of the direct export of vast quantities of oil to their foreign benefactor. Critical scholars concerned with emancipatory movements should likewise engage Nkrumah more substantially when seeking to describe, and to explain, the current power strategies of foreign corporations in Africa. Nkrumah's analysis can shed a critical light upon the apparent 'new scramble' for African resources, as undertaken by corporations from the USA, UK, China, and Middle Eastern states (among many others).

It is perhaps important to restate, however, that Nkrumah himself did not deny the need for certain regulated, limited forms of FDI in African countries. What he did call for was forms of intervention which were tied into genuine developmental state strategies, overseen by sovereign state ministries, and pursued in a fashion that preserved the wealth of Africa for Africans. This is clearly a form of development that is not found within programmes such as the NAFSN, or in terms of current oil arrangements in Ghana. It is also important to emphasise that Nkrumah did not examine the role of corporations in isolation from their donor counterparts. As this chapter has implied, there is a close connection between foreign corporations and donor institutions as they collectively act to pursue (and impose) certain policy preferences in Africa. The next two chapters therefore examine donor institutions and their challenge to African empirical sovereignty in the case of 'traditional' Western donors (such as the EU and UK DFID) and in the case of 'emerging powers' (such as China and Turkey). These chapters together raise further questions as to the potential relevance of the concept of neo-colonialism for making sense of mal-development in Africa today.

NOTE

1. For instance, he condemned mining companies which from his perspective exploited both Africa's natural resources and its ill-treated labourers.

REFERENCES

Acharya, U. (2013). Globalization and hegemony shift: Are states merely agents of corporate capitalism? *Boston College Law Review, 54*, 937–969.

Ackah-Baidoo, A. (2012). Enclave development and "Offshore corporate social responsibility": Implications for oil-rich Sub-Saharan Africa. *Resources Policy, 37*(2), 152–159.

ActionAid. (2015). *New alliance, new risk of land grabs: Evidence from Malawi, Nigeria, Senegal and Tanzania*. London: ActionAid.

Barrientos, S., Gereffi, G., & Rossi, A. (2011). Economic and social upgrading in global production networks—opportunities and challenges. *International Labour Review, 150*, 319–340.

Bloomberg. (2012). *Ghana signs $1 Billion loan with China for natural gas project*. Available at: https://www.icafrica.org/en/news-events/infrastructure-news/

article/ghana-signs-1-billion-loan-with-china-for-natural-gas-project-3080/. Accessed 3 July 2017.

Borras, S., Hall, R., Scoones, I., White, B., & Wolford, W. (2011). Towards a better understanding of global land grabbing: An editorial introduction. *Journal of Peasant Studies, 38*(2), 209–216.

Brooks, S. (2016). Inducing food insecurity: Financialisation and development in the post-2015 era. *Third World Quarterly, 37*(5), 768–780.

Cash, A. (2012). Corporate social responsibility and petroleum development in Sub-Saharan Africa: The case of Chad. *Resources Policy, 37*(2), 131–260.

The Chronicle. (2014, November 11). Exposed: $9.35 oil cash in foreign hands. *The Chronicle.* Available online at. http://www.ghanaweb.com/GhanaHomePage/NewsArchive/Exposed-935bn-oil-cash-in-foreign-hands-334332. Accessed 9 Feb 2017.

Collier, P., & Hoeffler, A. (2005). Resource rents, governance and conflict. *Journal of Conflict Resolution, 49*(4), 625–633.

DFID. (2015). *UK aid: Tackling global challenges in the national interest.* London: DfID.

EITI. (2017). *Royal Dutch shell.* Available online at. https://eiti.org/supporter/royal-dutch-shell-plc. Accessed 9 Feb 2017.

Gereffi, G., & Lee, J. (2016). Economic and social upgrading in global value chains and industrial clusters: Why governance matters. *Journal of Business Ethics, 133*(1), 25–38.

The Enquirer. (2010, January 20). The E.O. group's darkest secrets. *The Enquirer.* Available online at: http://www.ghanaweb.com/GhanaHomePage/NewsArchive/artikel.php?ID=175414. Accessed 9 Feb 2017.

European Parliament. (2015). *Study: The new alliance for food security and nutrition in Africa.* Brussels: European Parliament. Available online at: http://www.europarl.europa.eu/RegData/etudes/STUD/2015/535010/EXPO_STU(2015)535010_EN.pdf. Accessed 9 Feb 2017.

Fraser Institute. (2017). *Annual survey of mining companies, 2016.*

Frynas, J. G., & Paulo, M. (2007). A new scramble for African oil? Historical, political and business perspectives. *African Affairs, 106*(423), 229–251.

Global Witness. (2014). *A good deal better? Uganda's secret oil contracts explained.*

GRAIN. (2012). *Squeezing Africa dry: Behind every land grab is a water grab.* Barcelona: GRAIN.

GRAIN, Martinez-Alier, J., Temper, L., Munguti, S., Matiku, P., Ferreira, H., Soares, W., Porto, M. F., Raharinirina, V., Haas, W., Singh, S. J., Mayer, A. (2014). *The many faces of land grabbing: Cases from Africa and Latin America* (EJOLT Rep. No. 10), pp. 1–93. Barcelona: GRAIN.

The Herald. (2016, August 8). Develop regulations on discretionary powers in oil industry—Dr. Manteaw. *The Herald.* Available online at: http://

theheraldghana.com/develop-regulations-on-discretionary-powers-in-oil-industry-dr-manteaw/. Accessed 9 Feb 2017.

Hilson, G., & Maconachie, R. (2008). "Good governance" and the extractive industries in Sub-Saharan Africa. *Mineral Processing and Extractive Metallurgy Review, 30*(1), 52–100.

Holterman, D. (2014). The biopolitical war for life: Extractivism and the Ugandan oil state. *The Extractive Industries and Society, 1*(1), 28–37.

Kiwanga, G. (2014). Western corporations carve up Africa. *This is Africa*. 1st April 2014.

Kosmos. (2014). *Positive impact—corporate social responsibility report.* Available at: http://www.perotmuseum.org/media/files/Newsroom/2015/2015-07-09_Kosmos_Energy_Corporate_Responsibility_Report_2014.pdf. Accessed 3 July 2017.

Lanning, G., & Mueller, M. (1979). *Africa undermined: Mining companies and the underdevelopment of Africa.* Harmondsworth: Penguin.

Lungu, N. (2016a, July 4). This Mahama-Dagadu-Buah 2016 E&P bill is a vulture bill for oil companies. *The Voiceless.* Available online at. http://thevoicelessonline.com/6388-2/. Accessed 9 Feb 2017.

Lungu, N. (2016b, August 13). Mahama loses $6 Billion of Ghana's oil money and still claims "Remarkable economic achievements". *Ghana Web.* Available online at. http://www.ghanaweb.com/GhanaHomePage/features/artikel.php?ID=462322&comment=0#com. Accessed 9 Feb 2017.

McCaskie, T. (2008). The United States, Ghana and oil: Global and local perspectives. *African Affairs, 107*(428), 313–332.

McKeon. (2014). *The new alliance for food security and nutrition: A coup for corporate capital?* Amsterdam: Transnational Institute.

McMichael, P. (2015). The land question in the food sovereignty project. *Globalizations, 12*(4), 434–451.

Moyo, D. (2008). *Dead aid.* London: Allen Lane.

NAFSN. (2014). *About.* Available online at. https://www.new-alliance.org/about. Accessed 9 Feb 2017.

Nkrumah, K. (1963). *Africa must unite.* London: Heineman.

Nkrumah, K. (1965). *Neo-colonialism: The last stage of imperialism.* Sixth Printing—New York International Publishers, 1976.

Oakland Institute. (2016). *The unholy alliance: Five western donors shape a pro-corporate agenda for African agriculture.* Oakland: Oakland Institute.

Oram, J. (2014). *The great land heist: How the world is paving the way for corporate land grabs.* Johannesburg: ActionAid International.

Owen, T., Vanmulken, M., & Duale, G. (2015). *Land and political corruption in Sub-Saharan Africa.* London: London School of Economics.

Oxfam. (2013). Poor governance, good business. *Oxfam Media Briefing*, Ref: 03/2013, 7th February 2013. London: Oxfam.

Pan Africanist Briefs. (2014, April 4). Unilever, Monsanto take over African land and agriculture. *Pan Africanist Briefs*. Available at. https://www.newsghana. com.gh/unilevermonsanto-take-african-land-agriculture/. Accessed 9 Feb 2017.

Phillips, J., Haliwood, E., & Brooks, A. (2016). Sovereignty, the "Resource Curse" and the limits of good governance: A political economy of oil in Ghana. *Review of African Political Economy, 43*(147), 26–42.

Robertson, B., & Pinstrup-Andersen, P. (2010). Global land acquisition: Neo-colonialism or development opportunity? *Food Security, 2*(3), 271–283.

Rupp, S. (2013). Ghana, China and the politics of energy. *African Studies Review, 56*(1), 103–130.

Taylor, I. (2004). Blind spots in analysing Africa's place in world politics. *Global Governance, 10*, 411–417.

Taylor, I. (2008). Sino-African relations and the problem of human rights. *African Affairs, 107*(426), 63–87.

The Telegraph. (2013, March 22). Tullow oil apologies to Ugandan government over bribery allegations. *The Telegraph*. Available at: http://www.telegraph. co.uk/finance/newsbysector/energy/oilandgas/9949319/Tullow-Oil-apologises-to-Ugandan-government-over-bribery-allegations.html. Accessed 9 Feb 2017.

Tullow. (2015). *Corporate responsibility report: creating shared prosperity*. Available at: https://www.tullowoil.com/Media/docs/default-source/5_sustainabil-ity/tullow-oil-2015-corporate-responsibility-report.pdf?sfvrsn=2. Accessed 3 July 2017.

Turshen, M. (2002). Introduction to the African oil development debates. *Association of Concerned African Scholars, 64*, 1–5.

Vokes, R. (2012). The politics of oil in Uganda. *African Affairs, 111*(443), 303–314.

Woddis, J. (1967). *An introduction to neo-colonialism*. London: Lawrence and Wishart.

World Development Movement. (2014). *Carving up a continent: How the UK government is facilitating the corporate takeover of African food systems*. London: World Development Movement.

CHAPTER 3

Neo-Colonialism and Donor Interventions: Western Aid Mechanisms

INTRODUCTION

Neo-colonialism as a concept usefully focuses upon both corporate and donor forms of state penetration. As articulated by Nkrumah (1965: xv), foreign external influence—and control—may be exerted via forms of aid-giving. Donor aid is not necessarily a form of altruistic largesse (although in certain humanitarian scenarios it may well be) but can very often act as a lubricant for neo-colonial systems of policy co-optation. In this context, the chapter examines Western donor aid-giving to better understand whether Nkrumah's critique retains relevance in a modern understanding of 'development' interventions in Africa. It does this by focussing upon three forms of Western aid—namely traditional forms of project aid aimed at discrete policy initiatives; budget support whereby aid is directed towards support of government programmes; and so-called 'blending' aid initiatives whereby aid is combined to private sector resources to maximise poverty reduction. In this third category of aid, the chapter highlights the role of Development Finance Institutions (DFIs) including the erstwhile Commonwealth Development Corporation (now rebranded simply as CDC) and the European Investment Bank (EIB).

Through examination of these aid modalities, the chapter questions whether aid monies are being used for poverty reduction as per the normative claims of the donors themselves. Western donors emphasise that the ultimate goal of aid-giving is to alleviate hardship in developing

© The Author(s) 2018
M. Langan, *Neo-Colonialism and the Poverty of 'Development' in Africa*, Contemporary African Political Economy,
https://doi.org/10.1007/978-3-319-58571-0_3

societies, and to generate growth and livelihoods conducive to a better quality of living. At times Western donors also emphasise that there is a 'win-win' aspect to aid-giving, namely that the donor state itself might accrue certain benefits from development co-operation (see for example DFID 2015; *The Economist* 2017). This is often discursively framed in terms of security or enhanced opportunities for future trade, since aid for economic development will spur poorer countries to further integrate into globalised markets. Nevertheless, there is a discursive emphasis on poverty reduction and on the need to assist vulnerable citizens in Africa. Through critical interrogation of these aid channels, however, this chapter draws attention to the ways in which aid may in fact exacerbate conditions of ill-being in African developing countries. Namely, that certain forms of project aid might result in resource extraction with negative consequences for local people and their environment. That budget support arrangements might denude policy sovereignty on the part of recipient governments, with deleterious consequences for the well-being of African citizenries. And that blending exercises—with heavy intervention from DFIs—might pose a barrier to poverty reduction, rather than act as a pro-poor stimulus for economic growth and development.

The discussion is structured as follows. The chapter first contextualises the conceptual emphasis on donor aid as part of the study of neo-colonialism. This highlights Nkrumah's own writings amidst other critical scholars who aired fears about the role of aid monies in denuding popular sovereignty in African countries recently freed from formal Empire. These writings indicate that radical Africanist writers have historically highlighted the possible strategic aims of foreign donors in capturing policy-making processes in African states. This discussion also highlights how more modern writers such as Dambisa Moyo (2008) have also raised concern about the impact of aid on African development. Nevertheless, the chapter indicates that these more contemporary critiques of aid often do more to blame the 'failings' of aid on the apparent neo-patrimonial behaviours of local elites, rather than to highlight the underlying commercial and political objectives of foreign donors. This omission on the part of writers such as Moyo is seen as a significant failure—one which can be remedied via focus upon the concept of neo-colonialism. The chapter, after this discussion, examines the three aid modalities and provides a reflection on the usages of neo-colonialism as critique.

AID-GIVING THROUGH A NEO-COLONIAL, AND A NEO-PATRIMONIAL, LENS

Nkrumah (1965) usefully alerted African nationalists to the possibilities of Western aid monies in denuding genuine political and economic sovereignty. Nkrumah indicated that aid money, if regulated and controlled by a developmental state, might be used for industrialisation and for economic progress. Nevertheless, he expressed real concerns that the reality of aid-giving would be to enhance Western donors' policy influence and de facto political control at the expense of the autonomy of local elites. Namely, certain neo-colonial elites in Africa—with parallels to the concept of the comprador class—would abdicate their responsibility to govern in the interest of local citizens. They would instead rely upon the securities of foreign aid and acquiesce to external demands not necessarily conducive to the well-being of local peoples. Moreover, Nkrumah (1965: xv) commented on how aid monies operate as a 'revolving credit' whereby Western governments essentially recoup their 'investment' through the bringing about of policy change in African countries conducive to their own economic and commercial interests.

Importantly, this emphasis on the role of aid money in cementing foreign economic interests has historically been echoed by a number of radical Africanist writers. Notably, the Chairman of the Organisation for African Unity (OAU, now the African Union) issued a strong rebuke to Western aid donors at the beginning of the roll-out of Washington Consensus policies in the early 1980s. With some prescience, given the social impact of Western-supported structural adjustment programmes (SAPs) in that decade, the Chairman indicated that:

> The economic aids given by these developed nations are more of a dehy-drating agent than an economic advancement catalyst. The strings attached to most of the aids given to African nations and the interest charged... [are a] noose on the neck of Africa and a double gain for these nations. (cited in Udofia 1984: 364)

In a similar vein, Woddis (1967: 89) indicated that aid monies would not only be used to bring about economic policy change conducive to the extraction of raw material wealth, but would also be used to fund infrastructure projects conducive to this 'robbery'. With certain parallels to modern Aid for Trade initiatives (discussed in more detail in Chap. 5), he indicated that Western governments subsidised their own companies' 'loot' of Africa via the construction of better roads, railways and ports (thereby assisting the export of valuable goods to Europe and the USA). Aid was not necessarily a benefit to local peoples, but rather helped to perpetuate colonial patterns of trade that facilitated capital accumulation in the donor country (ibid.).

However, while radical analyses of aid-giving are sometimes apparent in the modern literature (see for example, Bracking 2009 on DFIs), nevertheless the majority of writings in leading journals and conferences now tend towards a neo-patrimonial prism. As discussed in Chap. 1, this dominant paradigm highlights the role of African elites in the misrule of their own societies. Aid-giving—via extraversion—is seen to be largely initiated by the appeals of predatory African rulers who then utilise foreign resources for the enrichment of their power networks. Contemporary critiques of aid monies thus often emphasise that foreign donors must insist upon good governance initiatives and human rights (see for instance Taylor 2008 and Armon 2007). In addition, many critiques advance the argument that aid money disrupts the efficient functioning of markets in Africa. Prominent authors such as Moyo (2008) contend that aid feeds into corrupt governance systems, with the result that local elites do not rely upon the successful cultivation of a local entrepreneurial class and taxation. Economic mal-governance in Africa is therefore enabled by aid-giving.

These neo-patrimonial—or in the case of Moyo herself, neo-liberal—critiques of aid-giving do bear a certain credence. Again a modern conception of neo-colonialism need not deny that African elites may welcome aid monies as a channel for lubricating their own patronage networks (as per Bayart's [2010]concept of extraversion). Nor must it deny that African elites might ignore the cultivation of local business people, instead having their rule buffered by foreign aid monies. However, a modern critique of neo-colonialism must highlight the strategic objectives of the donor community in promoting their own economic and corporate interests in Africa. Not only do African elites themselves have a vested interest in the perpetuation of regressive forms of aid, but the donors also have an interest (and an economic benefit) in maintaining such systems of influence within Africa. Moreover, critical focus on neo-colonialism can emphasise how aid initiatives are constructed in the first instance by the donor community. Rather than beginning with appeals from African elites, the majority of aid schemes originate in London,

Brussels, Washington (and in the next chapter, Beijing and Ankara). It is quite misleading therefore to rely upon essentialist visions of 'Big Men' leaders in African countries in helping to explain the preponderance of (misused) aid schemes. Rather, we must explicitly engage Western economic interests and motivations in cementing aid linkages with African recipients. This more critical approach can unveil the ways in which the West often benefits from its 'revolving credit', whether delivered in the form of project aid, budget support (programme aid), or indeed in terms of so-called 'blending' initiatives in conjunction with the major DFIs (Nkrumah 1965: xv).

The next sections thus interrogate three forms of Western aid-giving to problematize the pro-poor orientation of aid co-operation. In all three cases, the chapter indicates how Western corporate and economic interests are cemented via various channels of aid largesse. Accordingly, critical light is shed on the ideational aspect of 'development'—namely that these interventions are undertaken (and justified) on the basis that they are promoting a more egalitarian international system where poverty is being eradicated. When the material outcomes of aid-giving are examined closely, however, it becomes somewhat apparent that aid schemes often perpetuate inequalities and cement poverty in recipient African countries. Nkrumah's critique of aid-giving as part of neo-colonialism does appear to bear relevance in a contemporary understanding of North-South relations.

Project Aid and Western Economic Interests in Africa

Project aid is a category of donor assistance where money is levied towards a specific initiative, or project (such as construction of a highway). This is in contrast to budget support—or programme aid—where money is given towards a government's overarching (and multi-layered) national development strategy (Knoll 2008; Hauck et al. 2005). Project aid is thus a more discrete mechanism where donors support a particular initiative that they deem to bear fruit for poverty reduction. One prominent and illustrative example of a multi-donor project is the New Alliance for Food Security and Nutrition (NAFSN) which was partly discussed in the previous Chap. 2. The NAFSN brings together the UK's DFID alongside USAID (the development wing of the USA), and the World Bank to support agri-business opportunities. Rather than forming a 'new' initiative per se, however, the NAFSN in fact brings together a multitude of pre-existing agricultural schemes under a single policy umbrella. The UK's Independent Commission for Aid Impact (ICAI 2015: 28) finds that 'donors are rebranding ongoing projects as "New Alliance" commitments, while [recipient] governments are disappointed that the movement has not resulted in additional funding'. Nevertheless, the NAFSN is partly novel in the sense that it brings corporate partners to the very fore, being careful to involve companies such as Monsanto, Unilever and Syngenta in setting out an overarching vision of food production and agricultural development in Africa. The prominence of these corporate partners in NAFSN communications is something which outstrips that of many pre-existing donor agricultural 'aid' schemes.

Interestingly, the NAFSN can also be understood to fall into a specific project aid category—that of PSD initiatives in Africa. PSD schemes have gained particular significance in Western donor strategies since the late 1990s onwards. The apparent 'lost decade of development' of the 1980s, combined to sluggish growth rates in Africa in the early 1990s, encouraged donors to focus upon the stimulation of growth in private sector enterprises. Promoted by the Organisation for Economic Co-operation and Development (OECD), PSD initiatives became seen as a means of marrying free market strategies, as earlier encouraged under SAPs in the Washington Consensus, to pro-poor outcomes (OECD 2007; DFID 2008; European Commission 2003; USAID 2008). African countries would be able to translate free market reform into poverty reduction through the provision of donor PSD largesse within the Post-Washington Consensus (te Velde 2006; Brewster and Njinkeu 2008). Notably, the European Commission (2000) pledged fulsome support to PSD initiatives under its Cotonou Agreement with the African, Caribbean and Pacific (ACP) states. The Cotonou Agreement, signed in 2000, committed the EU to the stimulation of private sector business in Africa as a means of achieving economic growth and development. This was preceded by the 1996 Green Paper on ACP-EU relations in which the EU aligned itself to the OECD's rationale on the need for greater aid towards PSD initiatives in Africa (European Commission 1996). Interestingly, in the context of the more recent UN SDGs, Goal 8 specifically commits donor partners to PSD strategies as part of stimulating developing countries' economies (European Commission 2017). The NAFSN—with its focus on private sector growth within so-called agricultural corridors—can therefore be viewed as an example of a PSD aid initiative supported by Western donors.

As noted in the previous chapter, however, the NAFSN has been accused of supporting 'land-grabs' in African countries, with local villagers and governments often bypassed by NAFSN actors. Moreover, there is grave concern that NAFSN activities undermine food security objectives (ActionAid 2015; Brooks 2016; European Parliament 2015). This is due to the fact that subsistence farmers are often removed from land which latterly is used for cash crop agri-business ventures. Moreover, there are concerns that local citizens employed within the NAFSN agricultural corridors are not treated fairly either in terms of pay or in terms of working conditions (ibid.). It is important to note, however, that these findings are not confined to the NAFSN alone. In many cases, PSD initiatives sponsored by the EU, UK DFID or USAID have been found to exacerbate the economic and social problems of developing countries in Africa rather than to promote genuine forms of pro-poor growth. Notably, PSD aid under the ACP-EU European Development Fund (EDF) has supported dubious forms of European investment into African economies, with little tangible benefit for local citizens or communities (Langan 2009; 2011; 2011b; 2012). For example, the ACP-EU Centre for the Development of Enterprise (CDE) channelled PSD aid to export processing zone (EPZ) activities in Madagascar with questionable outcomes for the workers employed in low-waged employment. Rather than promote 'development', the CDE could be seen to effectively subsidise predominantly French investors within the EPZ textiles sector. The national government, meanwhile, did not benefit from taxation revenues given the EPZ status offered to foreign companies in this area. Workers, in addition to the low rates of remuneration, also faced poor working conditions (Langan 2011b; Nicita 2006).

UK DFID assistance to PSD initiatives in Africa, meanwhile, also underscores concerns about the misuse of project aid. The ICAI (2014; 2015) recently issued strong rebukes to DFID and queried whether its PSD activities are bringing about poverty reduction. The ICAI (2015: 11) noted that DFID had not acted to ensure the implementation or even recognition of a 'do no harm' principle to govern PSD aid-giving. Interestingly, the ICAI (2015: 14) also lamented the fact that DFID had to ostensibly abide by 'post-conditionality' criteria espoused in the Post-Washington Consensus. It called for DFID to be much more open about the ways in which its PSD monies might be channelled to UK business operations in developing countries in Africa, and beyond. The ICAI report recommended that DFID should work more closely with the Foreign and

Commonwealth Office (FCO) and UK Trade and Investment (UKTI) to maximise opportunities for supporting British companies through PSD project aid (ibid.).[1] Again, this recommendation was contextualised in terms of an antipathy towards 'strict' interpretations of post-conditionality and the non-tying of aid:

> A strict interpretation of the untied aid provision can lead to the unantici- pated situation where DFID… is precluded from working with UK busi- nesses. Our discussions with DFID, FCO and UKTI staff indicate that there are ways that each party can be helpful to the other. DFID is well- placed to provide analysis of economic developments, government strategy, and procurement opportunities to UKTI colleagues. The latter, in turn, can help DFID by providing business insights into bottlenecks and oppor- tunities. Each can provide the other with business contacts and introduc- tions (ibid.).

However, as chap. 2 noted, UK DFID has already delivered its PSD resources in a fashion that supports British commercial interests (with dubious returns for local citizens). DFID monies went towards the sup- port of lobbying groups that apparently cemented the position of an Anglo-Irish firm through the passing of the E&P bill. Numerous other examples can also be found where UK DFID has apparently channelled monies to the support of British business—ahead of entrepreneurs from recipient countries themselves, or from other developed nations. An OECD-commissioned report found that only 18% of DFID contracts in 2007 went to non-British firms *(The Guardian* 2012). Examples of British business beneficiaries of DFID spending include GRM International, a London-based company, which received over £677 million to manage and coordinate a food security programme. It additionally received over £25 million for a separate PSD initiative aimed at market development, with focus on Northern Nigeria. Rather than channel funds directly to small- and medium-sized enterprises (SMEs) in Africa, such monies went directly to UK-based companies on the ostensible grounds of implementing schemes that benefit local entrepreneurs (ibid.).

Another worrying example of UK DFID utilising project aid money in a manner that furnishes British companies but with dubious out- comes for local citizenries in Africa, is that of its support to water pri- vatisation. In Tanzania, DFID issued £444,000 to Adam Smith International—headquartered in London as an outgrowth of the Adam

Smith Institute—for public relations exercises (*The Guardian* 2007). This apparently included around £66,000 for 'study tours' (Action Aid 2004: 7). Meanwhile, the UK's Export Credit Guarantee Department (ECGD) lent its support to a British company, BiWater—headquartered in Dorking, UK—to undertake investments in City Water in Dar es Salaam (a privatised water entity) to run the Tanzanian capital's water system. ECGD's support comprised insurance for BiWater against 'risk of expropriation by the Tanzanian government, war, and restrictions on profit remittances' (ActionAid 2004: 7).

This UK DFID aid was granted despite grave concerns surrounding the commodification of water. Water privatization regularly enriches foreign investors while raising prices for local citizens already on the economic margins. This came to pass in Tanzania, where World Bank officials soon made clear that City Water (and its investors, including BiWater) would double tariffs for local consumers (ActionAid 2004: 14). Interestingly, the Tanzanian government—in the lead up to presidential elections—decided not to renew City Water's contract in 2005, leading to outcry from the major donors (including the World Bank and DFID). Nevertheless, donor influence remains a constant in the Tanzanian water sector, with the USA promoting a highly controversial dam project. US agencies have made clear that they expect the costs of the dam to be recouped through price rises of around 250% (Pigeon 2012: 53–54). Despite the Tanzanian government's apparent agency in ending the services of City Water in Dar es Salaam, there remain real challenges for country sovereignty owing to Western project aid. Pigeon (2012: 55) in fact contests the argument that the remunicipalisation of City Water in Dar es Salaam represented a truly 'sovereign' act:

> [Western donor] institutions impose conditions that shape the [water] system's structural evolution, both technically and ideologically... the remunicipalisation of water in Dar es Salaam is a *default situation created by the collapse of a private contract, not a strategic move planned by sovereign political institutions*. If political sovereignty is a condition for sustainability, then the limited choices imposed by donor conditionality must be seen as one of the biggest obstacles to solving Dar es Salaam's water woes in the long run (emphasis added).

Interestingly, a similar scenario has been witnessed in Ghana itself, where Nkrumah issued his many warnings about neo-colonial co-optation via Western aid monies. A multi-donor effort involving UK DFID, the World Bank and the International Monetary Fund (IMF) promoted private sector participation (PSP) in Ghana's urban water supply, with foreign companies being offered leases of up to 25 years for service provision. Companies involved in the tendering process included two UK firms, two French firms, the USA's Haliburton, as well as a Dutch firm—ARVL—which was awarded the water concession in Accra in 2006. Christian Aid (2001: 5) explain how this privatisation process has been facilitated by donor leverage, with the major aid-givers tying water privatisation initiatives to other forms of aid to the Ghanaian government:

> the decision to lease the urban water systems to foreign companies was largely driven by pressures exerted by donors and creditors. They set up and funded an autonomous body, the Water Sector Restructuring Secretariat... to carry out the privatisation... They funded and carefully selected pro-privatisation British and American firms to conduct a series of studies... [moreover] donors have demonstrated their preparedness to arm-twist the government by withholding critically needed investments in on-going programmes.

This privatisation initiative was met with much protest from Ghanaian civil society. For instance, the Integrated Social Development Centre based in Accra issued a full submission to the UK Parliament's International Development committee, outlining their fears. They noted that DFID had provided around £10 million for a publicity campaign about the benefits of privatisation but that this did not represent a genuine form of public consultation. Moreover, they noted the paradox that a Highly Indebted Poor Country (HIPC) would be obliged to take out loans for the improvement of national water supplies, whilst a private company contributed relatively little capital (despite accruing large profits for operating the existing services):

> The PSP proposal will bring US$140 million from the private sector but the estimated cost of rehabilitating and expanding the urban water infrastructure is approximately US$1.3 billion. There are serious concerns about the appropriateness of a HIPC country incurring additional external debt for rehabilitation of the water system when the majority of the revenues will accrue to foreign private companies. The rates of return required by the private sector companies, as well as other key financial information

on the PSP was not available in the public domain. (Select Committee on International Development 2002)

With further parallels to the Tanzanian situation, the privatisation of water in Accra effectively came to an end in 2011 when the Dutch operator decided not to seek contract renewal. TNI (2014) explain that this de facto remunicipalisation of water services again had less to do with the sovereign interventions of the government than with the wholescale failure of the water operator to meet basic levels of service:

> AVRL failed consistently throughout the contract period to meet its targets. Some of the significant failures included inability to reduce non-revenue water, inability to improve water quality, and consistently poor performance in six other target areas identified in a World Bank commissioned technical audit report. These facts, in addition to the unmet expectations of citizens and workers of the company, created the conditions for the contract to be discontinued.

Project aid thus helped to bring about the situation in which vital water resources were privatised in countries such as Tanzania and Ghana. Foreign corporations—including the UK's own BiWater benefited from such profitable arrangements—while water services stagnated, or indeed declined in quality. African governments, meanwhile, were pressured into such agendas via aid conditionality and leveraging. The eventual remunipalisation of water services in both cases owed less to the sovereign act of the African governments themselves than to the wholescale failure of the companies in question to provide a service able to meet basic standards and consumer expectations.

Budget Support and Western Donor Leverage

It is also important to recognise that Western donors regularly utilise budget support mechanisms by which to deliver aid within African governance systems. Budget support—which involves direct finance support from the donor to the recipient government treasury—is viewed by certain donors, such as the European Commission, as being a more progressive form of support than project aid. According to EU officials, in particular, budget support represents an opportunity for genuine partnership between donors and aid recipients (Langan 2015). Rather than project aid, which historically has been conditional upon acceptance of foreign firm involvement, budget support is viewed as a means of supporting a developing country to achieve its overarching economic and social policy agenda. In this vein, donors present budget support as being conducive to a 'post-conditionality' approach to development within the Post-Washington Consensus (Hayman 2011). Recipient governments and Western benefactors will be able—via budget support—to agree upon policies and work together for their effective implementation. By co-ordination among budget support donors, moreover, this aid mechanism is also viewed as a means of preventing duplication of aid efforts, as often occurred (occurs) with project aid (Langan 2015; Knoll 2008).

Despite the discourse of post-conditionality and partnership, however, there are concerns that budget support does not move beyond regressive forms of North–South relations (Knoll 2008; Alvarez 2010; Langan 2015; Hauck et al. 2005; IEG 2010 PAFt has been utilised to support premature trade liberalisation in Africa, to the detriment of local agricultural producers and domestic manufacturers. The Ghanaian Parliament, for instance, had agreed upon the raising of tariffs upon poultry imports to protect livelihoods and production in the local sector. However, their decision—and that of the government—was challenged by the IMF which directly intervened to make their displeasure known. Given the IMF's position as a major provider of budget support, alongside the World Bank and the EU, the Ghanaian government (under President Kufuor) capitulated to donor wishes. Christian Aid (2005: 32), in this context, usefully remark that it is:

> no wonder that the IMF, the senior of the two Washington-based institutions, is able to prescribe policies that Ghana has little choice but to follow. The Fund sits at the top of a pyramid of donors on whom Ghana relies for 45 per cent of its money. If Ghana steps outside a narrow, prescribed policy path, the IMF can withdraw its seal of approval – and with it the pyramid of funding that stands beneath, pitching Ghana into economic freefall.

This instance of overt intervention in the policy-making of the Ghanaian government by its donors (utilising the implicit, and at times explicit, threat of budget support withdrawal) was mirrored in the case of kerosene subsidies. Once more the Kufuor administration found that its policy to subsidise local prices for kerosene—to improve living standards and stimulate the economy—was found to fall foul of donor preferences.

Accordingly, the Multi-Donor Budget Support (MDBS) group took action to challenge the Trade Ministry, leading to a 'conflictual tug of war' in 2004/2005 (Gerster n.d). Eventually, as with the situation of poultry tariffs, the Kufuor government gave way to donor demands, leading to citizen riots in Accra at the price of this vital commodity rose. In addition, the Kufuor administration found that their intended President's Special Initiatives (PSIs)—which aimed to assist strategic business sectors—were also targeted by the budget support community. The PSIs were seen by donors to fall foul of free market norms and to instead artificially 'pick winners', despite the fact that such developmental state policies have witnessed major development gains in East Asia. Moreover, the Ghanaian government was overruled on the detail of the Performance Assessment Framework (PAF) upon which its use of budget support is assessed. An Overseas Development Institute (ODI) report, along with CDD, found that although the government:

> was invited to provide an initial proposal on the content of the 2007 PAF, some MDBS partners were reluctant to accept the government's priorities and sought to insist on their own priorities. (cited in Alliance 2015, 2007: 9)

Interestingly, a report by Ireland's development ministry (Irish Aid) concludes that budget support (in this Ghanaian situation) remains subject to traditional aid conditionalities despite the official discourse of post-conditionality. Budget support donors in Ghana utilise budget support as leverage for the government's abidance by their own free market outlook:

> Far-reaching and quite complicated [free market] reforms were made a condition of a variable tranche on the basis of rather limited evidence that the reforms were technically feasible and the government had the capacity to implement them. The budget-support donors appear to have slipped into something close to the traditional concept of buying reforms, rather than engaging constructively in the resolution of the technical and capacity problems. This failed for very traditional reasons. Thus, the new aid thinking recognises there are things that donors cannot influence with conditionality, but tends to act as if this were not the case. (Irish Aid 2008: 15)

Rather boldly, however, the Irish Aid report goes on to recommend that donors should continue to seek radical change within developing countries' governance systems. Making explicit reference to the 'neo-patrimonial state' in Africa and its perceived ills, the report rec-ommends that donors should continue to make strategic interventions in governance, as seen under the Kufuor administration. The Irish Aid publication states that donors must not become 'mere purveyors of finance' but must 'transform [African] institutions' and ensure 'institutional impacts' (Irish Aid 2008: 50). Indeed, such institutional impacts were witnessed in Ghana itself, to the chagrin of local poultry produc-ers dependent on government assistance to protect their livelihoods from cheap foreign imports (including from agriculturally focused countries such as Ireland).

Budget support disbursements in other African countries, mean-while, corroborate many of the concerns surrounding policy intrusion and government sovereignty as found in Ghana. Perhaps most notably, Mozambique has faced a '"united front" of donors, who are negotiat-ing from strength, as a harmonized bloc, with technical resources that outweigh those the government can marshal'. This donor bloc has—with parallels to Ghana—insisted upon the government's adherence to a strict PAF. This includes a commitment to PSD in keeping with a free market perspective on the benefits of open markets and liberalisation of tertiary services. In the case of Mozambique, moreover, parliamentary and civil society concern has been exacerbated by the fact that much of the donor budget support is not properly disclosed within official government com-munications. Budget support—despite its name—is kept 'off-budget', meaning that there is little proper scrutiny or oversight of donor funding in the country. Hodges and Tibana (2004: 43) explain that:

> This problem has been a matter of special concern to the [parliamentary] deputies who participate in the Planning and Budget Commission's mid-year monitoring missions to the provinces, where they have come face to face with the implications: the impossibility of monitoring execution of the investment component [that is, donor budget support component] of the budget in conditions where there is only a partial correspondence between the projects included in the approved budget and the projects actually being implemented on the ground.

Concerns about modern budget support disbursements are heightened in Mozambique by historical evidence. Earlier forms of de facto budget support under SAPs in the 1990s resulted in tariff liberalisation with respect to the sensitive cashew sector. This resulted in mass job losses for local producers as cheaper foreign produce entered the country at the World Bank's behest (based upon its core norms relating to free market policies) de Renzio and Hanlon (2007: 11) explain that the historical episode of cashew liberalisation set into motion a situation in which Mozambique's political elites began to shift from 'aid dependence' to 'aid subservience', with many elite individuals themselves benefiting from liberalisation processes that worked to the disadvantage of poorer producers and agriculturalists.

In the case of Ethiopia, widely seen as a recent economic success story in Africa, budget support donors and the government have also strongly disagreed on a number of sensitive policy issues including liberalisation of the fertiliser distribution system, opening of the financial sector to foreign banks, as well as liberalisation of the telecommunications sector to allow foreign companies' entry into telephone and internet provision (Furtado and Smith 2007: 11–13). The World Bank, among others, have emphasised to the Ethiopian government that adherence to free market norms are essential for the continued flow of aid monies. Interestingly, however, the Ethiopian government has (at least at time of writing) resisted in the implementation of these free market reforms. In particular, Prime Minister Desalegn has explained that the state-ownership of telecoms is essential since it brings the government annual revenues of $430 million, money which is then invested into the development of railways. Thus, while the government would anticipate $3 billion from the selling of telecoms licences in the short term, the long-term interest lies in the government's maintenance of its public ownership. This policy decision is to the chagrin of donors, and foreign operators who would profit from inclusion within the marketplace (*The Financial Times* 2013). Whitfield and Therkildsen (2011) explains that Ethiopia's apparent policy insulation from donor demands is aided by the fact that it has not faced the same proliferation of donor agencies witnessed in other states (such as Mozambique). Donor co-ordination has been less cohesive in the Ethiopian situation, combined to government elites influenced by a developmental state ideology promoted by the late Prime Minister Meles Zenawi. A combination, therefore, of weaker donor structures combined to ideological preferences on the part of local governing elites has given Ethiopia the space to resist (for the time being) some of the more controversial aspects of donors' free market preferences.[2] Nevertheless, the Ethiopian government has bowed to certain free market demands, particularly relating to market openness vis-à-vis trade regimes (as witnessed in its reluctant acquiescence to the EU's EPA in the region).

DFIs and 'Aid Blending' Initiatives

DFIs also play a major role as aid-givers in the Post-Washington Consensus, as pursued by Western actors. DFIs promote investment and job creation in developing countries through grants and loans to private sector agencies that might not otherwise invest in 'risky' climates within Africa. In many cases, the DFIs do expect to recoup monies to cover their expenses, citing the need for long-term sustainability of their operations (Bracking 2009). Many leading DFIs, including the UK's CDC and the EU's EIB emphasise that they make a vital pro-poor contribution to economic *and social* development in terms of how they catalyse capital injections into developing countries. Interestingly, there is also recent donor discussion of the apparent merits of aid 'blending'. This occurs when traditional donor, public aid, is mixed with private DFI capital within a particular scheme or project. The European Commission has been particularly enthusiastic about its ability to 'blend' aid with that of the EIB as part of the recently established Africa Investment Facility (AfIF), founded in 2015. The European Commission makes clear that a number of sectors will be positively impacted, including local entrepreneurs/SMEs:

> AfIF interventions should focus on the following sectors: energy, agriculture, transport, environment, water and sanitation, climate change, SMEs, information and communication technologies (ICT) and social services, support to private sector development, in particular Small and Medium Enterprises (SMEs).

Nevertheless, there are several grounds upon which to call into question the 'development' auspices of DFI interventions and aid blending for Africa. In keeping with a critical consideration of Nkrumah and the concept of neo-colonialism, such aid-giving can rightly be viewed as a form of 'revolving credit'. In particular, the activities of the EIB have drawn criticism from civil society organisations such as Counter Balance, as well as from the European Parliament itself (Langan 2014). Notably, the EIB has been vocally criticised for its investments into extractive industries, including copper mining in Zambia. The EIB has been seen to deliver its capital via private equity schemes to business operators who alleg-edly fall foul of core labour standards, environmental standards as well as transparent taxation norms. The European Parliament specifically raised concerns that the EIB has supported the activities of Glencore despite apparent taxation issues associated with the Mopani copper mine in Zambia (Langan 2014). Moreover, the European Parliament success-fully called for a moratorium on EIB investments into mining sectors in Africa, partly in response to its concerns surrounding the Zambian situ-ation (ibid.). This success, however, did not roll back almost one dec-ade of EIB investments into developmentally questionable sectors under the ACP-EU Cotonou Agreement (2000–2020). Many private sector enterprises have been supported in such sectors via EIB grants and loans, often with negative consequences for local workers and long-term devel-opment strategies (given the extraction of vital raw commodities with lit-tle taxation or skilled jobs in return).

It is also important to note that the EIB continues to invest in devel-opmentally dubious initiatives, notwithstanding the current moratorium on the mining sector. Notably, there are concerns that the EIB is sup-porting intensive agri-business with regressive consequences for local communities. With parallels to the European Commission's focus on food security via the NAFSN, the EIB emphasises its intent to continue supporting foreign direct investment into agri-business chains. Its 2015 Annual Report, for example, highlights the importance of intensive agri-business:

> This employs a high proportion of the population in many ACP countries. It is not a new sector for the Bank. We have long been active in this field. As a means to produce food for growing populations, and also a target sector for economic development and growth, its importance cannot be understated... The EIB is keen to invest throughout these value chains... It not only provides the means for established players to grow and to inno-vate, but it also enables the formal economy to expand by involving more people. (EIB 2015: 18)

Nevertheless, the dangers of such an approach can be illustrated with refer-ence to Feronia, a large agri-business operation in the DRC. In this instance it is the UK's CDC which is the largest DFI contributor, rather than the EIB itself. Collectively, the DFIs own around 91% of Feronia's shares, including $41 million from the UK CDC (operated under the umbrella of UK DFID). Feronia, meanwhile, stands accused of having illegally occupied land tracts without consent of the local apparently communities involved. Local chiefs have apparently condemned Feronia and argue that subsistence farming—and food security—will be drastically undermined if the company continues to deny access to the land that it now occupies:

> With all of our energy, we deplore and denounce this illegal occupation of our territories, an occupation that is without titles or rights and which has made us extremely poor and will end in our collective death if this manner of operating is not stopped. (RIAO-RDC et al. 2016: 6)

Civil society campaign groups also query DFI rationales that investments into Feronia result in job creation and social prosperity for local people. CDC, for example, pointed to its investments as having spurred wage increases for workers on the Feronia plantation. However, when such claims are investigated in detail, there are apparently serious grounds for concern:

> In September 2015, the CDC stated that the average wages for Feronia's plantation workers were increased by 70 per cent to an average of US$4 per day following its 2014 investment... However, pay stubs from "superior" workers (*maneouvres supérieurs*) at Feronia's Lokutu plantations show that wages throughout 2015 remained at only US$2 per day (1921.58 CDF). Moreover, Feronia managers and workers report that the wages for daily labourers, which constitute the vast majority of Feronia's plantation workers, are even lower—at no more than US$1.25 per day (ibid: 9).

Despite these ongoing concerns, CDC remains committed to its investment. Moreover, CDC (2015) makes explicit use of development discourse, emphasising the need for economic growth. This is notwithstanding low wages, land loss, as well as allegations of wider labour rights violations on the plantation. CDC discourse is very firm on the need for such pro-poor initiatives in the DRC:

> Agriculture is a long-term business and requires patient investment in order to scale up operations. Past economic and political instability has hindered investment in the agricultural industry, resulting in the decline of established plantations such as those owned by Feronia. However, with an increasing population and economic growth, there is a significant opportunity for patient investing to build sustainable businesses. CDC will provide

this long-term capital to Feronia, supporting growth and development to create a sustainable and profitable business that continues to contribute significantly to local employment and to local communities (CDC n.d).

Furthermore, CDC seeks to extend its agri-business investments beyond the DRC. Notably, in 2016, it provided significant funding to a meat enterprise in Zambia, with concerns being raised by civil society groups such as Global Justice Now (2016: 4):

> In 2016, CDC invested $65 million in Zambeef, one of the largest meat producers in southern Africa which is listed on the London Stock Exchange and exports in Africa and also to China, India, the UK and Italy. Zambeef is also one of the largest landholders in Zambia, with more than 100,000 hectares. Those supporting the company have previously been accused of facilitating the concentration of land in the country into just a few hands, while the vast majority of the population are subsistence farmers and have on average just 0.6 hectares per household.

It is important to note that the UK's CDC has also been criticised for investments in a number of other controversial sectors. Interestingly, in terms of the neo-patrimonialism discourse embraced by donors such as Irish Aid (and UK DFID), the CDC stands accused of having proffered funds to companies owned by James Ibori, a former governor of Nigeria once hailed as a future presidential contender. A whistleblower, Mr Oloko, brought to the British agencies' attention that these companies were apparent fronts for money laundering in Nigeria (*The Financial Times* 2012). At first, the CDC resisted all criticism but eventually, as proceedings went forth against James Ibori, it was forced to concede that it had acted improperly (Walker 2012). Asking for the UK government to acknowledge CDC complicity, a memorandum from numerous UK civil society groups, including Jubilee Debt Campaign, to the UK development minister lamented that:

> serious concerns have emerged over whether or not two CDC-backed private equity funds – Emerging Capital Partners Africa Fund II PCC (ECP Africa Fund II) and Ethos Fund V – complied with CDC's Investment Code. Both funds have invested in Nigerian companies reported to be "fronts" for the alleged laundering of money said to have been obtained corruptly by the former Governor of Nigeria's oil rich Delta State, James Ibori. Nigeria's Economic and Financial Crimes Commission (EFCC)

and law enforcement agencies in the UK have alleged links between these ECP- or Ethos-backed companies and Ibori and/or his associates. (Jubilee Debt Campaign et al. 2010)

It is interesting to note potential political implications, given that Ibori was seen to have apparently played a role in financing the election campaign of Yar'Adua, the one-time heir apparent to President Osabanjo. It appears possible, therefore, that UK tax-payer funds—via the CDC and its private equity investments—were used for influencing electoral campaigns in this oil-rich country (*BBC News* 2012). Rather than mitigating problems associated with the alleged 'neo-patrimonial state' in Africa, aid monies (in the form of CDC private equity investments) would be seen as a possible lubricant for opaque political dealings in Nigeria. The CDC, meanwhile, has also been accused of funding PSD initiatives that benefit a wealthy elite within African countries (as well as wealthy expatriates), with little meaningful impact for poverty reduction. Citing job creation in the construction sector, for example, the CDC has given large monies to the Garden City shopping complex in Nairobi Kenya (*The Guardian* 2015). While useful for local business elites, and for wealthy shoppers, many doubt whether this benefits poorer people or merely entrenches donor influence over the business (and political) class in the country.

Moreover, the recent discourse of aid blending has also come under intense scrutiny. A comprehensive report by Eurodad (2015) questions the 'development' credentials of such aid funding given the apparent shift from humanitarian spending to PSD initiatives. Given the existing evidence surrounding DFI behaviour—and investments into dubious agri-business and mining ventures—the report queries whether African civil society groups and parliamentarians ought to 'trust' the European Commission's intent to channel public funds to blending exercises. Eurodad (2015) point to the ways in which unregulated blending injections of capital might undermine locally owned industrial and economic growth strategies. They note that the EU must take care not to undermine developing countries' own priorities, and not to utilise blending monies as leverage for policy change that contradicts government's own priority agendas. In addition, they point to the potential dangers of blending finance being used as a means of subsidy for lucrative FDI (with major gains for European companies but little for local citizenries). In this vein, they recommend that only local enterprise should benefit from proposed investments, and that there must be clear and transparent taxation protocols observed by all parties.

Western Aid as Revolving Credit in Systems of Neo-Colonialism?

The concept of neo-colonialism places emphasis on the role of aid as a revolving credit in Africa. Donors provide aid as a means of maintaining skewed economic relations, often based along colonial patterns of trade (focused on raw materials and minerals). Moreover, the concept emphasises the way in which aid monies can be utilised to win favour of local political elites, and to bind them into systems of neo-colonial co-optation. It is clear from the discussion of project aid, budget support and DFI grants/loans (recently as part of blending) that the concerns raised by Nkrumah in the 1960s do resonate in the contemporary era. Western donors' use of project aid to embed corporate interests in initiatives such as the NAFSN gives rise to concerns about the misuse of aid to support agri-business interest at the expense of the food security of local people. Similarly, use of donor aid in the promotion of water privatisation (and to ensure government's acquiescence to such arrangements in the first instance) give further rise to concerns about developing countries' sovereignty, as well as the commodification of natural resources at the expense of local living standards. The use of budget support, meanwhile, to achieve so-called 'policy dialogue' with African recipients on a number of issues, including PSD and economic liberalisation in tertiary sectors, raises concerns about aid as policy leverage, diminishing African elites' decision-making autonomy. Consideration of DFI interventions in terms of agri-business interests as well as for natural resource extraction also raises several serious questions about the role of Western aid in embedding regressive forms of FDI, with little regard for workers' rights, environmental sustainability or legitimate taxation.

In this vein, it is useful to revisit the language and concept of neo-colonialism. Rather than focusing upon narratives of the so-called neo-patrimonial state in Africa, Nkrumah's analysis helps us to more clearly identify (and understand) the role of Western aid-giving after formal declarations of independence. Aid money—across a range of vehicles discussed above—is often utilised as a means of 'buying' political agendas and policy conformity on the part of recipient African governments (such as in Mozambique). On the other hand, it can also be used to discipline governments that appear to depart from donor preferences and free market norms. Note, for instance, the situation with the Kufuor government in Ghana in relation to kerosene subsidies, poultry tariffs and the PSIs. Notably, the MDBS successfully intervened across these policy issues to force the Ghanaian government to move away from developmental policies (since they contravened donor free market norms). As a result of such interventions, moreover, donors secured the interests of their own business community—for instance, in relation to valuable poultry exports from Western origins into Ghana, despite negative impacts for local industry and workers. The neo-colonial lens can also help us to more fully diagnose potential pathways for African development (discussed more fully in chap. 8). Namely, it points to the need for African strategies that move away from 'aid dependence' or indeed 'aid subservience'. Aid monies, from the vantage of Nkrumah's insights, can be seen often to do less for development in African states, than to entrench systems of North–South relations that retard growth and prosperity.

It is also important to note, from a critical constructivist angle, that donor language pertaining to aid-giving does regularly evolve in order to present such activities as being both benevolent and legitimate. As discussed, the language surrounding budget support is particularly interesting since on the one hand it appears to acknowledge dangers associated with conditional project aid, while emphasising that government-to-government aid will be free of conditionalities whatsoever. In this fashion, budget support has been presented as an ethical contribution to development in the Post-Washington Consensus, aligning to pro-poor concerns as embodied within the new UN SDGs (discussed in more detail in chap. 7). Similarly, donor language of 'aid blending' presents the mixing of donor aid with DFI funding as a 'win-win' for job creation and economic take-off within Africa. Rather than representing a conflict of interests between tax-payer money (public aid) and DFI private capital, this aid mechanism is presented as an innovative solution to poverty. Nevertheless, when examined in more detail, such initiatives are seen to support regressive forms of FDI, for instance in extractive industries and agri-business sectors. While the language of aid and development provides an ethical veneer, the material outcomes of such aid-giving do not necessarily align to ostensible normative goals relating to poverty reduction. On the contrary, the moral language of aid-giving might in fact work as a veil for regressive practices and damaging forms of economic relations that re-embed conditions of poverty in African countries.

It is clear that there are already coalitions of civil society groups and African parliamentarians who are questioning the efficacy of such aid arrangements—whether in terms of budget support, project aid or DFI investments. Moreover, the donor community's recourse to such moralising statements questions whether 'common sense' adherence to such practises is breaking down within North–South relations. The fact that donor language surrounding budget support has acknowledged perceived failings with project aid, for example, demonstrates that the regressive impact of Western aid is entering into policy and public consciousness. Western donors are increasingly unable to pursue 'business as usual' in Africa but must increasingly find new ways to justify their policies to sceptical African recipients, as well as to sceptical public audiences within Europe and the USA. While corporate interests continue to be bolstered by aid-giving—and policy leverage exerted in African governance systems—nevertheless Western donors are coming under increased pressure to legitimise their aid-giving apparatus. This is interesting from a critical constructivist standpoint concerned with African sovereignty and neo-colonialism. It points to donors' struggle to maintain the façade of benevolent 'development' interventions with regard to the material consequences of their aid in African states such as Ghana.

Conclusion

This chapter has examined Western aid interventions with an eye as to whether Nkrumah's warnings of neo-colonialism retain relevance in a contemporary setting. When examining project aid, budget support and DFI activities, it becomes clear that many of the concerns held by Nkrumah are pertinent for today's assessment of African states' relations with Western aid-givers. In the case of project aid, Western donors appear to often subsidise their own corporations' entry into African markets without due concern for the impact of such activities for local communities. Indeed, many of the project aid schemes—including the NAFSN—do more to perpetuate conditions of ill-being and forms of economic exploitation than to genuinely create conditions for pro-poor development (as per donor narratives). Moreover, in the case of budget support, many concerns arise about the diminution of African sovereignty and collapsing policy space. Most notably, in Ghana in the mid-2000s, the Kufuor administration found that its policy preferences for developmental state strategies (such as subsidies on kerosene and higher tariffs to protect import-competing sectors such as poultry) were effectively overridden by the demands of the MDBS. Meanwhile, countries such as Mozambique have capitulated to donor demands for wider market liberalisation in services such as telecommunications, despite the negative impact of such policies in historical terms (for instance, the collapse of Mozambique's cashew sector under liberalisation reforms in the 1990s). Moreover, DFI interventions—and now aid 'blending'—underscore how aid monies are often used more to support foreign corporate investment than to support genuine moral objectives associated with poverty reduction. Aid becomes less about pro-poor development, than about supporting corporate profit at the expense of workers' rights and environmental sustainability in Africa.

It is important to understand, however, that Nkrumah's focus on Western aid-givers must be balanced in a modern context with focus on the role of emerging powers in Africa. In particular, it is necessary to focus upon the role of China as an increasingly significant aid-giver, and to examine the material impact of such practices for sovereignty and poverty reduction. Perhaps paradoxically, Western donors themselves decry Chinese neo-colonialism in Africa, while maintaining that their own aid schemes empower African citizens and bring about social prosperity. The next chapter accordingly examines the role of China in Africa, with focus on aid for economic development. It underscores how aid supports Chinese companies' entry into African markets (with parallels to Western aid and the position of enterprises such as Feronia in the DRC). In order to guard against overt focus on China, however, the next chapter also points to the role of other emerging powers and the impact of their aid-giving. Specifically, it highlights the practices of Turkey in its 'neo-Ottoman' foreign policy phase initiated by former Prime Minister Davutoglu after EU accession stalled in 2007. Turkish aid is seen to have had a mixed record, with certain concerns surrounding neo-colonialism again coming to the fore.

Notes

1. This reticence about moving away from aid conditionality in the Post-Washington Consensus is also found in Koeberle and Masa (2015): 'although ex ante conditionality has often been criticised as corrosive and

ineffective, leading to volatility of resource flows, straining the donor-recipient relationship, and undermining the respective country's sovereignty, it is still a necessity'.

2. It is interesting to note here that East Asian states also successfully pursued developmental strategies and enjoyed degree of policy space free from donor interference. Henderson convincingly argues, however, that donor conditionalities prevailed in the mid-1990s. This precipitated the East Asian Financial Crisis of 1996/7 and—paradoxically—delegitimised the developmental state approach, despite the cause of crisis being the liberalisation promoted by the donor community (with particular regard to the housing bubble that sparked the crisis).

REFERENCES

ActionAid. (2004). *Turning off the taps: Donor conditionality and water privatisation in Dar es Salaam, Tanzania*. London: ActionAid.

ActionAid. (2015, May). *New alliance, new risk of land grabs: Evidence from Malawi, Nigeria, Senegal and Tanzania*. London: Action Aid.

Alvarez, R. (2010). The rise of budget support in European development co-operation: A false panacea. *FRIDE Policy Brief*, No. 31, January. Madrid: FRIDE.

Armon, J. (2007). Aid, Politics and Development. *Development Policy Review, 25*(5), 653–656.

Bayart, J. F. (2010). *The state in Africa: The politics of the belly*. London: Polity Press.

BBC News. (2012). James Ibori: How a thief almost became Nigeria's president. *BBC News*, 28 February 2012. Available at: http://www.bbc.co.uk/news/world-africa-17184075 Accessed 30 July 2017.

Bracking, S. (2009). *Money and power: Great predators in the political economy of development*. London: Pluto Press.

Brewster, H., & Njinkeu, D. (2008). Aid for trade and private sector development. In D. Njinkeu & H. Cameron (Eds.), *Aid for Trade and Development* (pp. 369–392). Cambridge: University Press.

Brooks, S. (2016). Inducing food insecurity: Financialisation and development in the post-2015 Era. *Third World Quarterly, 37*(5), 768–780.

CDC. (2015). *New investment from the UK government to help boost jobs in the world's poorest places*. London: CDC.

Christian Aid. (2001). *Water privatization in Ghana*. London: Christian Aid.

Christian Aid. (2005). *The damage done: Aid, death and dogma*. London: Christian Aid.

de Renzio, P., & Hanlon, J., (2007). Contested sovereignty in Mozambique: The dilemmas of aid dependence. *GEG Working Paper*, 2007/25. Oxford: University College Oxford.

DFID. (2008). *Private sector development strategy—Prosperity for all: Making markets work.* London: DfID.

DFID. (2015). *UK aid: Tackling global challenges in the national interest.* London: DfID.

The Economist. (2017, February 2). Priti patel does economics: DFID tries to justify its existence. *The Economist.*

EIB. (2015). *Annual report 2015 on EIB activity in Africa, the Caribbean and Pacific, and overseas territories.* Brussels: EIB.

Eurodad. (2015). *A dangerous blend? The EU's agenda to 'Blend' public development finance with private finance.* Brussels: Eurodad.

European Commission. (1996). *Green paper on the relations between the european union and the ACP countries on the Eve of the 21st Century.* Brussels: European Commission.

European Commission. (2000). *Partnership agreement ACP-EU signed in cotonou on 23 June 2000.* Revised in luxembourg on 25 June 2005—Brussels: European Commission, 2005.

European Commission. (2003). *European community co-operation with third countries: The commission's approach to future support for the development of the business sector.* Brussels: European Commission.

European Commission. (2017). *Trade—Countries and regions—West Africa.* Brussels: European Commission. Available at: http://ec.europa.eu/trade/policy/countries-and-regions/regions/west-africa/index_en.htm Accessed 7 Jan 2017.

European Parliament. (2015). *Study: The new alliance for food Security and nutrition in africa.* Brussels: European Parliament. Available online at: http://www.europarl.europa.eu/RegData/etudes/STUD/2015/535010/EXPO_STU(2015)535010_EN.pdf Accessed 9 Feb 2017.

The Financial Times. (2012, April 16). CDC is linked to Ibori fraud scandal. *The Financial Times.*

The Financial Times. (2013). Ethiopia's leader aims to maintain tight rein on key businesses. *The Financial Times,* 27 May 2013. Available at: https://www.ft.com/content/c0985378-c5ef-11e2-99d1-00144feab7de Accessed 30 July 2017.

Furtado, X., & Smith, W. (2007). *Ethiopia, aid and sovereignty* (GEG Working Paper 2007/28).

The Guardian. (2007). Tanzania's water scandal: The water margin. *The Guardian,* 16 August 2007. Available at: https://www.theguardian.com/business/2007/aug/16/imf.internationalaidanddevelopment Accessed 30 July 2017.

The Guardian. (2012). Why is so much UK aid money still going to companies based in Britain? *The Guardian,* September 21. Available at: https://www.theguardian.com/global-development/datablog/2012/sep/21/why-is-uk-aid-going-to-uk-companies Accessed 9 Feb 2017.

The Guardian. (2015, July 17). *CDC Criticised for Pouring Funding into Gated Communities.*

Hauck, V., Hasse, O., & Koppensteiner, M. (2005). *EC budget support: Thumbs Up or Thumbs Down?* Maastricht: ECDPM.

Hayman, R. (2011). Budget support and democracy: A twist in the conditionality tale. *Third World Quarterly, 32*(4), 673–688.

Hodges, T., & Tibana, R. (2004). *Political economy of the budget in Mozambique.* Oxford: OPM.

Irish Aid. (2008). *Good governance, aid modalities and poverty reduction: Linkages to a millennium development goals and implications for Irish Aid.* Dublin: Irish Aid.

ICAI. (2014). *DFID's private sector development Work.* London: ICAI.

ICAI. (2015). *Business in development.* London: ICAI.

Independent Evaluation Group (IEG). (2010). *Poverty reduction support credits: An evaluation of world bank support.* Washington: IEG.

Jubilee Debt Campaign and One World Action and Platform Remember and Saro-Wiwa Tax Justice Network and The Corner House and War on Want. (2010). *Memorandum to secretary of state for international development: Concerns over alleged corruption in CDC-backed companies in Nigeria.* London: Jubilee Debt Campaign.

Knoll, M. (2008). *Budget support: A reformed approach or old wines in new skins?* Geneva: UNCTAD.

Koeberle & Malesa. (2005). *World Bank Conditionality: Edited Collection 2005.* Washington: World Bank.

Langan, M. (2009). ACP-EU normative concessions from Stabex to private sector development: Why the European Union's moralised pursuit of a "Deep" trade agenda is nothing "New" in ACP-EU relations. *Perspectives on European Politics and Society, 10*(3), 416–444.

Langan, M. (2011a). Uganda's flower farms and private sector development. *Development and Change, 42*(5), 1207–1240.

Langan, M. (2011b). Private sector development as poverty and strategic discourse: PSD in the political economy of EU-Africa trade relations. *Journal of Modern African Studies, 49*(1), 83–113.

Langan, M. (2012). Normative power europe and the moral economy of Africa-EU ties: A conceptual reorientation of "Normative Power". *New Political Economy, 17*(3), 243–270.

Langan, M. (2014). A moral economy approach to the Africa-EU ties: The case of the european investment bank. *Review of International Studies, 40*(3), 465–485.

Langan, M. (2015). Budget support and Africa-European union relations: Free market reform and Neo-Colonialism? *European Journal of International Relations, 21*(11), pp.101–121.

Moyo, D. (2008). *Dead Aid.* London: Allen Lane.

Nicita, A. (2006 February). *Export-led growth, pro-poor or not? Evidence from Madagascar's textile and apparel industry* (World Bank Policy Research Briefing Paper, No. 3841). Washington, DC: World Bank.

Nkrumah, K. (1965). *Neo-colonialism: The Last Stage of Imperialism* (Sixth Printing—New York International Publishers, 1976).

OECD. (2007). *Business for development: Fostering the private sector—A development centre perspective.* Paris: OECD.

Pigeon, M. (2012). From fiasco to DAWASCO: Remunicipalising water systems in Dar es Salaam, Tanzania. In M. Pigeon, D. McDonald, O. Hoedeman, & S. Kishimoto (Eds.), *Remunicipalisation: Putting water back into public hands.* Amsterdam: Trasnational Institute.

RIAO-RDC, Africa Europe Faith & Justice Network, Entraide et fraternité, GRain sos faim, UMoYa urgewald, War on Want, & World Rainforest Movement. (2016). *Land conflicts and shady finances.* Kinshasa: RIADO-RDC.

Taylor, I. (2008). Sino-African relations and the problem of human rights. *African Affairs, 107*(426), 63–87.

TNI. (2014). *Post privatisation challenges of public water in Ghana.* Amsterdam: TNI.

te Velde, D. W. (2006). Aid for private sector development. In S. Page (Ed.), *Trade and aid: Partners or Rivals in Development Policy?* (pp. 117–140). London: Cameron may.

Udofia, O. E. (1984). Imperialism in Africa: A case of multinational companies. *Journal of Black Studies, 14*(3), 353–368.

USAID. (2008). *Securing the future: A strategy for economic growth.* Washington DC: USAID.

Walker, A. (2012, February 28). James Ibori: How a thief almost became Nigeria's President. *BBC News.*

Whitfield, L., & Therkildsen, O. (2011). What drives states to support the development of productive sectors.

Woddis, J. (1967). *An introduction to Neo-colonialism.* London: Lawrence and Wishart.

CHAPTER 4

Emerging Powers and Neo-Colonialism in Africa

INTRODUCTION

Nkrumah's analysis—written at the height of the Cold War—focused mainly on the external influence of Western aid donors and their corporate entities in the promotion of neo-colonialism in Africa. Given his experience of European Empire in the continent, and the perceived aggression of the USA (witnessed in the overthrown of Lumumba in the Congo Crisis), Nkrumah concerned himself with the critique of Western diminution of African sovereignty via inequitable trade, investment and aid arrangements. In the contemporary era, however, it is of course necessary to consider the potential relevance of the concept of neo-colonialism beyond the core of Western donors, corporations and Western-led global governance institutions such as the World Bank. There is much scholarly focus now on the role of Chinese interventions in Africa, as part of a wider literature on the rise of the 'BRICS' (Brazil, Russia, India, China and South Africa).[1] More recently, there is also now a focus on the potential role of other emerging economies such as President Erdogan's Turkey within the region. In this context, there are fears that African sovereignty and policy space for genuine pro-poor policies are being compromised by external elements in both government and corporate form.

Accordingly, this chapter pays attention to the potential relevance of Nkrumah's writings for making sense of Chinese and Turkish involvement in Africa. China is highlighted as the leading 'BRIC' nation in the

© The Author(s) 2018
M. Langan, *Neo-Colonialism and the Poverty of 'Development' in Africa*, Contemporary African Political Economy,
https://doi.org/10.1007/978-3-319-58571-0_4

region, and Turkey as an example of a non-BRIC emerging economy. Chinese interventions are examined in the context of its own industrialisation strategies, and its adjacent need for raw materials and energy supplies from African origins. This is contextualised in terms of Chinese discourse concerning win–win cooperation and South-South solidarity (Mohan and Lampert 2013: 110). Interestingly, given the focus on neo-colonialism, it also highlights a Chinese discourse concerning protection of state sovereignty in trade and aid dealings within African regimes. In the case of Turkey, meanwhile, the chapter examines President Erdogan's and (erstwhile) Prime Minister Davutoglu's intention to demonstrate their 'virtuous power' through humanitarian intervention and trade exchange with 'fragile states', notably Somalia. This is contextualised in terms of the normative discourse of the Turkish benefactor, with reference to the neo-Ottoman foreign policy pretensions of Erdogan's rule. In both these Chinese and Turkish cases, the chapter problematizes 'development' interventions in terms of regressive impacts upon genuine policy autonomy within African societies (as well as negative impacts for labour rights, the environment and for poverty reduction more broadly).

The discussion is structured as follows. The chapter first highlights the literature surrounding Chinese intervention in Africa. It notes the irony that the language of neo-colonialism is in fact embraced by many Western audiences in their own depiction of Sino-African relations, despite the taboo that exists when the concept is invoked in the critique of the West's own trade and aid affairs. The chapter then provides some empirical examination of the impact of Chinese policies, with emphasis on Angola and Zambia given the importance of these states within Beijing's wider African strategy. The chapter then outlines the neo-Ottoman discourse—and ambitions—of the Erdogan regime in Africa. It problematizes Turkish interventions and, with parallels to China, notes Turkish interest in energy supplies. In both cases, the chapter explores ways in which Nkrumah's writings bear relevance for the contemporary analysis of African relations with emerging powers in the global market economy.

CHINA AND 'WIN-WIN' COOPERATION AS PART OF SOUTH-SOUTH TIES?

There is a wide gap between the language utilised by the Chinese authorities to portray, and to legitimise, their interventions in Africa as compared to the discourse embraced by many detractors in the West to describe their efforts (Zoumara and Ibrahim 2013: 2). There is a distinct irony here that the language of neo-colonialism, whilst almost entirely taboo in the current discussion of Western policies, is heartily embraced by Western media and politicians alike with regards to Sino-African affairs. As part of this 'China Threat' discourse, Beijing is viewed as a neo-coloniser, unconcerned with human rights and solely focused on satiating its appetite for raw materials (such as copper and oil). On the other hand, official Chinese policy discourse represents linkages in Africa as the epitome of win—win cooperation between mutually respectful and sovereign geopolitical blocs. In contrast to the meddling of the West, China is perceived as a level-headed actor able to engage African countries for mutual industrialisation and infrastructure-led development.

It is important to recognise, however, that China is not in fact a 'new' actor within Africa, despite the proliferation of debates surrounding its current interventions in the region. The Communist Party under Mao Zedong focused heavily on African relations as part of the demonstration of the People's Republic of China's (PRC) status on the global stage, particularly after the break with the Soviet Union. It was Mao who coined the concept of the 'Third World' and who emphasised the need for South–South engagement to carve out a distinct geopolitical space insulated from the two superpowers (USA and Soviet Union). Perhaps mostly famously, the PRC offered technical assistance to Julius Nyerere's Tanzania for the successful construction of a large-scale railway system to connect the country to neighbouring Zambia (Zeleza 2014: 148). This stood as a physical testament to Sino-African friendship in the context of the Cold War. Moreover, the Communist regime in Beijing successfully courted the diplomatic support of many African governments in support of the 'One China' policy in relation to the disputed status of Taiwan. It was the support of African governments, including that of Nyerere, which enabled the PRC to win diplomatic recognition in the UN in 1971, and to take the UN Security Council seat theretofore held by the Republic of China (ROC) (Zheng n.d: 271).

There is perhaps, therefore, a degree of historical amnesia in the way in which certain Western sources portray China as a new actor that threats to change the 'rules of the game' in Africa. Niu (2016: 199) explains that the 'China Threat' theory presents China as a foe that wishes to up-end existing types of Western-led development strategies in favour of a mercantilism unburdened by human rights or democratic concerns. Moreover, the China Threat theory—advanced through such rhetorical devices as the 'China cough'—emphasises that local living standards and environmental integrity are undermined by dirty development interventions undertaken by state-led Chinese companies in Africa. These deprecating themes are echoed within official policy discourse too. Taylor and Xiao (2009: 714–715) document how European diplomats have portrayed China as a dangerous 'other' within Africa, given its implicit challenge to the European sphere of influence:

> [the] Parliamentary State Secretary in the German Development Ministry, has declared that "Our African partners really have to watch out that they will not be facing a new process of colonization in their relations with China"... while South Africa's former President Thabo Mbeki warned in December 2006 that "the potential danger . . . was of the emergence of an unequal relationship, similar to that which existed in the past between African colonies and the colonial powers. China can not only just come here and dig for raw materials and then go away and sell us [Africa] manufactured goods".

Anxiety regarding a shift from European influence is also captured within the academic literature. For instance, Alden has considered the possibility of an Africa 'without Europeans' in a more Sino-centric global order (Large 2008: 56).

Again, however, these 'China Threat' narratives are fiercely contested by the authorities in Beijing. They emphasise that China was itself the victim of colonial pretensions in the past, that it remains a developing country, and that it is committed to respectful and mutually beneficial relations with African partners. Beijing maintains, moreover, that Chinese policy is a superior and less denigrating form of intervention than offered by the West. For example, the Chinese embassy in South Africa emphasises that relations are built on 'sincerity... equality and mutual benefit; solidarity and common development', with an implied rebuke to Western actors who might not share such sentiments (cited in Edoho 2011: 106). Furthermore, the Chinese white paper on relations with Africa published in 2006—coinciding with the Forum on Chinese and African Cooperation (FOCAC) where the PRC promised to double aid to Africa to $1 billion by 2009—emphasised norms of solidarity and state sovereignty (Cisse 2012: 2). These norms build on the historical approach of the Communist Party in the Cold War era. Zhou Enlai's "Eight Principles" of aid, issued in 1963/1964, emphasised the need for 'mutual help' and for assistance to allow 'recipient countries [to] develop independently'. In the contemporary era, however, some of the more overt ideological notions of the Third World and the 'Bandung Spirit' have been downplayed in favour of a more practical business concern.[2] Zheng (2010: 275) convincingly argues that:

> It is notable that Chinese foreign and economic policies today are no longer determined by ideological concerns, and besides political consideration, economic and financial gains are significant and conspicuous factors in the formation of state policy. Given that China has embraced capitalism economically, most of its business operations should be first and foremost based on a quest for profit. Thus it is reasonable to argue that self-interest and impulse for profit are the driving forces for this new Sino-African partnership.

The material impact of this focus on growth and trade within Sino-African ties is borne out in terms of empirical data concerning their economic relations. Since the inauguration of FOCAC in 2000, China dismantled tariffs on 190 import lines from 28 least-developed African states—improving market-entry into China for certain African producers. In 2004, there was notable increase in trade flows between the parties with the total volume reaching a record level of US $29.46 billion (Edoho 2011: 115). This represented an increase of 59.8% as compared with the level of volume recorded in 2003. Chinese exports to Africa accounted for US $13.82 billion of this 2004 total figure, while Chinese imports from African sources accounted for US $15.65 billion (ibid.). China's imports included the value of raw materials (such as copper and iron ore as facilitated by Chinese FDI). Moreover, China's import values from Africa in 2004 represented an increase of 87.1% compared to 2003. This trend towards greater volumes of commodities entering China from Africa continued until 2011. The recent reverse of the trend has been attributed to falling world commodity prices and a shift in Chinese consumption. Chinese exports into Africa, meanwhile, constitute the largest source of tradeable goods entering the region as of 2016. Nevertheless, Chinese exports to Africa fell somewhat in 2014 due to global market conditions (Dollar 2016: 20). They have since recovered according to the *Financial Times* (2015), which makes clear that while Africa enjoyed a trade surplus with China from 2010 to 2015, that China now enjoys

Table 4.1 Sino-African trade by key tradeable goods and commodities from 2014–2015

China's imports from Africa	Value US million
Minerals, fuels, lubricants and related materials	53,470
Commodities and transactions, n.e.s	26,591
Crude materials, inedible except fuels	17,923
Manufactured goods	14,514
Africa's imports from China	
Machinery and transportation equipment	42,830
Manufactured goods	28,185
Miscellaneous manufactured articles	18,562
Chemicals and related products, n.e.s	7621
Food and live animals	2746

Source Derived from the Financial Times (2015) graphic of UNCTAD yearly figures

the larger balance of trade between the two blocs. Furthermore, minerals and fuels continue to dominate China's imports from Africa, and machinery and transportation equipment continue to dominate African imports from Chinese origin. This is demonstrated in Table 4.1.

It is interesting to note that certain African countries remain extremely dependent on China in terms of their total exports to international partners. Eritrea, the Central African Republic, Angola, Sudan, Mauritania and the DRC all send 40% or more of their total exports to China. Many other African states remain relatively dependent, such as Zambia and Liberia which send approximately 28 and 27% of their total exports to China, respectively (*Financial Times* 2015).

China and Neo-Colonialism in Africa: Sovereignty Matters?

While the 'China Threat' discourse deployed by Western actors wrongly paints China as the 'other' in contrast to the apparently virtuous interventions of Europe and the USA, nevertheless, it would be misguided to maintain the opposite stance—namely that China's interventions somehow represent an unmitigated opportunity for African development. It is instructive to examine whether China does violate African popular, empirical sovereignty in terms of self-government based on national interests. China's use of trade and aid to sway certain African elites towards policy positions that advance Chinese mercantilist interests, and which improve Chinese firms' profitability, can be examined via Nkrumah's lens of neo-colonialism. China's pursuit of energy and raw materials, as well as its offensive trade interest in opening up African markets for consumption of Chinese hardware, has raised concerns about its undue political and economic influence. These fears have especially come to light in countries that—to date—have experienced a relative dependence on Chinese aid and investment. The cases of Angola and Zambia are prominent in this regard within much of the policy and academic literature.

The latter case—Zambia—is perhaps most useful to examine given its 'cause celebre' status as an African state that has witnessed both fierce civil society and party political opposition to perceived Chinese leverage and neo-colonial influence. Michael Sata, while campaigning as the presidential candidate for the Patriotic Front (PF), expressed grave concerns about the neo-colonial ambitions of the Chinese in terms of Zambia's natural resource wealth. As part of his populist appeals to the citizenry, he reflected that European colonialism had at least attempted to improve the well-being of its subjects, whereas the neo-colonialism apparently pursued by the Chinese was not tempered by any humanitarian aspirations with regards to Africa's people. Sata's rhetoric emerged as a response to substantial Chinese interventions within the mining sector. Investors under the China Nonferrous Mining Co. Group (CNMC), for instance, took control over the Chambishi Copper Mine in 1998. This facility had previously ceased production in 1988 as Washington Consensus reforms took hold (with 1 year 1997–1998 it being unsuccessfully owned by a Canadian-led consortium). By 2006, under Chinese ownership, the Chambishi mine produced around 50,000 tonnes of copper concentrates from 800,000 tonnes of ore (Naidu and Davies 2006: 78). Meanwhile, CNMC investors undertook plans to build an industrial processing zone alongside the mine. This would ostensibly ensure that some processing activities occurred in Zambia itself. The Chambishi Multi-Facility Economic Zone (MFEZ) was successfully established, focussed upon the production of copper-related products (Brautigam and Tang 2011: 83).

Such notable Chinese investments drew ire from Michael Sata during his election campaign in 2006. This owed in large part to concerns that Chinese firms were exploiting Zambian employees in hazardous, low paid and casualised work (Okeowo 2013; Human Rights Watch 2011). This included the Chambishi operations itself, where 52 workers were killed during an explosion at a Beijing Research Institute of Mining and Metallurgy plant surrounding the mining activity. In July 2005, meanwhile, four Zambian workers were shot by a Chinese manager while protesting their low levels of pay (Spilsbury 2012: 257–258). In this vein, Sata referred to the Chinese as 'infesters' not 'investors' (cited in Carmody and Kragelund 2016: 11). This line of argument was maintained by other influential politicians within the PF. The party's deputy leader, Guy Scott, stated that 'the Chinese are no longer welcome. They are seen as cheats and our government as crooks for allowing them to get away with it' (cited in Sautman and Hairong 2009: 750). Michael Sata also notably engineered the expulsion of Lukasa's mayor from the PF, since she had agreed to a Chinese official visit to the city (ibid.). The Zambian citizenry themselves—while not electing Sata until later elections in 2011—were clearly influenced by his populist appeal against Chinese leverage. Rioting broke out in Lukasa and the Copperbelt region, with individuals attacking facilities and businesses identified with Chinese investors.

Importantly in terms of the concept of neo-colonialism and its focus upon relations between external donors and local political elites, Michael Sata, when President from 2011 to 2014, enacted a volte-face. Soon after taking office, he stated in October 2011 that 'I promised to sort the Chinese out… they are also [now] going to sort me out and so we are going to use them to develop'. This clear allusion to Chinese influence upon his presidential programme was tangibly witnessed in terms of his erstwhile attempts to improve taxation income upon mining activities. Carmody and Kragelund (2016: 16) explain that the pressure of Chinese companies—alongside other foreign investors—pressured the government into a wholescale retreat on the issue:

> the power of the Zambian government vis-`a-vis the largescale mining companies soon turned out to be an illusion. The proposed amendments to the mining tax regime were retracted because of uproar among the mining companies who threatened to cut jobs, delay investments, and close down operations if they were implemented. The Zambian government therefore backtracked key aspects of the mining tax regime.

Eventually, the government settled on a minor 3% taxation increase on open mining, while capitulating entirely on the issue of underground mining (ibid.). Meanwhile, the Sata government largely failed to improve labour standards and payment levels in the sector, despite its electoral foundations being built on such concerns. For instance, the Mines Safety Department (MSD) within the Ministry of Mines—admittedly both before and during the Sata administration—was seen to collude with foreign investors. A report by Human Rights Watch (2011) made clear that the MSD faced allegations of corrupt dealings. The report also outlined the institutional limitations of the Ministry of Labour:

> Zambia's Mines Safety Department (MSD) in the Ministry of Mines is supposed to ensure compliance with health and safety regulations. But understaffed, underfunded, and facing allegations of corruption—it provides little effective regulation of mining companies. The Ministry of Labor appears equally weak in protecting those in the copper industry, endorsing collective bargaining agreements that appear inconsistent with Zambian law.

A former minister of mines—Maxwell Mwale—was notably imprisoned by Zambia's judiciary in 2015 for corrupt dealings in the award of mining concessions to a Chinese enterprise (Reuters 2015). This was an extremely rare case in which an elected official was successfully held to account, underlining the potential agency of law courts vis-à-vis foreign influence upon domestic elites. The institution of the Presidency itself—under Sata—is also seen to have been undermined by external influence, not least the fact that the President before his death in October 2014 accepted Chinese assistance to cover his medical costs in an Israeli facility (*The Telegraph* 2014). Shortly before his death, he memorably praised Chinese investment in the country and referred to Zambia and China as 'Siamese twins'—a radical departure from his election promises and original political discourse (Syampeyo et al. 2014).

The situation of Angola equally underlines concerns about the economic—and political—influences of Chinese interventions in terms of African sovereignty and genuine self-governance. In this case, the Dos Santos presidency has regularly been accused of colluding with Chinese oil and infrastructure firms to secure its own political ascendancy. This has been described as a 'reverse democratization process' in which the state itself is being privatised by a corrupted domestic elite in the favour of Chinese foreign investors:

Angola now faces a reverse democratization process: the comeback of a de facto one-party system that emulates the Chinese model but without the basic human development that China provides to its own. The concentration of power in the presidency has turned Sino-Angolan relations into a new stream for looting. The ruling elite around Dos Santos can maximize their profits while allowing the Chinese to acquire core prerogatives of sovereignty in what French academic Béatrice Hibou describes as "the privatization of the state." (Morais 2011)

This de-democratization has been buttressed by Chinese aid in the form of infrastructural assistance, particularly in the run up to elections, as well as (allegedly) Chinese monies for Dos Santos' direct electoral campaigning (Carmody and Owusu 2007: 514; Morais 2011).

Interestingly, in terms of Nkrumah's focus on both corporate and government-led interventions, the situation of China in Angola demonstrates a firm alliance between authorities in Beijing and Chinese firms. A separation between the two appears blurry—with the government directing the operations of its business investors within this strategic African petroleum state. There is particular concern about the close affiliations between the PRC and the Chinese Investment Fund (CIF), constituted as a private firm. The CIF, based in Hong Kong, has led on the majority of major infrastructure developments undertaken in Angola. It appears to act as a 'go-between' vis-à-vis the Angolan Presidency and the Chinese Communist Party (Marques de Morais 2011). Human Rights Watch (2010) note that CIF credit lines have benefitted corrupt politicians, who in return assist China in securing oil concessions. Moreover, Human Rights Watch notes that Dos Santos dismissed the head of his External Intelligence Services when the official threatened to unveil senior politicians who had appropriated CIF funding (ibid.). In addition, Chatman House has documented the personal connections between the Board Chairman of CIF—Xu Jinghua—and Angolan/Chinese political elites. Xu Jinghua is understood to have forged bonds with Angola during the civil war by assisting in the provision of weapons to the government. He is also understood to stand behind the operations of China Sonangol International and its oil investments, not only in Angola itself but also in Gabon, Guinea, Tanzania and Zimbabwe. Given his alleged links to Chinese security services, Xu Jinghua is also understood to have assisted Zimbabwe's intelligence division to bolster the regime of Robert Mugabe (Ovadia 2013: 245).

Throughout Africa, meanwhile, there is concern that cheap imports of Chinese agricultural and manufacturing commodities are depressing local production, leading in many instances to the retraction of industry, or its disbandment. Whilst African consumers may benefit from cheaper goods in the marketplace there are concerns about quality and safety, combined to problems associated with stagnation or indeed retraction in the wider economy (for instance, in terms of the recent decline of the Ghana cedi in international exchange values, which does much to increase prices for consumers). In the case of Ghana's textiles sector, for instance, Tsikata et al. explain that:

> Chinese textiles are displacing domestic textiles products and in some cases forcing the closure of some textiles plants; this has many dire consequences especially in relation to job losses, loss of revenue and loss of research and development capacity in the textile industry in Ghana. (cited in Ademola et al. 2009: 498)[3]

Chinese aid has also been directed to large infrastructure projects in Ghana. With parallels to Western aid, much of this has been directed to road building, helping to establish an enabling environment for business including Chinese oil companies and gold prospectors (Tsikata et al. 2008: 27). Chinese aid has also been directed to prestige projects, such as the construction of the new National Theatre (ibid.). As noted in Chap. 2, the John Mahama government also negotiated a $3 billion loan from Chinese authorities in return for Ghanaian oil supplies. Such forms of Sino-Ghana ties query whether Chinese aid and loans benefit the Ghanaian people, or whether it provides short-term monetary injections, while forestalling genuine economic advancement for the country through disadvantageous trade links combined to regressive FDI in lucrative extractive industries.

Accordingly, there is merit in examining whether Nkrumah's analysis of neo-colonialism is fruitful in diagnosing relations between Chinese firms—and authorities in Beijing—and local African elites. Taylor and Xiao (2009) argue that 'Sino-African relations are processed not of colonization but of globalization and the somewhat chaotic reintegration of China into the global economy'. Beyond the energy sector, they argue, Chinese firms compete with one another without direct input from political authorities in Beijing. Moreover, Taylor (2008: 70–71) himself has focussed upon the 'patrimonial' regime in Africa, noting that this form of political structure finds itself in sync with Chinese benefactors who ask few questions about human rights and democracy. As noted, there are also commentators, such as Niu (2016), who decry the 'China Threat' discourse in terms of how it portrays China as a dangerous 'other'. These lines of argument notwithstanding, the consideration of Chinese interventions in the oil and mining sectors do raise valid questions about neo-colonialism in Africa. Nkrumah's prescient focus on the role of aid monies as lubricant for alliances between foreign actors and domestic elites helps us to conceptualise, and make sense of, the role of bodies such as CIF in Angola and its closeness to the Dos Santos presidency. Furthermore, Nkrumah's focus on the pressures applied by foreign companies and external governments upon African leaders is borne out in the example of Michael Sata in Zambia. Despite his initial intent to raise taxation revenues, to discipline foreign investors on violations of labour standards, and to ensure a greater share of Zambia's natural resource wealth for its own citizenry, Sata soon alluded to the pressure placed upon him by Chinese companies and the Beijing authorities. His attempts to raise taxes on underground mining operations floundered amidst economic threats from (predominantly) Chinese investors in the sector. Key government ministries, including the Ministry of Mines, were also implicated in corruption (similar to the case of Angola and the CIF). Sata himself, meanwhile, apparently accepted subsidies from the Chinese authorities for his medical treatments in Israel.

Nkrumah's warnings about the co-optation of local African elites therefore are highly relevant in the examination of Chinese involvement in Zambia. His concerns about the neo-colonial situation in which African citizenries might find themselves also bears true in the case of Angola where an authoritarian regime—maintained in office through Chinese aid—agrees to the export of its natural resource wealth despite concerns about the long-term viability of its 'development' model. Angolan elites mortgage their natural resource wealth for short-term benefits from Chinese firms. Popular sovereignty—understood as the self-government of the citizenry within a nation-state—is denuded by the interventions of Chinese economic interests which maintain predatory elites. As Kolstad and Wiig (2011: 46) remark in relation to Chinese—and Western—interventions, 'exploiting resources and weak institutions appears to be the name of the investment game in Africa'.

The so-called situation of 'neo-patrimonialism' can be understood, in this vein, as a symptom of neo-colonialism rather than as an alternative paradigm for making sense of development failings. The literature on neo-patrimonialism and the resource curse often emphasises the role of 'Big Men' politicians in perpetuating underdevelopment. This literature does little, however, to correctly interrogate the role of external elements- such as China—in the maintenance of so-called neo-patrimonial regimes in political power. If it were not for the interventions of China in Angola, its predatory elites would soon be swept from the echelons of the state due to popular protest. In Zambia, for instance, citizen riots in Lukasa and the Copper Belt came about as a result of the perceived abuse of the country's economic situation and political institutions by a 'rapacious' China. Such popular unrest would in many cases likely unseat predatory regimes if not for their ability to fall back on the aid and investment of their foreign benefactors, and de facto enablers. The language of the neo-patrimonial state in Africa does more to obscure the political realities and alliances connecting internal elites to their foreign counterparts in Beijing (and London, and Washington). It does not clearly pinpoint the fundamental causal factors that maintain conditions of poverty and underdevelopment in Africa.

It is important, however, to avoid the 'othering' of China as per the 'China Threat' discourse. China is not alone in the perpetuation of conditions of mal-governance and ill-being. Western actors—as well as other emerging powers—facilitate their own economic and political interests via aid and trade to the detriment of African sovereignty. Accordingly, the chapter now examines the role of Turkish involvement in the region, with emphasis on the Horn of Africa, given the immediate focus of the Erdogan regime upon Somalia. It does this to move beyond the 'othering' apparent within the China Threat thesis and to demonstrate how other emerging powers also entrench systems of neo-colonial relations—with much resonance for concerns expressed by Nkrumah in the 1960s.

VIRTUOUS POWER TURKEY IN AFRICA: NEO-OTTOMANISM AND NEO-COLONIALISM

Turkish elites have begun what might be described as a re-entry into Africa. In wake of stalled EU accession negotiations in 2006, the Erdogan regime—with the activism of the erstwhile Foreign Minister and later Prime Minister, Ahmet Davutoglu—sought to create a legitimate space for Turkish influence within the region. While the immediate foreign policy focus of Erdogan's Justice and Development Party (AKP) had been within the Middle East, AKP elites soon turned to Africa after the onset of the Syrian Civil War and the outbreak of the Somali famine during the Ramadan Festival in 2011. Turkey's worsening relationship with the Bashar al-Assad regime, and latterly with other Arab regimes (such as General el-Sisi's Egyptian dictatorship), has done much to frustrate Turkish ambitions in its immediate neighbourhood. Accordingly, AKP elites have increasingly emphasised (sub-Saharan) Africa as a region in which the Turkish nation put a 'neo-Ottoman' foreign policy into practice. Namely, a foreign policy which draws upon the cultural legacies of the Ottoman Empire with an eye to soft power, as well as material gains for the Turkish state. Dealing with poorer countries such as Somalia (in wake of the 2011 famine) will apparently enhance the reputation and clout of 'neo-Ottoman' Turkey as an independent actor on the global stage. It will also be a means of tangibly demonstrating the altruism of the AKP government, and more broadly, of the Turkish people themselves.

Interestingly—and with parallels to Chinese official narratives—AKP elites' construction of their foreign policy role in Africa has drawn sharp contrasts between Turkish and Western actors, particularly the EU. Davutoğlu sought to emphasise the anti-colonial credentials of this 'neo-Ottoman' foreign policy in contrast to that of the West:

> Stretching hundreds of years back, our history tells us that the wellbeing of Africa and Turkey cannot be separated from each other. Within a relationship based on equality, mutual respect, cooperation and common stance against adversaries, the rise of African and Turkish civilizations were always closely linked ... when our ties and defences were weakened due to many reasons including imperialism, colonialism, conflicts or inner strife, we were both weakened and fell back behind other nations.

Going further, Davutoğlu made clear that Turks and Africans share a similar culture, underpinned by the Ottoman state's historical influence. He states that 'we are proud of this... culturally we see ourselves as African' (cited in Bilgiç and Nascimento 2014: 2). Davutoğlu further claims that the 'the great powers' are dismayed that Turks should 'even go to Africa', since it strikes at their own influence in the region (cited in Hashemi 2014: 82). This defiant discourse has been mirrored by (then)

President Gül. With parallels to Davutoğlu, an anti-colonial—and arguably anti-Western—tone is struck:

> We [Turks] have never run after only our own interests. We know that states, which only looked after their own interests in the past engendered major damage to Africa. The international community should know that we could only be equal partners in Africa. (cited in Rudincová 2014: 209)

This implicit denunciation of Western imperialism has been augmented by Gül with more direct language. Speaking to Ghanaian officials, the former President of Turkey made clear that:

> We are different from Europeans. We do not take away your raw materials. We invest and also bring along technology and qualified workforce. We have done so in other African countries. We have already begun to do so in Ghana as well (ibid.)

Gül has also referred to Turkey's intent to bring a 'clean slate with a humanist approach' in its dealings with African countries, alluding to the murkier histories of other (Western) powers in their own relations with the region (cited in Ali 2011: 66).

Interestingly this anti-colonial, anti-Western tone has filtered down to Turkish business, media and civil society. An influential article in *Insight Turkey* by Abdirahman Ali, for example, lavished praised upon the Erdoğan government for its humanitarian intervention in Somalia. Ali made clear that the altruism of Turkey marked a clear contrast from the machinations of Western powers:

> Turkey's approach is a radical contrast to the security-driven approach of the US and is also very different from the strings-attached European style… The Turkish model on the other hand, is groundbreaking and fundamentally centrist, in that it avoids the imperialist tendencies of the US and Europe, all the while establishing "a moral" standard anchored in protecting human rights and helping the weak. (Ali 2011: 72)

This anti-Western perspective is even underlined in the statements of Turkish business entrepreneurs, demonstrating the 'common sense' nature of the 'virtuous' neo-Ottoman foreign policy:

Somalis do not want Western companies in their markets. They think, 'our problems started because of America and *other countries*'. They want to continue without America and the *other countries*. (cited in Harte 2012: 31, emphasis added)

Given the origins of the neo-Ottoman turn in the wake of stalled EU accession, this particular theme is of much interest. Emphasis on the benevolence of Turkey plays a double role. It legitimises Turkish foreign policy intervention on the basis of its enlightened nature—that is to promote 'win-win' cooperation among equals (again with certain parallels to China's own discourse in the region). Second, it does much to delegitimise the EU's role in the region (opening up greater space for Turkish action) as well as distancing Turkey from the need to join such an 'imperial' EU entity. In this way, AKP elites not merely open up opportunities for trade and aid linkages in Africa. But they also assuage domestic opinion on the issue of (stalled) EU membership, and thereby challenge European elites themselves both to rethink their conduct towards Turkey, and to Africans. Indeed, within the utterances of AKP officials, there is the distinct implication that Turkey itself has been the 'victim' of EU policies in the past. Turkey and Africa, standing together, are seen as a solid bloc able to warn off encroachments from possible imperial powers, such as the EU.

Significantly, however, this negative tone is balanced by more positive themes. In particular, there is emphasis on the ability of Turkey to develop friendly relations with African states that are home to significant Muslim populations. The past role of the Ottoman Empire as the seat of the Caliphate, and its subsequent influence on the development of the Islamic world, is positively invoked. Notably, Turkey has enhanced its role within the Organization for Islamic Conference, inviting African dignitaries to take part (Özkan and Akgün 2010: 538). Additionally, Turkish elites have emphasised the development mission of the Turkish state via the Turkish Co-operation and Co-ordination Agency (TIKA). Turkish assistance is emphasised as having increased dramatically in the period of the Erdoğan governments. A TIKA report from 2013, for instance, remarks that Turkish overseas aid rose from $85 million in 2002 to $3.3 billion in 2013. In terms of African countries, Turkish aid has reached substantial proportions, standing at $749.47 million in 2012 and $782.73 in 2013 (TIKA 2012, 2013). This is matched by increases in terms of Turkish trade with sub-Saharan Africa, which 'reached

$7.5 billion in 2011, a 72% increase from the year before and a ten-fold increase since 2000' (Özkan and Orakçi 2014: 344). It is also augmented by the expansion of Turkish embassies throughout the region, as well as an increase in the number of aviation routes to Africa from Turkey (ibid.).

Crucially, Turkey has utilised interventions in Somalia as a 'showpiece' for its potential humanitarian clout. In the wake of the 2011 famine, the Erdoğan government sought to demonstrate the potency of its more assertive neo-Ottoman stance. This emphasised the normative values of Turkey in juxtaposition with the perceived neglect of Somalia by self-interested Western entities. It also underscored the material capabilities of Turkey as an emerging economy, tangibly demonstrated in terms of aid and trade assistance. A visit to the war-torn nation by Erdoğan himself in 2011 was a particular highlight. It at once demonstrated the ability of Turks to take advantage of cultural affinity to offer friendship to (Muslim) people in Africa. It also underlined the apparent ethical qualities of the leader, as well as of the Turkish state.

Significantly this intervention has also been utilised to reinforce the neo-Ottoman theme that Turkey is a virtuous power *in contrast to* the West, and the EU institutions. Erdoğan took the opportunity in a UN General Assembly Address to highlight colonialism as the historical foundation of Somalia's recent plight:

> We should not only look into the picture of today, but also the shameful history that has led Somalia into the arms of this great tragedy. Indeed, beneath the tip of this huge iceberg lie great crimes against humanity. In that respect the situation in Somalia has also revealed the deep wounds inflicted by the colonialist mentality which kept Africa under its hegemony for centuries. As this old colonial mentality ignores places where it has no interest, it is now watching millions of children die in need of a morsel of bread. (Erdoğan 2011)

Importantly, this discourse was materially buttressed by TIKA aid, private donations, as well as trade. Private Turkish donations to Somalia alone amounted to more than $365 million in 2011 (Harte 2012: 27). Moreover, by 2014, the Turkish state had delivered around $500 million in aid (Özkan and Orakçi 2014: 348). 'Virtuous Power Turkey' also extended 1200 scholarships to Somali youth as a means of building in concern for that country's long-term progress (Harte 2012: 27).

Interestingly, narratives of the activism of the Turkish state were also matched by language pertaining to the activism (and heroism) of Turkish aid workers and NGOs. Humanitarian action on the part of Turkish citizens was contrasted by AKP elites with the perceived inaction of EU officials who maintained headquarters in the distant Kenyan capital, Nairobi. Most striking, however, this discourse was repeated by Somali leaders. Notably, the President of Somalia juxtaposed the humanitarianism of the Turks with the uncaring attitude of 'other powers':

> Turkey did not hold back, waiting for stability before it invested... where other international partners chose to plan their interventions from elsewhere [such as the EU based in Nairobi], Turkey put its people on the ground in Somalia. (cited in i24news.tv 2015)

Interestingly, the Somali government has also endorsed the historical image of a benevolent Ottoman Empire. For instance, the Somali President recently welcomed Erdoğan back to the country in 2015, noting that 'the friendship between Turkey and Somalia is long—beginning in the sixteenth century with ties between the Ottoman Empire and the Abel Sultanate' (Radio Muqdisho 2015).

It is important to restate, however, that Turkey does not intend to limit itself to partnership with this one African country. Already, Turkish embassies have made strategic linkages with African officials beyond the Horn of Africa. Moreover, President Gül made trade and aid objectives known to his Ghanaian counterparts in the West of Africa. More recently, President Erdoğan has engaged East African countries as part of a 2016 tour. Turkey—in its neo-Ottoman phase of assertive, humanitarian diplomacy—is giving largesse to Somalia as a means of launching a wider African policy. As Harte states 'with its unrivalled on-the-ground rebuilding effort and generous scholarship program, Turkey is using Somalia as the first great display of "virtuous power"' (Harte 2012: 28).

Furthermore, AKP elites envisage a sustained Turkish challenge to a wider 'world-system' dominated by the EU and other Western powers (Haşimi 2014: 126–128). Turkey is thus portrayed as a great emerging power of its own accord. Specifically, Turkey seeks to 'put the traditional world on notice' and to challenge regressive forms of Western, and EU, interventions in the Global South (Ali 2011: 65). It is important, however, to contextualise Turkish constructs in terms of consequences for

African citizens, with potential resonance for the concept of neo-colonialism as put forth by Nkrumah. The next section therefore, considers, whether Turkish claims to promote humanitarian aid and trade linkages in Africa should be tempered with concerns about the impact of AKP largesse for genuine sovereignty and citizen well-being in recipient states. Moreover, it highlights potential implications for the EU given the manner in which it has been so fiercely contrasted with the 'virtuous' nature of Turkish foreign policy.

TURKEY'S DEVELOPMENT INTERVENTIONS: A NEO-COLONIAL FORCE WITHIN AFRICA?

A constructivist perspective allied to critical discourse analysis may challenge power asymmetries that are either veiled, or downplayed, through language (Fairclough 2009; Fairclough et al. 2009; Van Djik 1993; Wodak 2002). Accordingly, it is important to question whether there might be disjuncture between stated Turkish objectives and material policy outcomes, with reference to the concept of neo-colonialism. This is not to deny the contributions of Turkish aid in wake of famine in Somalia, for instance. But it is to question whether there may be negative repercussions of particular forms of Turkish interventions that are hidden, or rationalised, by dominant forms of official policy discourse. Indeed, it is notable that Turkish elites have spoken of their intent to provide assistance as a *precursor* to enhanced business linkages in Somalia, and beyond (Kagwanja 2013). The stabilisation of Somalia is understood as a form of enlightened altruism in which the Turkish benefactor will gain trading access to an important regional hub (ibid.) As such, Somalia is understood as a staging post for greater Turkish economic involvement in Africa. Note for example (then) President Gül's visit to Ghana. Moreover, the Turkish government has made clear its intent to 'double its trade volume with all African countries, currently at $16 billion in a "few years"' (Harte 2012: 31).

Specifically, there are grounds on which to doubt whether Turkish FDI will necessarily have positive consequences for ordinary workers and communities. For example, in Somalia there has been recent condemnation of Turkish investment in ports facilities. Workers have protested local job losses amidst the arrival of Turkish managerial class to operate the facilities in a more 'professional' manner. Also there is concern that

Turkish investors will use imported machinery to the detriment of local peoples. In the words of one port worker:

> the [Somali] government deliberately handed over the port to the Turkish company without considering our right to work and earn an income... Turkey wants to use its lifts instead of the thousands of porters. (Reuters 2014)

Moreover, there are those (not least the terror group, Al Shabab) who question Turkish motives in terms of oil reserves within Somalia's Puntland province. With certain parallels to the Chinese case explored earlier in this chapter, there is general recognition that Turkey, as an emerging economy, has substantial geopolitical interest in Africa to underpin its own national energy security. The Puntland province alone could produce 10 billion barrels of oil, while Turkey currently imports around 600,000 barrels per day (Yurdusev 2004: 31). There are therefore concerns about Somalia's loss of a vital resource, environmental degradation, as well as the likely treatment of Somali workers by Turkish energy companies. Incidents such as the 2014 mining disaster in Soma and the lack of protection of *Turkish* workers' rights increase fears that Turkish FDI may not entail progressive results for poorer workers in *Somalia*. Moreover, concerns about Turkey's motives in the region are not confined to Somalia. As Özkan and Orakçi (2014: 343) remark of officials in Africa more widely:

> Some view Turkey as concerned mostly with its own economy and industries, and many associate Turkey with a self-interested approach to trade. For this reason, many African countries have been suspicious of Ankara's manoeuvres over the past decade.

Furthermore, with clear relevance for the application of the concept of neo-colonialism, there are grave fears about the impact of Turkish aid policy in terms of exacerbating 'corrupt' government in Africa. Notably, the decision of the Turkish government and TIKA to give monies to recipient states without following standard international development reporting protocols potentially lends itself to the subsidisation of Somali (and wider African) elites without due anti-graft measures (Murphy and Woods 2014: 3). This is amplified by the fact that—as demonstrated above—certain African personnel have engaged in deliberate extraversion

(Bayart 2004). That is, they have made deliberate appeals to external donors as a means of lubricating domestic patronage networks. In the case of Turkey, Somali officials have deliberately complimented the humanitarian self-image of AKP elites as a means of levering in greater aid flows from their benefactors in Ankara. As Murphy and Woods (2014: 3) remark 'Somalis [in government institutions] have played the development game a long time, and they know how to play it well'. Accordingly, there is the fear that 'naïve' or perhaps more properly, self-interested, Turkish officials are lubricating the patronage networks of the authoritarian Somali government to secure access to energy resources without due concern for corruption issues.

Additionally, there is concern that Turkey is merely following the EU (and other emerging economies such as China) as a neo-colonial actor in a 'new scramble' for African markets. Notably, Turkish elites are vigorously pursuing free trade agreements (FTAs) with African countries including the DRC, Seychelles, and Cameroon (Shinn 2015). A recently signed FTA with Mauritius is notably based upon the EU's own interim EPA with this African nation (owing largely to Turkey's status within the EU's Customs Union) (Mauritius Chamber of Commerce and Industry 2016). This FTA will likely prove a boon to Turkish entrepreneurs, but will pose a serious challenge to local business people who will have to compete with (often) cheaper foreign manufacturers. Turkey is thus seen to follow a mercantilist instinct, one which may 'kick-away-the-ladder' of development by depressing domestic entrepreneurial growth in Africa. Rather than departing from the machinations of an 'imperial' EU (or of rival emerging economies such as China), Turkey is instead seen as yet one more player in the new scramble for African markets.

Perhaps most alarmingly, there is also concern about the provision of Turkish arms to African governments that are largely divorced from democratic accountability to the wishes—and material needs—of their own citizenries. In the case of Somalia, the Turkish state signed a 2014 agreement to build fully equipped military bases, and to train government forces (Ryan 2014). In terms of sub-Saharan Africa more broadly, Turkish military firms Aselsan and Turkish Aerospace Industries have seen impressive revenue gains. Aselsan's revenues grew from around $800 million in 2012 to approximately $1 billion in 2013. This was coupled to rising revenues for Turkish Aerospace Industries which increased from around $650 million in 2012 to just under $800 million in 2013 (Young 2014). Such trends not only raise alarm in terms of the AKP elite's support of African governments with dubious human rights records. They also raise questions in terms of Turkish arms falling into the possession of radical militias, whether deliberately or accidentally, through capture of state equipment. In the case of Syria, there has already been widespread allegation that AKP elites consciously supported ISIS forces as a means of destabilising their erstwhile ally, Bashar al-Assad.

In the African context, there are parallel concerns expressed by secular civil society activists that AKP elites are embroiling themselves in similar civil conflicts. Altintas (2015) notes that there are 'harrowing claim[s] that Turkey has armed jihadist groups in Nigeria', namely Boko Haram. In this Nigerian context, there are specific allegations that a Turkish airline carrier has been forced to channel arms, despite the apparent protestations of its managerial echelons (Rubin 2014). It is also interesting to note that the Turkish ambassador to Chad, Ahmet Kavas, publicly expressed his reservations about French action in neighbouring Mali in 2014 to tackle al Qaeda in the Islamic Maghreb (Kredo 2013). Fears have been raised that Turkish armaments have fuelled Islamist insurgencies in Chad and Mali, in addition to the cases of Nigeria and Syria. The creeping militarisation of Africa via Turkish defence firms—whether in terms of arms to de jure states, or to radical Islamist groups—is a clear cause for concern and does much to undermine the apparent 'ethical' tone of Turkish foreign policy. It also raises fears that Turkey is indeed a neo-colonial player in the region, intervening in the sovereign affairs of African nations for both ideological (Islamist) as well as economic (energy) motivations.

At an ideational level there is also concern that Turkish interventions might perpetuate—and are part motivated by—an Orientalism exhibited on the part of AKP elites, and within the wider Turkish population. There is already a perception in certain quarters of Turkish society that African states are 'weak' and are 'embarrassingly incompetent'(Ali 2011: 68). More widely, 'Sub-Saharan Africa has been perceived to be a distant and unfamiliar area with a variety of problems such as hunger, civil wars and disaster'(Rudincová 2014: 201). In this context, there is scope for AKP elites to portray themselves as the humanitarian 'saviour' of weaker polities in Africa, and to publicly justify stark levels of political and economic intervention on the basis of the alleged incompetency of African officials. At the level of post-colonial imaginaries, this element of AKP discourse threatens to perpetuate stereotypes of African nations as tragic containers of human misery. With parallels to the neo-patrimonialism literature, AKP discourse largely blames African countries for their own dilemmas, while promising that foreign intervention will do much to rectify underdevelopment (notwithstanding loss of natural raw materials through extractive processes in provinces such as Somalia's Puntland province). Such narratives do much to impinge upon African agency—further marginalising African states on the international stage. Following Edward Said (1979), it leaves African societies vulnerable to regressive forms of external intervention on the grounds of their implied 'barbarity' or lack of capability.

Interestingly, there are potentially major implications of the neo-Ottoman entry into Africa for the European project. As explained, AKP elites have deliberately drawn upon colonial histories to portray Europe (rather convincingly) as a neo-colonial entity concerned solely with resource extraction, and trading interests. It is necessary to highlight that there is a potential paradox in Turkish discourse here as the EU is simultaneously condemned for its neo-colonial incursions in Africa, while also being condemned for being too remote in cases such as Somalia. Nevertheless, Turkish elites counter that the EU involves itself only when its neo-colonial interests will be served. When certain countries are too unstable, then these countries are left to suffer humanitarian crises whose very origins can be traced back to European colonialism (Erdoğan 2011).

The emergence of Turkey as a development player in the region is a clear challenge to EU-Africa trade and development ties. This might be dismissed by certain European officials as mere hyperbole stemming from AKP elites' frustration with stalled EU accession talks. Nevertheless, there is a real jeopardy for the EU that these confrontational, anti-colonial narratives gain wider traction within African governments, particularly in 'moderate' states such as Ghana which have heretofore largely acquiesced to EU policy preferences (for instance, on the issue of EPAs). There is substantial evidence which lends credence to the neo-Ottoman thesis that EU institutions are perpetuating poverty in certain African states through regressive aid and trade linkages. The role of the EIB, for instance, has been roundly condemned for environmentally and socially damaging activities in countries such as the DRC, Zambia and Mozambique (Counter Balance 2009; Friends of the Earth 2006; "The European"; Brynildsen and Nombora 2013). The role of EU budget support, meanwhile, has been seen to sway African officials towards disadvantageous EPAs (see Chap. 2 for more on donor budget support, and Chap. 5 for more on ACP-EU EPAs). Accordingly, Turkish language relating to European neo-colonialism may fall upon fertile soil. African governments—offered material and discursive support from Ankara—may increasing concur with neo-Ottoman sentiments that 'Europe only thinks of itself; its aim is to exploit other countries. We should not expect help from Europe and we have to awaken ourselves'(Şemsettin Günaltay cited in Hashemi 2014: 89). Of course, however, these African elites should also be wary of Turkey, particularly in light of its energy demands, as well as its corporations' interest in the arms trade.

EMERGING POWERS AND NEO-COLONIALISM IN AFRICA: REFLECTIONS ON THE CHINESE AND TURKISH CASES

There are clear discursive overlaps in China's and Turkey's respective representations of their (legitimate) involvement in Africa. Both China and Turkey emphasise their own experiences of imperial predation at the hands of Western powers. Both China and Turkey highlight their role as emerging economies able to assist other 'Southern' nations to obtain development objectives. Moreover, both countries (and their elites) emphasise that their aid and trade assistance is not encumbered by the conditionalities often imposed by Western actors. Moreover, there is also clear parallel between China and Turkey in terms of their desire to secure vital energy supplies through alliances with African regimes with dubious records in terms of the well-being of local citizenries. While Chinese and Turkish officials claim to promote the sovereignty and territorial integrity of their African partners, their aid often supports isolated domestic elites to maintain power and to perpetuate a divorce between African politicians and their own peoples.

In this situation, it is necessary to engage the concept of neo-colonialism to better understand—and to critique—the impact of Chinese and Turkish interventions in Africa. Nkrumah's analysis once again provides us with a toolkit for the examination of both trade and aid linkages between these external elements and their 'partner' states in Africa. Nkrumah's focus on both the corporate and government pursuit of neo-colonial ambitions in the region is useful when examining the role of Chinese (and Turkish) companies in securing energy goals and policy leverage (for instance with regards to the failed tax increase on Zambian mining operations under Michael Sata). His analysis helps us to conceptualise how political and corporate elites seek to denude genuine self-governance in Africa for their own strategic purposes.

Moreover, it is again necessary to reflect on how the neo-patrimonialism literature can skew our attention away from the external influences upon African regimes and towards (oftentimes) essentialist portrayals of Africa's 'Big Men' and their wrongdoings. It is perhaps obvious that strongmen leaders such as Angola's Dos Santos are complicit in their nation's own development failings. Nevertheless, it is wholly necessary to consider how such regimes are supported, maintained and encouraged by foreign actors who benefit from collaboration. Working with the Dos Santos regime to secure oil contracts—lubricated by the CIF—ensures that China can fulfil its own demand for energy supplies (while undermining the material basis for African countries' longer term well-being). While states such as Angola or Zambia may witnesses certain minor advances in terms of infrastructure projects, their elites' extraversion perpetuates corrosive forms of government. On a final note, it is worth reflecting on debates about African agency (to be explored in more detail in Chap. 8). The ambition of the Sata government in Zambia to raise taxation upon the mining industry may be viewed as an attempt to secure a certain restoration of political power within the presidency vis-à-vis external elements. Nevertheless, this should not be mistaken as an attempt to break with relations of neo-colonialism per se. Rather than seek to exert full sovereign authority (for instance, in terms of the nationalisation of the resource wealth of the country), the Sata regime sought (rather unsuccessfully) to renegotiate certain terms of Chinese investment. As Carmody and Kragelund (2016: 17–18) argue:

> what we have witnessed is power or "agency at the margins".... Londsdale refers to this situation as "agency in tight corners." The central agency employed, however, involved reproducing the extant structure of the actor-network, despite the formal right to assert full sovereignty over "national" resources such as copper. Thus, Zambia arguably reproduced the hegemony of transnational capital through a slight renegotiation of the contract of extraversion to facilitate legitimation.

With parallels to Nkrumah, Carmody and Kragelund do not deny scope for limited renegotiation of the status quo. What they do cast doubt upon, however, is the capacity—or willingness—of regimes in resource-rich nations to fundamentally recast power relations between themselves and external benefactors. Rather than seek to transform and overcome relations of neo-colonialism, such African elites are structurally constrained and enact 'agency in tight corners'. This constrained agency is now considered in Chap. 5 in relation to trade agreements. With emphasis on EU negotiations for EPAs with African sub-regions (such as ECOWAS), it points to the structural limitations which certain African elites face when dealing with their donor 'partners'.

Notes

1. Interestingly in terms of South Africa, Bond (2004, 2016) points to its position within a 'sub-imperialism'. He points to President Mbeki's championing of the New Economic Partnership for African Development (NEPAD) as evidence of the way in which South African elites have embraced neo-liberal norms, leveraging their political status vis-à-vis the traditional donor community, while advancing their economic interests within other African countries.
2. The Bandung Spirit refers to the Bandung Conference which established South–South development co-operation.
3. It is interesting to note also that Chinese textiles have challenged African exports in other markets, notably in terms of the USA after the end of the Multifibre Agreement—see Brautigam and Tang (2014: 79).

References

Ademola, O. T., Bankole, A.-S., & Adewuyi, A. (2009). China-Africa trade relations: Insights from AERC scoping studies. *European Journal of Development Research, 21*(4), 485–505.

Ali, A. (2011). Turkey's foray into Africa: A new humanitarian power? *Insight Turkey, 13*(4), 65–73.

Altintas, E. B. (2015, September 3). What is Turkey doing in Africa? *The Daily Zaman.*

Balance, Counter. (2009). *Coherence for development? Development check of the financing activities of the European Investment Bank.* Brussels: Counter Balance.

Bilgiç, A., & Nascimento, D. (2014). *Turkey's new focus on Africa: Causes and challenges.* Oslo: NOREF.

Bond, P. (2004). Bankrupt Africa: Imperialism, Sub-Imperialism and the politics of finance. *Historical Materialism, 12*(4), 146–172.

Bond, P. (2016). BRICS banking and the debate over sub-imperialism. *Third World Quarterly, 37*(4), 611–629.

Brautigam, D., & Tang, X. (2011). African Shenzhen: China's special economic zones in Africa. *Journal of Modern African Studies, 49*(1), 27–54.

Brautigam, D., & Tang, X. (2014). Going global in groups: Structural transformation and China's special economic zones overseas. *World Development, 63,* 78–91.

Brynildsen, O., & Nombora, D. (2013). *Mining without development: The case of Kenmare moma mine in Mozambique.* Maputo: CIP and Eurodad.

Carmody, P., & Kragelund, P. (2016). Who is in charge? State power and agency in Sino-African relations. *Cornell International Law Journal, 49*(1), 1–23.

Carmody, P., & Owusu, F. (2007). Competing hegemons? Chinese versus American geo-economic stategies in Africa. *Political Geography, 26,* 504–524.

Cisse, D. (2012). *FOCAC: Trade, investments and aid in China–Africa relations.* Stellenbosch: Centre for Chinese Studies, Stellenbosch University.

Dollar, D. (2016). *China's engagement with Africa: From natural resources to human resources.* Washington: Brookings Institute.

Edoho, F. (2011). Globalization and marginalization of Africa: Contextualization of China–Africa relations. *Africa Today, 58*(1), 102–124.

Erdoğan R. T. (2011, September 22). Statement by Recep Tayyip Erdoğan at 66th UN General Assembly. *Voltaire Network,* New York.

Fairclough, N. (2009). Language and globalisation. *Semiotica, 173*(1), 317–342.

Fairclough N., Mulderrig J., & Wodak R. (2009). Critical discourse analysis. In T.A. van Djik (Ed.), *Discourse studies: A multidisciplinary introduction.* London: SAGE.

Financial Times. (2015, February 9). China's policy dilemma deepens on record trade surplus. *Financial Times.* Available at: http://blogs.ft.com/beyond-brics/2015/02/09/chinas-policy-dilemma-deepens-on-record-trade-surplus/. Accessed 13 July 2017.

Friends of the Earth International. (2006). *The European Investment Bank in the South: In whose interest?* Amsterdam: Friends of the Earth.

Harte, J. (2012). Turkey shocks Africa. *World Policy Journal, 29*(4), 27–38.

Hasemi, S. A. (2014). The Ottoman response to the Western storm: Lessons for Neo-Ottomanism in Turkey. *The Quarterly Journal of Political Studies of Islamic World, 2*(8), 81–96.

Haşimi, C. (2014). Turkey's humanitarian diplomacy and development cooperation. *Insight Turkey, 16*(1), 127–145.

Human Rights Watch. (2010). *Transparency and accountability in Angola.* New York: Human Rights Watch. Available at: https://www.hrw.org/report/2010/04/13/transparency-and-accountability-angola. Accessed 25 Mar 2017.

Human Rights Watch. (2011). *You'll be fired if you refuse: Labour abuses in Zambia's state-owned copper mines.* New York: Hyman Rights Watch. Available at: https://www.hrw.org/report/2011/11/04/youll-be-fired-if-you-refuse/labor-abuses-zambias-chinese-state-owned-copper-mines. Accessed 25 Mar 2017.

i24news.tv. (2015, January 26). Turkish President Erdoğan Visits Somalia.

Kagwanja, C. (2013, June 29). Turkey in Somalia: Building relations using brotherhood, aid and dialogue. *The East African.*

Kolstad, I., & Wiig, A. (2011). Better the devil you know? Chinese foreign direct investment in Africa. *Journal of African Business, 12*(1), 31–50.

Kredo, A. (2013, February 27). Turkish tweet turns heads. *The Washington Free Beacon.*

Large, D. (2008). Beyond dragon in the bush: The study of China–Africa relations. *African Affairs, 107*(426), 45–61.

de Marques Morais, R. (2011, March/April). The new imperialism: China in Angola. *World Affairs.* Available at: http://www.worldaffairsjournal.org/article/new-imperialism-china-angola. Accessed 25 Mar 2017.

Mauritius Chamber of Commerce and Industry. (2016). *Mauritius-Turkey free trade agreement (FTA).* Port Louis: MCCI.

Mohan, G., & Lampert, B. (2013). Negotiating China: Reinserting African agency into China–Africa relations. *African Affairs, 112*(446), 92–110.

Murphy T., & Woods A. (2014, February). Turkey's international development framework—Case study: Somalia. *IPC-Mercator Policy Brief.* Istanbul: Istanbul Policy Centre.

Naidu, S., & Davies, M. (2006). China fuels its future with Africa's riches. *South African Journal of International Affairs, 13*(2), 69–83.

Niu, Z. (2016). China's development and its aid presence in Africa: A critical reflection from the perspective of development anthropology. *Journal of Asian and African Studies, 51*(2), 199–221.

Okeowo, A. (2013, June 12). China in Africa: The new imperialists? *The New Yorker.*

Ovadia, J. (2013). Accumulation with or without dispossession? A 'both/and' approach to China in Africa with reference to Angola. *Review of African Political Economy, 40*(136), 233–250.

Özkan, M., & Akgün, B. (2010). Turkey's opening to Africa. *Journal of Common Market Studies, 48*(4), 525–546.

Özkan, M., & Orakçi, S. (2014). Viewpoint: Turkey as a "Political" actor in Africa—As assessment of Turkish involvement in Somalia. *Journal of Eastern African Studies, 9*(2), 343–352.

Radio Muqdisho. (2015, January 25). The President: We welcome our Turkish friends back to Somalia. *Radio Muqdisho.*

Reuters. (2014, October 23). Somali port set for facelift with Turkish Help. *Reuters.*

Reuters. (2015, February 27). Update 3—jailing of Zambian ex-minister prompts calls for action on graft. *Reuters.* Available at: http://www.reuters.com/article/zambia-corruption-idUSL5N0W11YE20150227. Accessed 13 July 2017.

Rubin, M. (2014, March 20). Tape suggests Turkey supports terror. *Commentary.*

Rudincová, K. (2014). New player on the scene: Turkish engagement in Africa. *Bulletin of Geography: Socio-economic Series, 24,* 197–213.

Ryan, G. (2014, December 12). Ottoman Brethren: Turkey's role in Somalia's recent development. *Polity.org.za.*

Said, S. (1979). *Orientalism.* New York: Random House.

Sautman, B., & Hairong, Y. (2009). African perspectives on China-Africa links. *The China Quarterly, 199,* 728–759.

Shinn, D. (2015). *Turkey's Engagement in Sub-Saharan Africa: Shifting Alliances and Strategic Diversification.* London: Chatham House.

Spilsbury, L. (2012). Can Michael Sata tame the dragon and channel Chinese investment towards development for Zambians? *Journal of Politics and International Studies, 8,* 238–278.

Syampeyo, Y., Chibuye, J., & Chinga, A. (2014, June 20). Sata Defends China. *Daily Mail Zambia.*

Taylor, I. (2008). Sino-African relations and the problem of human rights. *African Affairs, 107*(426), 63–87.

Taylor, I., & Xiao, Y. (2009). A case of mistaken identity: "China Inc." and its "imperialism" in sub-Saharan Africa. *Asian Politics and Policy, 1*(4), 709–725.

The Telegraph. (2014, October 29). Michael Sata—Obituary. *The Telegraph.*

TIKA. (2012). *Turkish development assistance 2012.* Ankara: TIKA.

TIKA. (2013). *Turkish Development Assistance 2013.* Ankara: TIKA.

Tsikata, D., Pokuaa, A., & Aryeetey, F. (2008). *China-Africa relations: A case study of Ghana: A draft scoping study prepared for the African economic research consortium.* Accra: Institute of Statistical, Social and Economic Research—University of Ghana.

Van Djik. (1993). Principles of critical discourse analysis. *Discourse and Society, 4*(2), 249–283.

Wodak, R. (2002). Aspects of critical discourse analysis. *ZfAL, 36,* 5–31.

Young, A. (2014, August 5). Turkey is boosting weapons exports with a focus on Africa: Here's who benefits. IbTimes.com.

Yurdusev, A. N. (2004). *Ottoman diplomacy: Conventional or unconventional?.* London: Palgrave.

Zeleza, P. T. (2014). The Africa–China relationship: Challenges and opportunities. *Canadian Journal of African Studies, 48*(1), 145–169.

Zheng. (n.d.). *Neo-colonialism, ideology or just business? China's perception of Africa.* Boulder: University of Colorado.

Zheng, L. (2010). Neo-colonialism, ideology or just business? China's perception of Africa. *Global Media and Communication, 6*(3), 271–276.

Zoumara, B., & Ibrahim, A. F. (2013). China-Africa relations looking beyond the critics. *Pambazuka,* No. 166. Available at: http://pambazuka.org/en/category/features/87735. Accessed 7 Jan 2017.

CHAPTER 5

Trade and Neo-Colonialism: The Case of Africa–EU Ties

Introduction

Nkrumah (1963: 182–183) warned that neo-colonialism would involve the continuation of asymmetric trade between Africa and foreign nations, particularly those that had historically colonised the continent. While African countries had gained formal independence, aid monies and corporate pressure would be utilised to cajole African elites into trade arrangements that did not suit the long-term interests of their citizenries. This was echoed by Sekou Touré (1962: 149) who warned that Association trade and aid arrangements between Africa and the newly established European Economic Community (EEC) would maintain Africans' subordinate position as 'hewers of wood and drawers of water'. Touré and Nkrumah both warned that the EEC would ensure that African countries continued to supply its members with raw materials and energy, while ensuring that African states remained open markets for value-added consumer goods produced in Europe.

These stark predictions about the continuation of (neo)colonial patterns of trade deserve scrutiny in the context of Africa's current trade relationships with external actors. The EU has notably gained the recent agreement of West African Heads of Government in July 2014 to the terms of a free trade deal (the EPA). As of December 2016, this regional EPA has been provisionally applied in Ghana and Ivory Coast and will likely be rolled out across the whole of West Africa once remaining dissenters (such as Nigeria) give way to the full ratification and

© The Author(s) 2018   119
M. Langan, *Neo-Colonialism and the Poverty of 'Development'*
in Africa, Contemporary African Political Economy,
https://doi.org/10.1007/978-3-319-58571-0_5

implementation of the agreement. From the perspective of the European Commission (2002, 2005, 2007), the EPA ensures 'reciprocal' free trade between the blocs in which African countries continue to enjoy low tariff access to European markets (notwithstanding the Common Agricultural Policy [CAP]) while liberalising their own tariffs vis-à-vis goods from the EU member states.[1] The EU's granting of an EPA Development Programme (EPADP) with €6.5 billion of Aid for Trade monies will apparently ensure that the EPA is a 'win-win' for both parties (European Council 2010, 2014). Namely, the EPADP will help African signatories to adjust to the pressures of free trade and to support their own sectors to become more competitive in globalised markets (Langan and Price 2015).

There is much scepticism in West Africa, however, as well as other sub-regions of the ACP bloc where EPAs are being implemented, that free trade deals with Europe do not benefit nascent, emerging sectors. There is concern that import-flooding of cheaper European produce in sectors such as poultry, tomato agro-processing, carpet manufacturing and cotton-textiles will mean that local industries collapse (Bagooro 2011; Solidar 2008; ActionAid 2004). Earlier forms of tariff liberalisation resulted in foreign goods undercutting local production, leading to job losses and social hardship amidst retrenchment in key emerging sectors (ibid.). Trade liberalisation is therefore viewed by certain trade union and civil society groups as a barrier to diversification and value addition in developing economies. With parallels to the words of Touré above, African countries will remain dependent on exports of raw materials since their own nascent agro-processing and manufacturing sectors will collapse under the weight of EPAs/FTAs. In the context of the West African EPA, prominent groups such as the National Association of Nigerian Traders (NANTS 2010) have lobbied their governments to forestall implementation of the agreement, while alternative policy solutions are devised. The European Commission, meanwhile, has made clear that middle income West African countries will default to the Generalised System of Preferences (GSP) should a regional EPA not come into force (CONCORD 2015). This threat of a GSP default would mean higher tariffs for African export industries. For instance, higher tariffs would impact the cocoa sector in Ghana and Nigeria which have diversified into 'origin grindings'—that is, the processing of the raw cocoa beans into cake, butter and paste—for value-added export to Europe (World Cocoa Foundation 2012).

In this context, the chapter focuses upon the EU's EPA with West Africa in order to consider whether certain elements of Nkrumah's warning regarding neo-colonial systems of trade (and aid) remain relevant in the contemporary era. It first outlines the history of Africa–EU Association dating back to the signing of the Treaty of Rome in 1957. This draws attention to the then contributions of figures such as Nkrumah and Touré to the debates about the merits of this post-colonial/neo-colonial relationship between Africa and the newly established European supranational project. The chapter then examines the current ACP–EU Cotonou Partnership Agreement (2000–2020) and underscores the European Commission's pursuit of 'reciprocal' free trade via EPAs. Thereafter, the chapter examines the likely meaning of the West African EPA for import-competing sectors (such as poultry and tomato agro-processing), as well as for export-oriented sectors such as cocoa processing. The chapter also points to 'pay fish and go' agreements that remain outside of the EPA's purview, and that undermine the European Commission's claim to have realised pro-poor trade relations with former colonies. The chapter's concluding sections then revisit the relevance of Nkrumah and the concept of neo-colonialism while providing a summary of concerns regarding the West Africa–EU EPA.

History of Africa's 'Association' with the European Union

African countries have been 'Associated' with the European supranational project since the inception of the EEC under the Treaty of Rome in 1957. French diplomats—as part of their negotiations with other would-be EEC member states such as West Germany—insisted that then French colonies in Africa should be granted preferential terms of trade with the Common Market (Kawasaki 2000; Brown 2002). They insisted that joint European aid agencies should also be constructed to share the costs of development in Francophone Africa. France was successful in its insistence upon this Association between the EEC and its African territories. As a result, France's African colonies did receive low tariff access to the European market as compared with British African possessions (at that time outside of the Association arrangements since the UK did not join as a founding member in 1957). The European Development Fund (EDF) was also established to pool European aid monies for collective projects in the African territories (Van der Lee 1967: 198; Fredrichs 1970: 246).

Importantly, however, there soon came a push for 'reciprocal' free trade arrangements as this explicitly colonial relationship gave way to the era of decolonisation. Under the Yaoundé Accords (1963–1975) between the EEC and the Associated African States and Madagascar (AASM), European officials pushed for gradual tariff liberalisation on the part of the AASM group. AASM exporters would maintain their preferential access to the Common Market as compared with non-Associated developing countries. Nevertheless, they themselves would have to ensure that European exporters, in return, would be able to access the AASM bloc's consumers as part of reciprocal free trade arrangements (Brown 2002: 42). Meanwhile, EDF monies grew in terms of per capita contributions to AASM 'development' despite early controversies such as European aid towards 'white elephant' infrastructure projects (Robson 1965; Soper 1965). Even at this early stage of Association, many commentators queried whether reciprocal free trade and EDF monies would promote development per se, or instead lock-in poorer states into (neo) colonial patterns of trade and production (Ogikbo cited in Soper 1968; Nkrumah 1963; Touré 1962).

Significantly, this reciprocal free trade arrangement was replaced by the Lomé Conventions (1975–2000) which—at least in their first iteration—were inspired by the UN debates for a New International Economic Order (NIEO). Informed by the dependency school's critique of asymmetric trade and aid arrangements, the first Lomé Convention ostensibly sought to usher in a more egalitarian partnership between the EEC and the newly constituted African, Caribbean and Pacific (ACP) group (Zartman 1976; Gruhn 1976, 1993). The ACP bloc—with Francophone and Anglophone African states now united in a single negotiating entity following the UK's accession to the EEC—successfully pushed for NIEO-style concessions. Most notably, the first Lomé Convention promised that trade would be non-reciprocal, in the sense that there would not be pressure laid upon ACP economies to undertake tariff dismantling. EEC officials nominally recognised that African states might retain tariffs to protect their own emerging sectors while their competitive muscle grew. In addition, the Lomé Conventions established the System for the Stabilisation of Export Earnings (STABEX), as well as the System for the Stabilisation of Mineral Earnings (SYSMIN). These price support schemes sought to compensate African producers for any sharp downturns in international commodity prices in sectors such as cocoa and timber (*The Courier* 1975: 7). This represented a tangible policy response to the dependency school's critique (*The Courier* 1979: 4). African countries ostensibly would be able to stabilise their raw material production while at the same time using such earnings to diversify into agro-processing and manufacturing. This push towards value addition would also be supported under Lomé via the creation of the Centre for the Development of Industry (CDI). This would operate alongside the Centre for Technical Support to Agriculture (CTA) and provide capacity building assistance to ACP states' parastatals and private sector enterprise. The Lomé Conventions, in light of these NIEO-inspired concessions, were hailed by both African and European signatories as being revolutionary in character (Frey-Wouters 1980; Ravenhill 1985).

In their operation, however, the Lomé Conventions soon gave way to free market impulses as the Washington Consensus emerged from the late 1970s into the 1980s in response to the 'debt crisis'. SAPs were implemented in many African economies bringing about privatisation of industries (for instance, parastatals in the textiles sector), deregulation (for instance, with regards to minimum wages) and liberalisation with regards to FDI and import tariffs (for example, tariffs upon second-hand clothing imported from Europe) (European Council 1988: 95; Brown 2004: 21; Kenyan Association of Manufacturers 2016). Importantly, EU aid monies under the EDF became linked to African countries' acquiescence to, and roll-out of, structural adjustment (Mailafia 1997: 96). Indeed, the European Commission gave vocal support to the World Bank's and the IMF's own policy prescriptions with regards to African growth and development (Brown 2004: 21; European Council 1988: 95). In many cases, this involved austerity measures regarding day-to-day government expenditure, resulting in shrinking welfare services. The fallout of structural adjustment has been linked, moreover, to certain cases of social instability and unrest in Africa. Bracking (1999), for example, convincingly makes the link between the increasing authoritarianism of President Mugabe in Zimbabwe and social protests precipitated by his government's acquiescence to the donor community's austerity measures. The Lomé Conventions, in addition, were seen to fall short of their NIEO foundations with regards to the STABEX, SYSMIN and CDI/CTA programmes (Kokole 1981: 458; Ravenhill 1984: 537). Promised monies were often not forthcoming or else disbursed to developmentally dubious initiatives (such as French investments in a Malagasy export processing zone criticised for its treatment of women workers) (Langan 2011b, 2012).

The current Association framework—the Cotonou Partnership Agreement—emerged from the end of the Lomé Conventions and the EU's solidification of its free market footing in terms of development paradigms (much removed from the principles of the NIEO). The European Commission's (1996) Green Paper on the future of ACP–EU ties made clear that a free market approach to ACP development would be consolidated. This was contextualised in terms of the end of the Cold War and the need for both blocs—in a post-colonial era—to recognise each other's responsibilities 'less ambiguously' (European Commission 1996: 11). Significantly, the European Commission demanded upon a return to explicitly reciprocal free trade ties. With parallels to the Yaoundé Accords, African countries would now be expected to dismantle their own tariffs upon European products in order to qualify for continuing low tariff access to consumers in the EU member states. This shift to 'reciprocal' trade has met with uncertainty and concern by African partners as discussed in the next section.

THE COTONOU AGREEMENT AND THE EPAs: WHITHER 'PRO-POOR' TRADE AND AID TIES?

The signing of the Cotonou Agreement (2000–2020) gave rise to negotiations for the EPAs themselves. The EPAs would realise reciprocal free trade between the EU and sub-regions of the ACP bloc. Rather than negotiate as a single unit—what Nyerere described as a 'trade union of the poor'—ACP countries would now negotiate in sub-regional blocs such as the Economic Community of West African States (ECOWAS) and the Southern African Development Community (SADC) (cited in Whiteman 1998: 32). This was itself condemned by ACP civil society groups as constituting a 'divide and rule' tactic on the part of the European Commission. Moreover, it was condemned for potentially bringing about a 'hub and spokes' situation in which sub-regions of the ACP bloc competed against one another to access European markets on more favourable terms than their perceived rivals (Babarinde and Wright 2013: 98).

The content of the EPA themselves has been fiercely condemned by civil society groups such as SEATINI Uganda (2017), the aforementioned NANTS (2010) from Nigeria, as well as European trade justice groups including Oxfam (2008) and Traidcraft (2004, 2005). In short, there is deep concern that tariff liberalisation will undermine emerging

African manufacturing industries and agro-processing sectors. That is, reciprocal free trade will result in job losses and deindustrialisation amidst the import-flooding of cheap European consumables to the detriment of local production. Any net gain to individual consumers (in terms of cheaper shopping bills) will be whittled away by the wider economic hardships felt by unemployment and lack of economic diversification as value-added sectors collapse amidst the weight of foreign imports. There is also much concern that African governments will lose valuable tariff revenues which can account for as much as 35% of total treasury receipts in less developed countries such as Uganda and Senegal (Olanyo 2008). Berthelto and Gadry (2014: 1) explain that the West African region can expect:

> A progressive annual loss of import duties and value added tax up to € 2.5 billion in year 20 (based on 2012 imports from the EU)… These budget losses would be of €1 billion for the poorest countries – the 12 Least Developed Countries or LDCs out of the 16 Western African States.

Lower tariff revenues will, in turn, result in lower government spending levels, including on essential services such as education and health (with reminiscence of Fanon's [1961] austerity regimes).

The European Commission, in partial response to these concerns, has promised that it will furnish African signatories with additional Aid for Trade assistance upon their agreement to an EPA (Langan and Scott 2011). Aid for Trade will ostensibly ensure that African countries can support their viable import-competing sectors to cope with the competitive pressures emanating from tariff liberalisation. Additionally, Aid for Trade monies might be used to enhance productivity within export-oriented sectors (such as cut-flowers in Uganda) to bolster overall economic performance and to ensure that the EPA results in 'win-win' outcomes for both European exporters and for their ACP counterparts. Notably, in the case of the West African EPA, provisionally in effect in Ghana and Ivory Coast (as of December 2016), the European Commission has promised to disburse €6.5 billion via the EPADP instrument (European Council 2010, 2014). Importantly, however, the EPADP will not constitute 'new' money as originally demanded by West African negotiators (EuropAfrica 2011: Langan and Price 2015). Instead, it will be 'recycled' from existing aid commitments under the EDF. This has prompted concerns about the potential diversion of humanitarian aid to private sector development (PSD) initiatives. Furthermore, the figure of €6.5 billion represents a significant drop from the €9.5 billion originally requested by West African negotiators (Langan and Price 2015: 276).

Additionally, the European Commission has promised that African signatories will be able to make use of a 'sensitive goods basket' to shield their most vulnerable sectors from the impact of tariff liberalisation. This ostensibly will ensure that import-flooding is restricted in important economic areas where African officials feel their producers would be at a distinct disadvantage at their current level of development. However, given the limited percentage of overall commodities that may be placed into this sensitive goods basket, there is narrow scope for African governments to meaningfully protect their manufacturing industries. Owing to food security concerns, the majority of goods placed into this basket will be agricultural commodities—leaving little space for protection of sectors such as textiles, soap manufacturing or carpet production (Nwoke 2009: 10). Civil society groups are therefore sceptical that the sensitive goods basket will properly redress the widespread concerns about the impact of the EPAs upon African diversification and economic development (NANTS 2010). Moreover, they point to the historical discrepancy that European countries (and others) reached their own current levels of economic prosperity through use of protectionist trade policy tools which are now being denied to African governments. Following the work of Ha Joon-Chang (2003), many have expressed the fact that the EU appears to be 'kicking away the ladder of development' by preventing African countries from using protectionist tariffs to grow their emerging sectors, despite Europe's use of these own policies in the past—and indeed today under instruments such as the Common Agricultural Policy (c.f. Nairobi Statement on the EPAs cited in Social Watch 2012).

Interestingly, the EU has also utilised budget support monies to enhance governance capacity in ACP countries under the Cotonou Agreement. As discussed in Chap. 3, this form of aid represents a government-to-government financial transfer, or in this case, a transfer from the EU supranational project to individual ACP countries. For example, EU budget support monies have been disbursed to both Ghana and Uganda under the 10th EDF, with aid being channelled into government treasuries to bolster overall development plans (Whitfield and Jones 2009; Gerster n.d; Human Rights Watch 2011). Controversially, however, such budget support has included sectoral support to trade ministries to assist with their personnel and capacity constraints. Somewhat paradoxically, therefore, trade officials in countries such as Uganda have been partly financed by the European Commission (via budget support), while at the same time having to negotiate with the EU on extremely controversial issues of EPA trade liberalisation (European Commission 2007: 8–12, 24, 27). This raises the clear prospect of aid as leverage—as predicted by Nkrumah (1963, 1965)—with budget support being used to bring about what the European Commission opaquely terms 'policy dialogue' with ACP governments. In terms of sovereignty therefore, there are doubts whether trade officials in states such as Uganda are beholden more to their EU benefactors than to the economic needs of their producers and citizenries. Civil society groups such as SEATINI Uganda (2013) continue to protest their government's apparent capitulation to a regressive trade deal while being unable to counteract the impact of EU donor aid upon governmental outlooks on the EPA.

Despite the major concerns of civil society groups and, at times, African governments about the impact of 'reciprocal' trade liberalisation, the European Commission has consistently promoted a pro-poor development discourse when explaining the need for the EPA. The then EU Trade Commissioner, Peter Mandelson, who was responsible for launching the EPA negotiations in the immediate period following on from the signing of the Cotonou Agreement in 2000, played an active role in the construction of this discourse. Emphasising the universal benefits of free trade and the need for ACP countries to deal with the realities of economic globalisation, Mandelson regularly emphasised that the EPAs would be 'win-win' for Europe and for the sub-regions of the ACP bloc. In the case of negotiations with West African countries, for example, Mandelson insisted that the trade agreement would fulfil poverty reduction obligations while also respecting sustainability:

> The 21st century offers new challenges ... whether in Europe, West Africa or wherever. We must face them together. We need to act now if we are to create a world where people's prospects are no longer blighted by poverty and underemployment... The Economic Partnership Agreement['s]... objective is to make West Africa an economic magnet that attracts investment and stimulates private enterprise, a hive of economic activity that guarantees sustained growth and drives more sustainable economic, social and environmental development. The Agreement will build on the already considerable achievements of regional integration in West Africa. (cited in European Commission 2005: 1)

However, when the detail of the likely impact of the EPA are considered in more detail with regard to import-competing sectors (tariff liberalisation) and export-oriented industries (Aid for Trade), there is much ground to doubt the development discourse as espoused by figures such as Commissioner Mandelson.

IMPORT-COMPETING SECTORS AND THE EPA

Food (in)Security?

The EPA has been condemned for 'kicking away the ladder of development' from African countries by denying them the policy space to protect their emerging sectors from cheaper European imports (c.f. Chang 2003). The European Commission has been insistent in the negotiations that tariff barriers must be dismantled in order that African states may continue to enjoy low tariff access to European consumers. Should African countries such as Ghana refuse to initiate such tariff liberalisation, however, the European Commission emphasises that they will default to the GSP. This trade footing would see European tariffs rise on goods originating from ACP developing countries, leading to potential hardship for export-oriented sectors who would then find themselves at a relative competitive disadvantage compared to current access offered under Cotonou.[2]

It is import-competing sectors, however, that stand to bear the burden of tariff liberalisation within Africa should the EPA be implemented in the various sub-regions of the ACP grouping. For example, the West African Heads of State and Government agreed in July 2014 to the principle of the EPA as negotiated with the EU since 2000. The terms of this region-wide EPA are now in provisional application in Ivory Coast (since September 2016) and Ghana (since December 2016). These two countries have fully ratified the EPA within their domestic legislatures and have cleared the way for implementation of the EPA's provisions. However, certain West African countries—most notably, Nigeria—have yet to fully ratify the agreement. There is therefore uncertainty on the part of the European Commission (and other West African countries such as Ghana) whether the regional EPA will be stillborn. To complicate matters even further, Nigeria defaulted to the GSP in 2008 when it failed to meet the original EPA deadline of 31st December 2007. Certain countries such as Ghana, however, safeguarded their low tariff access after 2008 by signing what were termed 'interim' EPAs on a unilateral basis with the EU (despite the protestations of other West African states who did not acquiesce to EU demands) (Langan and Price 2015).

In this West African context, there are thus major concerns that import-competing sectors will be negatively impacted by the EPA. In terms of agro-processing sectors, the European Commission's own Sustainability Impact Assessment (SIA) indicates that there will be import surges in relation to onions (16% increase in volume), potatoes (15%), beef (16%) and poultry (18%) as West African states lower their tariffs (PriceWaterhouseCoopers 2007: 20). This is at the same time as the CAP subsidises European agro-production, for instance, with $39.4 million being allocated to EU millet production alone (Patel 2007). In this context, discourse surrounding 'win-win' trade contrasts with the EU's own use of protectionist policies (the CAP) while insisting upon tariff liberalisation within developing countries. Interestingly, in the context of the July 2014 agreement on the principles of the West African EPA, the European Commission (2014) has promised that it will withdraw export subsidies upon its agricultural produce destined for West African markets. It is not year clear, however, whether this will meaningfully mitigate the anticipated import surges documented in the SIA. Indeed, West African countries are being compelled to reduce their tariffs on agricultural imports to 35% which represents a dramatic concession compared to the permissible WTO tariff schedule of up to 99% tariffs.

Interestingly, the poultry sector is highly illustrative of the potential impact of EPA import surges upon West African agro-processing sectors. A publication by European NGOs, including APRODEV et al. (2007: 2), explain that Cameroon alone lost around 120,000 jobs in the poultry sector at the height of earlier import surges in the 2000s. The report reflects on the personal experiences of those affected and explains that locally produced poultry cannot compete against cheap European imports. In addition, the report notes that much of the imported European chicken is not safe for consumption by the time it reaches the Cameroonian shopper due to lack of proper refrigeration:

> In recent years, the massive exports of frozen chicken pieces from Europe have ruined domestic markets in West Africa. Cameroon's small farmers simply cannot compete with the low prices of imported poultry… they do not have the money for new chicks and they can no longer pay back their loans… The frozen chicken pieces from Europe are jeopardising the health of the population…there is no guarantee of a closed refrigeration chain. (ibid.)

This stark picture is corroborated by Bagooro (2011: 9–13) who states that Ghana lost the equivalent of 200,000 jobs in the poultry sector as a result of import surges in the country. Indeed, Ghana's domestic poultry sector supplied 95% of total domestic requirements as of 1992. By 2002, however, it only supplied 11% of the local market. The scale of Ghanaian job losses felt within this decade of decline reflects the fact that imports can not only impact upon the jobs of workers in poultry farms but can also negatively affect 'local grain producers, who supply chicken feed to the agro-industry (Pannhausen 2006: 26). Meanwhile, the Ghanaian parliament's attempts to ban—or at least to raise tariffs— on foreign poultry imports have been successfully challenged by the donor community. Issah (2007: 8) explains that the parliament voted in 2003 to raise poultry tariffs from 20 to 40% (and rice from 20 to 25%), falling well within WTO rules which permit tariffs up to the ceiling of 99%. Despite the decision of the Ghanaian legislature, however, the Kufuor government rescinded the tariff escalation after only four days of implementation 'as a result of the influence of the International Monetary Fund' (ibid.: 25). This reversal was challenged in court by local civil society groups, with the judiciary finding that the government was acting unconstitutionally in refusing to heed the earlier parliamentary vote. Amidst these legal proceedings, however, a second parliamentary vote was then held in 2005, with the government narrowly securing enough support to repeal the 2003 decision under intense IMF pressure (ibid.: 9).

The entrenchment and locking-in of tariff liberalisation under the West African–EU EPA raises major concerns that the current malaise of local production will be exacerbated, leading to yet further job losses for workers in poultry farms and grain production. Issah (2007: 23) provides a compelling case, noting that the EPA may prove the final straw for struggling agro-processing sectors while denying African governments tariff revenues to underwrite basic welfare services:

> Farmers fear that Economic Partnership Agreement (EPA) will likely to be the last stroke to "break the camels' back" of large parts of Ghanaian agriculture. Furthermore, the revenue loss for the state of Ghana caused by lower tariffs will probably mean diversion of resources from important sectors such as health and education, and the citizens might be tax burdened which will further increase the vulnerability of millions more to violations of their Right to Food and other human rights. (ibid.)

It is also worth noting that the EU itself maintains 'managed trade' in terms of its own poultry sector, utilising varying tariff levels to protect EU poultry producers from foreign competition from countries such as Brazil and the USA. ActionAid Ghana (2013: 34) point out that the:

> EU uses tariff protection as its principal market management tool while Ghana is bound under IEPA [the interim EPA since 2008] from adjusting its tariffs to manage its poultry industry. For instance, it is reported that in 2005, import tariffs imposed by the EU maintained its domestic poultry prices 11.5 to 13.1% higher than would have been the case in the absence of tariff protection.

The EU, in this manner, is again seen to be 'kicking away the ladder of development'—by depriving West African countries of the policy space to protect their nascent industries, while the European Commission itself utilises these same policies to safeguard EU member state producers (c.f. Chang 2003).

Perhaps most importantly, the potential collapse of sectors such as poultry in a post-EPA environment raises questions about food security in West Africa. Local civil society groups and trade unions have notably raised concerns about the meaning of import dependence for the food security of vulnerable populations (Bagooro 2011). They note that the World Food Crisis of 2006–2008 was precipitated by major price rises in key food commodities on global markets. In this context, they argue that it is vital for countries such as Ghana to retain domestic food production capacities and not to rely too heavily on imports prone to price volatility. The Third World Network Africa, for example, makes clear that the EPA (when combined to the CAP and subsidised production in Europe) will pose 'major unfair competition against West African producers of poultry, tomatoes, beef, cereals...' (ibid.). They explain that not only livelihoods but food security will be jeopardised as a result of the EPA's 'shrinking of the policy space' to safeguard Ghanaian agriculture from influx of cheaper foreign commodities (ibid.).

Deindustrialisation?

Furthermore, there are concerns that the EPA will have negative implications for emerging manufacturing sectors, in terms of provoking deindustrialisation. As mentioned, NANTS (2010) in the Nigerian context has been vocal about the potential meaning of premature tariff dismantling for value addition and industrialisation. Ken Ukaoha, the President of this prominent Nigerian trade association, states in explicit terms that:

> The real dangers of the EPA, if implemented in its current form, are legion and cut across all facets of the economic life of Africa. Nigeria's main grouse with EPA stems from the fact that it would lead to de-industrialisation, exposure to undue competition, loss of jobs and revenue, capital flight, increase in poverty and in some way, loss of sovereignty and disintegration of the region. (cited in Alli 2015)

In this vein, there is major concern that local industries such as apparel, soap manufacturing, carpet manufacturing, cement, steel and iron products, quicklime and confectionary production will be negatively impacted by influx of cheaper European manufacturers after the EPA initiates extensive tariff dismantling (Adenikinju and Alaba 2005; Ghana Ministry of Trade/TRAQUE 2006). Whereas tariffs have to date enabled certain emerging sectors to consolidate themselves in the domestic and regional market, EPA implementation will see cheaper European competition enter the country, leading to industrial collapse and job losses. In the case of Nigeria alone, it is predicted that the value of imports of EU manufactured goods will increase by around $600 million (Nwoke 2009). This not only underscores the clear commercial advantage accruing to the EU in terms of its balance of trade with West African states after EPA implementation. It also underscores how local producers will lose domestic market share to European manufacturers, given the technological and financial advantages that producers in the EU member states currently enjoy.

It is important to note that this EPA tariff liberalisation again represents a consolidation of free market norms promoted in West Africa since the onset of SAPs in the Washington Consensus. In this context, civil society's current concerns about livelihood losses and industrial collapse appear rooted in historical evidence. For instance, Nigeria lost around 30,000 jobs in the textiles sector alone as SAP policies led to liberalisation with regards to foreign imports (Enterplan 2005: 40). Such historical deindustrialisation was also witnessed in other West African countries, notably Ivory Coast and Senegal. Civil society campaigners against the implementation of the EPA have used these examples to articulate their concerns about 'second generation liberalisation' in the timeframe of the Cotonou Agreement. Mutume (2007) writing in the UN's *African Renewal* magazine notes, for example, that:

> Campaigners... cite examples of earlier trade liberalization measures. In 1986 Côte d'Ivoire cut tariffs by 40 per cent, resulting in massive layoffs in the chemical, textile, footwear and automobile assembly industries. Senegal lost one-third of manufacturing jobs between 1985 and 1990 after reducing tariffs from 165 per cent to 90 per cent. The campaigners are calling for EU-ACP trade relations that support the weaker partners' pursuit of economic development. [not further tariff reductions]

In addition, there are concerns that efforts at regional integration in West Africa will be negatively affected by the implementation of the EPA. Namely, that tariff liberalisation towards European goods will displace existing inter-regional trade between the West African countries themselves. Nigeria, in particular, sustains an important trade in manufactured goods with its ECOWAS neighbours and may face challenge for such markets from cheaper European merchandise in the post-EPA environment. Interestingly, the CTA (established under the Lomé Conventions as a means of spurring diversification in ACP economies) notes on its website that Nigerian manufacturers are concerned about higher quality and cheaper products entering the regional market from the industrialised EU member states:

> The fear of manufacturers is that by directly or indirectly acceding to the EPA, Nigeria could reverse the little progress already made in the manufacturing sector. They say opening the door to European products will certainly stifle local products that cannot compare or compete with better packaged and higher quality European products. They add that the EPA remains an agreement between two unequal halves. (cited in Business Day 2014)

Importantly, these fears are also echoed by Nigerian government officials—accounting in part for Nigeria's current failure to ratify and fully implement the West African EPA (despite the agreement of Heads of Government in July 2014). For example, the Nigerian Commerce Minister, Aliyu Modibo Umar, queried why the strict terms of 'reciprocal' free trade under Cotonou's EPAs would spur economic growth in West Africa when the more developmental approach of the non-reciprocal Lomé Conventions had failed to stimulate value addition:

If 30 years of non-reciprocal free market access into the EU did not improve the economic situation of the ACP, how can a reciprocal trading arrangement achieve anything better?" Instead, he [Umar] argues, simply liberalizing trade will "further widen the gap between the two [blocs] and probably destroy the little development that some ACP countries have managed to achieve over the past years." (cited in Mutume 2007)

The European Commission, however, insists that the EPA will result in pro-poor outcomes. EU officials emphasise that the EPADP can be used to bolster sectors that possess a comparative advantage vis-à-vis European competitors. Indeed, they emphasise that the EPADP monies can boost capacity in export-oriented sectors, creating new jobs and improving export earnings for governments in the region. The next section thus examines whether the EPA might bode well for exporters in West Africa, especially given the availability of the EPADP and its Aid for Trade assistance.

Export-Oriented Sectors and Aid for Trade Under the EPADP

The European Commission emphasises that while some import-competing sectors might suffer under the effects of the EPA that, on the whole, West African economies will flourish by realising their comparative advantages in export-oriented sectors. Namely, that while European imports may lead to contraction within uncompetitive sectors (such as poultry) that nevertheless West African governments can promote export industries, ensuring new job creation and improvements to the overall balance of trade. Moreover, the European Commission promises here that the EPADP and its Aid for Trade monies will provide tangible resources to enhance productivity in competitive sectors prioritised by West African countries themselves. The EPA itself therefore is not seen as a mercantilist instrument favouring European commerce, but is instead viewed as a win–win opportunity for pro-poor growth in African states.

It is important to restate, however, that the €6.5 billion EPADP monies made available to West African signatories of the regional EPA does not constitute 'new' money per se. It is recycled from existing aid commitments under the EDF, including humanitarian aid which may now be diverted towards private sector capacity building. Furthermore, the

EPADP must be contextualised as a short-term aid instrument which only partially compensates West African governments for their long-term loss of tariff revenues once EPA liberalisation has been implemented. As Berthelto and Gadry (2014: 1) make clear, West African countries by year 20 of EPA implementation are likely to lose around €2.5 billion *annually*. The limited contributions of the EPADP, therefore, are far outweighed by the negative revenue consequences of EPA tariff dismantling, with local governments effectively deprived of resource earnings while accepting short-term Aid for Trade from the EU donor. The premise that the EPADP represents a radical contribution to West African private sector capacity is wholly flawed.

There is also genuine scepticism on the part of West African private sector stakeholders and civil society whether Aid for Trade resources promised under the EPADP will reach the business community. Managers in the cocoa processing sectors in both Ghana and Nigeria, for example, expressed their concerns that government elites might misuse monies for their own patronage networks rather than meaningfully disburse EPADP finances to the private sector itself. This fear was echoed by a trade justice activist who pointed to the need for a *direct* form of disbursement, that is, from the EU directly to the business community:

> If the EU gave EURO 5 billion to manage the cost of adjustment, this money, by the time it gets to the industries, will have shrank in weight and in volume. The only way is for the beneficiaries to apply for the money directly and to target how the money will be used [rather than allowing West African governments to disburse EPADP monies]. (civil society activist cited in Langan and Price forthcoming)

Previous experience of Aid for Trade disbursements in other ACP subregions also lead to significant doubts whether the EPADP will meaningfully enhance export productivity in West Africa. For example, private sector actors in Uganda's flower industry have complained that previous EU monies under the APEX programme were disbursed in such a manner as to leave little tangible funds for business capacity building (Langan 2011a: 1229). Specifically, the EU's Aid for Trade assistance was filtered through a chain of local commercial banks who charged high interest rates. By the time the funds then reached the business community, private sector actors were being subject to 'Shylock' loans, according to one manager of a Ugandan flower farm (ibid.). The prospect that EPADP monies too might be offered in the form of loans via intermediary banks raises serious doubts that the funding will materially assist export sectors in West Africa.

Additionally, private sector actors in receipt of EU Aid for Trade in Uganda under the 10th EDF reported that much capacity building assistance came with strict timeframes for the use of the monies. Paradoxically, this resulted in situations where EU aid meant for building the human capacity of sectoral business associations had to be returned to the donor due to the fact that the money could not be allocated in the required timeframe (due to the very lack of capacity that the aid was meant to redress). The Ugandan Floriculture Exporters Association (UFEA) brought this paradox to the fore when discussing how they had had to return money to the EU. A manager there explained that:

> For flowers we had a project directly implemented with UFEA which ended two years ago to do strategic planning and training and capacity building... there were some problems, procedure related problems ... the money came back. One of the information things about EDF [is that] maybe it's not suited to private sector things because some of the procedures are quite [complex]. (cited in Langan 2011a: 1231)

There is also evidence that where Aid for Trade monies have been disbursed to ACP recipients, that the aid has regularly gone towards de facto subsidy of European investments in developmentally dubious sectors. For example, the CDE—originally established under the Lomé Conventions—disbursed €333,000 in 2005 to one textiles cluster in Madagascar alone during the operation of the 10th EDF in the initial years of the Cotonou Agreement. From 2005 to 2008, this EPZ in fact received over €1,800,000 from the CDE together with the French development agency (AFD) (Langan 2011b: 1230–1232). The EPZ accommodates a number of manufacturing units owned by European investors, serving multinational clients such as JC Penny. However, there have been concerns that workers in such EPZs are underpaid and often experience harsh working conditions. Indeed, the CDE's own policy documentation boasts that Madagascar's production costs are the 'lowest in the world' as part of the rationalisation of private sector funding in this ACP country (ibid.). The question arises in this context whether the Aid for Trade funding was genuinely conducive to poverty reduction through livelihood generation, or whether in fact it provided de facto subsidies to European commercial interests without much concern for low-paid Malagasy workers (ibid.). Based on this historical experience of EU Aid for Trade, the ability of the EPADP to translate into pro-poor growth in a post-EPA environment must be queried.

To corroborate this point, it is illustrative to consider existing EU Aid for Trade to the fisheries sector in West Africa. The European Commission's (2006) report *Making Trade Work for Development: Aid for Trade* makes clear that funding has been prioritised for fisheries, among other export-oriented sectors. This is likely to be repeated under the EPADP itself given its focus upon bolstering production in existing export industries, of which fisheries stands as one of the most lucrative. In the 2006 report, the European Commission lauds Aid for Trade as having assisted countries such as Benin to access European consumers. Namely, that Aid for Trade has provided technical assistance to the industry in order to help it cope with stringent 'SPS' hygiene requirements that relate to consumer standards. As part of a wider pro-poor discourse concerning EPAs and the role of Aid for Trade therein, the European Commission (2006: 44) explains that its Aid for Trade has:

> provided targeted assistance to fish-exporting countries… [the technical support] helped lift the export ban on shrimps from Benin to the EU in February 2005…. The [shrimp] sector employs some 400 000 people out of a total population of 8.4 million. Support was also provided to the other fish-exporting countries in the region. Activities included the upgrading of laboratories so as to meet the required standards for export… Another activity included support to bringing national regulations into compliance with EU sanitary requirements on fishery products.

Worryingly, however, the fisheries sector in West Africa is dominated by European supertrawlers as part of 'pay-fish-and-go' agreements. Namely, the EU has negotiated a series of fisheries access agreements with ACP countries, allowing European factory ships to operate within their territorial waters. Fish is then processed on board the ships, and the final product imported into EU member states to supply European consumers (Greenpeace 2012). This of course raises serious questions not merely about the presence of European fishing vessels in African waters, but queries the 'development' contributions of Aid for Trade assistance in this economic sector. The European super trawlers do not generate significant livelihoods for local West Africans. Moreover, they undermine food security in the region by facilitating the export of African fish stocks to European countries. Instead of protein-rich stocks going towards the satiation of hunger in West Africa, the pay-fish-and-go agreements ensure that this valuable commodity goes to European populations (with little of the trade revenues returning to West African in either the form of jobs or taxation). A Greenpeace (2012: 4) report documents this situation in the case of Senegal and laments that:

> Senegalese children will grow up never having known a foodstuff and basic source of protein that their parents, and grandparents, had access to for years. Jobs, which were once a birthright for many Senegalese, have been lost as the local fishing industry has collapsed as the fish are caught off-shore and taken abroad by giant factory ships.

This stark view of the regressive impact of European investments into the fisheries sector in West Africa is shared by Gegout (2016: 2197) who explains that job creation is limited, and that the presence of the super trawlers acts as yet another 'push' factor for migration:

> foreign companies do not necessarily create employment in coastal areas. Multinational corporations make low usage of local processing facilities. As a result, poor people lose their employment in the traditional fish industry, and can no longer own their ships. In an ironic twist some fishers earn more from transporting migrants to European coasts than from fishing. Some Senegalese fishers have even migrated to Europe.

The use of existing 'Aid for Trade' again queries whether the EPADP will itself bring about the pro-poor economic growth envisaged within the European Commission's 'development' discourse. The EPA, therefore, in the absence of a genuine level playing field, might accurately be said to be perpetuating (neo)colonial patterns of production and trade.

AFRICA–EU TRADE: THE EPAs AS A PRODUCT, AND ENTRENCHMENT, OF NEO-COLONIALISM?

Nkrumah (1963, 1965) warned that foreign powers would seek to maintain African countries in a position of economic subordination—as providers of raw materials and as markets for value-added manufactures. In order to perpetuate (neo)colonial patterns of trade, foreign donors would utilise aid as leverage for asymmetric trade arrangements. This would also be combined to corporate pressures (for example, either promises of FDI, or threats of divestment of existing assets). The contemporary phase of ACP–EU Association under the Cotonou Agreement—with the European Commission's vigorous pursuit of EPAs—can be understood through Nkrumah's lens of neo-colonialism. Namely, the EPAs—through the imposition of reciprocal free trade and concomitant tariff dismantling—can be seen as both a product, and entrenchment, of neo-colonialism.

In short, the EPAs effectively 'kick away the ladder of development' from African economies by denying them necessary policy space to protect (and most importantly grow) their own nascent agro-processing and manufacturing sectors (c.f. Chang 2003). By insisting upon extensive tariff liberalisation, the EPAs facilitate the import-flooding of African markets with cheap, often subsidised, European goods. As discussed in the above sections, this threatens food security in the various sub-regions of the ACP bloc, as well as deindustrialisation. Moreover, the European Commission's promises of Aid for Trade to ostensibly 'level the playing field' are found wanting. Aid for Trade monies fail to adequately compensate African economies for the long-term implications of lost tariff revenues historically used to support essential services including health and education. Aid for Trade revenues are not guaranteed to effectively reach private sector stakeholders in essential export sectors that might involve value addition and skilled job creation. Instead, Aid for Trade monies are regularly directed towards sectors (such as fisheries) whose current structures do not bode well either for livelihood generation or for taxation revenues. Aid for Trade in many circumstances can best be described as 'boomerang aid' in which EU funding subsidies European commerce, and hence their profit margins (such as those of European super trawlers).

Accordingly, the EPAs can be understood as a device through which the European Commission entrenches (neo)colonial patterns of trade and production between the EU member states and their ACP counterparts. As Nkrumah predicted, aid is used as a leveraging device in this process. Aid for Trade—such as pledges under the EPADP—is used as a means of securing African elites' acquiescence to inequitable trade deals. Aid is promised on the condition of a transition to 'reciprocal' free trade even in circumstances in which private sector stakeholders fear that the monies may be misused by predatory political elites for graft.

Moreover, Aid for Trade helps to entrench the commercial interests—and influence—of European investors, as discussed in terms of the fisheries sector in countries such as Senegal. At the same time, the European Commission utilises the threat of African countries' default to the GSP (which would see their tariff access to EU consumers become less preferable) as a means of additionally securing their compliance with EPA free market norms.

It should also be noted that these EPA negotiations have coincided with the EU's increasing preference for use of budget support aid mechanisms (as discussed in Chap. 3). This has included support to 'capability building' initiatives for individual trade ministries. Certain countries' trade negotiators (such as those in Uganda) have therefore benefitted from EU aid support to their civil service capacities. Simultaneously, they are negotiating with the same very benefactor on the terms of a highly controversial free trade agreement. This clearly echoes the scenarios envisaged by Nkrumah in his critique of neo-colonialism where he predicted that aid would be used to influence decision-making within corridors of African government. Popular sovereignty is clearly brought into question where trade negotiators are potentially compromised by the need to satisfy the commercial interests of the benefactor to maintain lines of aid support to their ministry.

Altogether, ACP–EU trade relations under the Cotonou Agreement are usefully explored through the lens of neo-colonialism. The EPAs have been pursued—despite African government reservations and civil society protests—as a means of accomplishing the European Commission's desire to secure on-going access to lucrative markets for European member states' manufactures and agro-processing exports. Free market norms—as initially pursued under SAPs and tied aid mechanisms—are now being cemented through recourse to Aid for Trade, and the threat of a default to the GSP. As Nkrumah predicted, many African governments have capitulated to foreign policy pressures despite the fact that the repercussions of the EPA will be severe in terms of food security, deindustrialisation and lost tariff revenues. (Neo)colonial patterns of trade in which African economies remain subordinate suppliers of raw materials and importers of high value European commodities are therein secured. This is despite the fact that European countries historically utilised protectionist policies to reach their current levels of development. And moreover that the EU, through current mechanisms such as the CAP, continues to manage its own production systems, while demanding that African economies adhere by the strictest interpretations of free market policies (as embodied by the EPAs). Conditions of poverty are entrenched through inequitable trade deals that leave little scope for the generation of value-added sectors that historically support higher paid skilled jobs.

CONCLUSION

This chapter has examined the EU's pursuit of EPAs with African countries—notably those of the West African negotiating bloc—under the Cotonou Agreement. The European Commission emphasises that its trade policy is commensurate with development objectives in Africa. Actors such as Peter Mandelson have regularly claimed that the reciprocal liberalisation arrangements will be 'win-win', securing livelihoods and bolstering economic growth for African partners. They point to the EU's provision of Aid for Trade assistance (as embodied in instruments such as the West African EPADP) as evidence of Europe's willingness to make free markets work for the poor. While recognising that certain import-competing sectors in Africa may suffer as a result of EPA tariff dismantling, the European Commission explains that African countries will increasingly realise their comparative advantage in more productive sectors. Thus, while there may be short-term pain, African economies—on the whole—will benefit from the market liberalisation agenda laid out in the terms of the EPA. Combined to Aid for Trade resources, the EPA will be an opportunity for African countries to 'successfully integrate' into globalised markets. At the same time, the European Commission also emphasises that any African country that fails to ratify and fully implement an EPA will be subject to the terms of the (less preferable) GSP. Countries such as Nigeria that failed to ratify an EPA by the original deadline of 31st December 2007 already have suffered the default to GSP, with deleterious consequences for export sectors dependent on low tariff access to European consumers (such as the cocoa processors in that ACP country).

As the above discussion illustrates, the material realities of EPA implementation do not necessarily conform to the EU's pro-poor development discourse, quite the opposite. As expressed by African civil society, trade unions and (at times) African political elites—the EPAs bring the prospect of yet more premature tariff dismantling within ACP economies. This will likely have regressive consequences for productivity—and thus livelihoods—within import-competing sectors such as poultry and tomato agro-processing that historically are reliant upon domestic, and regional, consumers for their viability. Faced with import-flooding of subsidised European agricultural produce and cheap manufactures, local production and businesses will suffer. This has historically been demonstrated under SAPs which initiated what can accurately be termed 'first generation' liberalisation, contrasted with the 'second generation' liberalisation now imminent under EPAs. Industries such as textiles greatly suffered in the 1990s as cheap European competition surged into local markets, undercutting African producers. Moreover, the EPA will mean reduced tariff revenues for African governments despite the fact that these represent significant resources for welfare expenditure, particularly in least developed countries such as Senegal. Lost tariff revenues will far outstrip any promised Aid for Trade assistance. For example, the West African EPADP at €6.5 billion will be outweighed by long-term tariff revenues losses in the region (predicted to constitute around €2.5 billion in lost receipts in the twentieth year of EPA implementation).

In these circumstances, Nkrumah's analysis of, and warnings about, neo-colonialism maintain relevance in the contemporary period of African relations with foreign actors. In the case of Africa-EU trade relations, the EPAs threaten to perpetuate African economies' subordination to the commercial interests of the industrialised EU member states. Faced with import-flooding and tariff liberalisation, African countries will continue to remain dependent on the export of raw materials while failing to meaningfully diversify into value-added sectors. The scope for African agency to reject the EPAs in their entirety, meanwhile, is restricted by the EU's use of aid as leverage in its negotiations with political elites in countries such as Ghana. Promised EPADP monies, for example, provide a sweetener for elites' acquiescence to European demands despite the long-term repercussions of trade liberalisation for their citizenries. As private sector stakeholders acknowledge, Aid for Trade monies can—in many circumstances—do more to augment the status of political elites than to effectively enhance productivity. Moreover, the allocation of Aid for Trade monies can often do more to entrench European investments in lucrative sectors such as fisheries, than to meaningfully assist African entrepreneurs and local livelihoods. In these circumstances, Nkrumah's protests against foreign influence and trade asymmetries appear prescient in our current phase of Africa–EU trade ties. European influence in other areas—such as security—further cement this view, as discussed now in the next chapter.

NOTE

1. The CAP artificially subsidises European production which makes the realisation of a 'level-playing field' particularly difficult when EU donors insist on ACP countries' adherence to strict free market norms (of which the CAP itself falls foul).
2. It should be noted that the European Commission has promised that least developed ACP countries, such as Uganda, will be able to continue non-reciprocal trade via the Everything But Arms (EBA) scheme. Thus if they do not sign and ratify an EPA then they can continue to access European consumers at low tariffs. In practice, however, this does not offer much assurance. First, such countries would be liable to 'graduation' measures whereby EBA access would be stripped if they rose to middle income status (as measured by World Bank indicators). Second, these least developed countries are often cajoled by their middle income peers to sign up to a regional EPA to ensure market cohesion within their sub-region (e.g. implementation of a common external tariff). Third, certain least developed countries—such as Uganda—have become avowed champions of the EPA agenda, finding that EU budget support monies constitute a large proportion of their day-to-day governance costs (and wishing to secure continuing aid largesse from their benefactors in the European Commission).

REFERENCES

ActionAid. (2004). *Trade traps: Why EU–ACP economic partnership agreement (EPAs) pose a threat to Africa's development*. London: ActionAid.

ActionAid Ghana. (2013). *Ghana under the interim economic partnership agreement*. Accra: ActionAid Ghana. Available at: http://www.ghanaweb.com/GhanaHomePage/economy/artikel.php?ID=301006. Accessed 25 Mar 2017.

Adenikinju, Adeola, & Alabam, Olumuyiwa. (2005). *EU–ACP economic partnership agreements: Implications for trade and development in West Africa*. Ibadan: University of Ibadan.

Alli, F. (2015, May 29). West Africa: The real dangers of EPA to Ecowas—Ukaoha, *Vanguard*. Available at: http://allafrica.com/stories/201505291475.html. Accessed 25 Mar 2017.

APRODEV, EED, ACDIC, & ICCO. (2007). *No more chicken please: How a strong grassroots movement in Cameroon is successfully resisting damaging chicken imports from Europe, which are ruining small farmers all over West Africa*. Brussels: APRODEV. Available at: http://aprodev.eu/files/Trade/071203_chicken_e_final.pdf. Accessed 24 July 2017.

Babarinde, O., & Wright, S. (2013). Africa–EU partnership on trade and regional integration. In J. Mangala (Ed.), *Africa and the European union: A strategic partnership* (pp. 123–148). London: Palgrave.

Bagooro, S. (2011, August 25). *Report of the National Civil Society Forum on the EPA*. Accra: Third World Network-Africa.

Berthelot, J., & Gadrey, J. (2014, November 27). *A worse TTIP for Africa where the EU shoots also itself in the foot*. Paris SOL, Alternatives Agroécologiques et Solidaires. Available at: https://www.sol-asso.fr/wpcontent/uploads/2014/12/A_worse_TTIP_for_Africa_where_the_EU_shoots_also_itself_in_the_foot.doc. Accessed 25 Mar 2017.

Bracking, S. (1999). Structural adjustment: Why it wasn't necessary and why it did work. *Review of African Political Economy, 26*(80), 207–226.

Brown, W. (2002). *The European union and Africa: The restructuring of North–South relations*. London: I.B. Tauris & Co.

Brown, W. (2004). From uniqueness to uniformity? An assessment of EU development aid policies. In K. Arts & A. Dickson (Eds.), *EU development co-operation: From model to symbol* (pp. 17–41). Manchester: Manchester University Press.

Business Day. (2014). Nigeria: Manufacturers fear harmful impact of EPA on local industries. *Business day*. Available at: http://brussels.cta.int/index.php?option=com_k2&view=item&id=9360:nigeria-manufacturers-fear-harmful-impact-of-epa-on-local-industries. Accessed 25 Mar 2017.

Chang, H. J. (2003). *Kicking away the ladder*. London: Anthem Press.

CONCORD. (2015). *The EPA between the EU and West Africa: Who really benefits? Convergence of EU policies for development*. Brussels: CONCORD. Available at: http://www.concord.se/wpcontent/uploads/Spotlight_2015-TRADE-EPA-April_2015-EN.pdf. Accessed 25 Mar 2017.

Coopers, Pricewaterhouse. (2007). *Sustainability impact assessment of the EU–ACP economic partnership agreements: Summary of key findings, policy recommendations and lessons learned*. London: Pricewaterhouse Coopers.

der Van Lee, J. (1967). Association relations between the European economic community.

Enterplan. (2005). *Capacity-building in support of preparation of economic partnership agreement*. London: Enterplan.

EuropAfrica. (2011, November 29). *Joint statement by the West African civil society platform on the Cotonou agreement*. Accra. Rome: EuropAfrica.

European Commission. (1996). *Green paper on the relations between the European union and the ACP countries on the eve of the 21st century*. Brussels: European Commission.

European Commission. (2002). *Making globalisation work for everyone: The European union and world trade*. Brussels: European Commission.

European Commission. (2005). *EU strategy for Africa: Towards a Euro–African pact to accelerate Africa's development*. Brussels: European Commission.

European Commission. (2006). *Making trade work for development: Aid for trade, a selection of case studies from around the world*. Brussels: European Commission.

European Commission. (2007). *Towards an EU aid for trade strategy—The commission's contribution*. Brussels: European Commission.

European Commission. (2014). *West African leaders back European partnership agreement with the EU*. Brussels: European Commission. Available at: http://europa.eu/rapid/press-release_IP14-827_en.htm. Accessed 1 Mar 2014.

European Council. (1988). 1244th meeting of the council, development co-operation. Brussels 31 May1988. In *council of the European communities, press releases, presidency: Germany, January–June1988, meetings and press releases May 1988*. Brussels: European Council. Available at: http://aei.pitt.edu/3265/01/000378_1.pdf. Accessed 8 Oct 2009.

European Council. (2010). *Council conclusions of 10th May 2010 concerning the EPA development programme(PAPED)*. Brussels: European Commission.

European Council. (2014). *Council conclusions of 17th March 2014 on the West African EPA development programme (PAPED)*. Brussels: European Commission.

Frey-Wouters, A. (1980). *The European community and the third world: The Lomé convention and its impact*. New York: Praeger.

Friedrichs, D. (1970). Association problems of African states. *Intereconomics, 8*, 246–248.

Gegout, C. (2016). Unethical power Europe? Something fishy about EU trade and development policies. *Third World Quarterly, 37*(12), 2192–2210.

Ghana Ministry of Trade/TRAQUE. (2006). *Ghana–EU Economic Partnership Agreement*. Accra: Ghana Ministry of Trade. Available at: http://www.traqueghana.org/files/03-EPA-Presentation.pdf. Accessed 25 Mar 2017.

GreenPeace. (2012). *The Plunder of a Nation's Birthright*. Amsterdam: Greenpeace. Available at: http://www.greenpeace.org/africa/Global/africa/publications/oceans/ThePlunderOfANationsBirthright.pdf. Accessed 25 Mar 2017.

Gruhn, I. (1976). The Lomé convention: Inching towards interdependence. *International Organization, 30*(2), 241–262.

Gruhn, I. (1993). *The evolution of African–European relations*. Washington: European Community Studies Association.

Human Rights Watch. (2011). *You'll be fired if you refuse: Labour abuses in Zambia's state-owned copper mines*. New York: Hyman Rights Watch. Available at: https://www.hrw.org/report/2011/11/04/youll-be-fired-if-you-refuse/labor-abuses-zambias-chinese-state-owned-copper-mines. Accessed 25 Mar 2017.

Issah. M. (2007). *Right to food of tomato and poultry farmers: Report of an investigative mission to Ghana*. Accra: Send West Africa. Available at: http://germanwatch.org/handel/ffm-ghana.pdf. Accessed 25 Mar 2017.

Kawasaki, S. (2000). *Origins of the concept of the Eurafrican community*. Tokyo: Tokyo Kasei University. Available at: http://www.kasei.ac.jp/library/kiyou/2000/2.KAWASAKI.pdf. Accessed 8 Oct 2009.

Kenyan Association of Manufacturers. (2006). *Manufacturing in Kenya: A survey of the manufacturing sector*. Nairobi: KAM.

Kokole, O. (1981). Stabex anatomized. *Third World Quarterly, 3*(3), 441–459.

Langan, M. (2011a). Uganda's flower farms and private sector development. *Development and Change, 42*(5), 1207–1240.

Langan, M. (2011b). Private sector development as poverty and strategic discourse: PSD in the political economy of EU–Africa trade relations. *Journal of Modern African Studies, 49*(1), 83–113.

Langan, M. (2012). Normative power Europe and the moral economy of Africa–EU ties: A conceptual reorientation of "Normative Power". *New Political Economy, 17*(3), 243–270.

Langan, M., & Price, S. (2015). Extraversion and the West African EPA development programme; Realising the development dimension of ACP–EU trade? *Journal of Modern African Studies, 53*(3), 263–287.

Langan, M., & Price, S. (forthcoming). West Africa–EU trade and cocoa agro-processing: Assessing business stakeholders perspectives on 'Pro-Poor' private sector development.

Langan, M., & Scott, J. (2011). The aid for trade charade. *Cooperation and Conflict, 49*(2), 143–161.

Mailafia, O. (1997). *Europe and economic reform in Africa: Structural adjustment and economic diplomacy*. London: Routledge.

Mutume, G. (2007). Africans fear 'Ruin' in Europe trade talks. *African Renewal, 21*(2) online. Available at: http://www.un.org/en/africarenewal/vol21no2/212-africans-fear-ruin-in-trade-talks.html. Accessed 25 Mar 2017.

NANTS. (2010). *The EU–West Africa economic partnership agreement (EPA) negotiations*. Abuja: NANTS.

Nkrumah, K. (1963). *Africa must unite*. London: Heineman.

Nkrumah, K. (1965). *Neo-colonialism: The last stage of imperialism*. Sixth Printing—New York International Publishers, 1976.

Nwoke, Chibuzo. (2009). *EU–ECOWAS economic partnership agreement: Nigeria's role in securing development-focus and regional integration*. Lagos: Nigerian Institute of International Affairs.

Olanyo, J. (2008, March 28). Uganda: Civil society vow to stop EPA. *The Monitor*. Available at: http://allafrica.com/stories/200803281270.html. Accessed 25 Mar 2017.

Patel, M. (2007). *Economic Partnership Agreements between the EU and African Countries: Potential development implications for Ghana*. Oxford: Realising Rights.

Pannhausen, C. (2006). *Economic partnerships and food security: What is at stake for West Africa?* Bonn: German Development Institute. Available at: https://www.die-gdi.de/uploads/media/Economic_Partnership_Agreements_and_Food_Security.pdf. Accessed 25 Mar 2017.

Ravenhill, J. (1984). What is to be done for third world commodity exporters? An evaluation of the stabex scheme. *International Organization, 38*(3), 537–574.

Ravenhill, J. (1985). *Collective clientelism: The Lomé convention and North South relations*. New York: Columbia University Press.

Robson, P. (1965). Africa and EEC: A quantitative note on trade benefits'. *Bulletin of the Oxford University Institute of Economics, 27*(4), 299–304.

SEATINI Uganda. (2013, March 7). *MUDESA with support from and in conjunction with SEATINI–U is organising a students' dialogue at Makerere University*. Kampala: SEATINI Uganda.

SEATINI Uganda. (2017). *SEATINI statement on the EPA's inherent dangers and the way forward*. Kampala: SEATINI Uganda. Available at: http://www.seatiniuganda.org/publications/downloads/121-seatini-statement-on-epas-inherent-dangers-and-way-forward/file.html. Accessed 25 Mar 2017.

Solidar. (2008). *Economic partnership agreements—The case of Nigeria*. Brussels: Solidar.

Soper, T. (1965). Independent Africa and its links with Europe. *African Affairs, 64*, 25–31.

Soper, T. (1968). Review of Ogikbo, P. N. C., Africa and the common market. *African Affairs, 67*, 259–260.

The Courier. (1975). Lome´ Dossier. Reprinted from *The Courier*, Special Issue No. 31, March 1975. Brussels: European Commission. Available at: http://aei.pitt.edu/1776/01/Lome_dossier.pdf. Accessed 8 Oct 2009.

The Courier. (1979). ACP–EEC Convention Lome II. *The Courier*, Special Issue No. 58 November. Brussels: European Commission. Available at: http://aei.pitt.edu/1777/01/Lome_II_dossier.pdf. Accessed 8 Oct 2009.

Touré, S. (1962). Africa's future and the world. *Foreign Affairs, 41*, 141–151.

Traidcraft. (2004). *EPAs—The hidden dangers*. Available at: http://www.traidcraft.co.uk/temp/radA276C.pdf. Accessed 8 Oct 2009.

Traidcraft. (2005). *Why more free trade won't help Africa: Through the lens of Kenya*. Available at: http://www.traidcraft.co.uk/temp/radF74F6.pdf. Accessed 8 Oct 2009.

Whiteman, K. (1998). Africa, the ACP and Europe. *Development Policy Review, 6*(1), 29–37.

Whitfield, L., & Jones, E. (2009). Ghana: Breaking out of aid dependence? Economic and political barriers to ownership. In L. Whitfield (Ed.), *The politics of aid: Strategies for dealing with donors* (pp. 185–216). Oxford: Oxford University Press.

World Cocoa Foundation. (2012). *Cocoa market update*. Washington: World Cocoa Foundation.

Zartman, I. W. (1976). Europe and Africa: Decolonization or dependency? *Foreign Affairs, 54*(2), 325–343.

CHAPTER 6

Security, Development, and Neo-Colonialism

INTRODUCTION

The concept of neo-colonialism, as put forth by Nkrumah, identified the potential for military incursions and violent conflict in Africa after de jure independence had been achieved by many 'sovereign' states. He warned that neo-colonialism, as a system, would provide the 'breeding ground for limited wars' which would likely escalate 'despite the desire of the great power blocs to keep it limited' (1965: xi). Nkrumah referenced here the potential for the superpowers in the Cold War to utilise African territories as sites of proxy warfare. As witnessed in countries such as Angola during its long civil war, African states did in fact become sites of ideological great power division. Washington and Moscow interfered in, and at times actively promoted, local conflicts to serve their own political and commercial interests in Africa.

Nkrumah's concerns about the linkages of neo-colonialism to war and conflict in Africa may appear anachronistic in a post-Cold War context. The real-politicking and proxy wars which Nkrumah correctly predicted in the Cold War setting may appear a phenomenon of the past in the twenty-first century. However, when the recent literature on the 'securitisation of development' is considered alongside that of Nkrumah's writings on neo-colonialism, there appears to be a modern day parallel to the Cold War conflagrations which he warned against. The impact of the 'war on terror' combined to international reliance on African energy supplies (for instance, in the Gulf of Guinea) has ensured that

© The Author(s) 2018   149
M. Langan, *Neo-Colonialism and the Poverty of 'Development'*
in Africa, Contemporary African Political Economy,
https://doi.org/10.1007/978-3-319-58571-0_6

Africa remains the potential site of conflicts which are exacerbated, and perhaps even prompted by, great power concerns. For example, French interventions—more recently pursued under the umbrella of the EU itself (EURFOR)—have prompted major concerns about the violation of African state sovereignty in the name of security and anti-terror. The recent French intervention in Mali, in particular, raises concerns that Paris remains focused upon exerting a (neo)colonial prerogative in its 'backyard' (despite Westphalian norms of sovereignty). The circumstances in which conflict arose in Mali also raise questions about the long-term implications of French aid conditionalities and policy prescriptions for state stability in Africa. There is concern that the Tuareg-led revolt in the north was in part provoked by donor 'development' initiatives that (further) isolated ethnic minority groups from central government. Such issues are interesting to explore with direct reference to Nkrumah. Again his writings potentially offer much insight into contemporary African affairs, as they did in the 1960s.

Furthermore, the recent 'securitisation of development' debate is important to consider not only in terms of the outbreak of war and civil strife in African states vis-à-vis conditions of neo-colonialism. Donor initiatives aimed at stemming migration flows to Europe also raise concerns about de facto violations of African state sovereignty (and the co-optation of local elites as a result of external power politicking). The European Commission, in particular, has sought to sign migration partnership agreements with a number of African states to deal with the 'push' factors that have motivated poorer individuals to attempt Mediterranean sea routes to the European mainland. These donor migration initiatives have created what might accurately be termed 'security states' in Africa which monitor their own populations and curtail civil liberties to prevent movement of people. Moreover, they raise issues about how donor security concerns influence the use of aid monies, especially in terms of creeping conditionalities. Altogether the securitisation of development vis-à-vis migration raises additional questions about contemporary aspects of neo-colonialism in Africa.

The chapter is structured as follows. It first examines emerging concerns about the securitisation of development in terms of recent literature on Western donor aid-giving and policy interventions in Africa. This addresses issues surrounding the 'war on terror' as well as energy supplies originating from African countries such as Mali and Niger. It makes clear that there are critical voices that have raised important questions about the potential violation of state sovereignty and of Westphalian norms. The second section then provides a case study focus on French interventions in the Sahel region, with emphasis on the Malian intervention. It examines French geopolitical motivations in the sub-region, as well as the impact of French policies and aid in the lead up to civil strife. Accordingly, the chapter frames whether such conflicts and foreign intervention might be usefully understood in relation to Nkrumah's thesis on neo-colonialism. The third section then draws attention to 'securitisation' in terms of the prevention of migration (as per current donor priorities). It assesses the European Commission's recent push for migration partnership agreements and considers, again, whether Nkrumah's warnings about the co-optation of local elites by external elements might be useful in helping to make sense of contemporary North–South affairs. Finally, the concluding sections reflect on potential applications of the concept of neo-colonialism given the creeping securitisation agenda that is unfolding within donor policy towards Africa.

THE SECURITISATION OF DEVELOPMENT?

African countries played a key part in the Cold War in terms of proxy conflicts between the superpowers. The material support of military dictatorships such as Mobutu in Zaire (now the DRC) by Western governments, for instance, reflected a geopolitics that emphasised the need to prevent African states from sliding into the 'wrong' ideological camp. Moreover, foreign interference in civil wars in territories such as Angola reflected great power strategies of supporting different local factions in the hope of installing compliant regimes. This was of course predicted by Nkrumah (1965: xi) when he wrote about the onset of neo-colonialism and the 'breeding ground' for limited wars which would ensue as a result of great power interference.

Nevertheless, there is a need to reflect on more contemporary conflicts within Africa, and whether great power intervention continues to fuel violence and instability in so-called 'fragile states'. While the Cold War continues to capture Western public imagination of African conflicts given its ideological hues, there remain a number of current conflict zones whose predicament can potentially be traced (in part) to external power politicking. Accordingly, there has recently been a growth of literature surrounding the idea of the 'securitisation of development' (for instance, see Abrahamsen 2005; Ferguson 2005; Carmody 2005; Keenan 2008; Bagoyoko and Gibert 2009; Keukeleire and Raube 2013; Fisher and Anderson 2015; Amosu 2007). Namely, that Western donors, in particular, have responded to the onset of the 'war on terror' by increasingly viewing Africa as a hazardous site of likely extremism and insecurity. Drawing upon colonial era imaginaries of the 'dark continent', many Western officials have established discourse in which African countries are viewed as inherently unstable and dangerous zones of barbarism (Charbonneau 2008). In this vein, the (in)famous Cheney Report, issued within US government circles after 9/11, emphasised that Africa would have to be securitised (Keenan 2008: 17). This would apparently pre-empt the outbreak of Islamic extremism, particularly in those countries in proximity to the Sahel that possess significant numbers of Muslims. Not only would North African Arab states come under increased US scrutiny, but so too would 'development' interventions in sub-Saharan Africa bend to a securitisation agenda.

Importantly, this securitisation agenda has also been understood in relation to increasing energy reliance on African countries, especially on the part of interventionist states such as the USA and France. The discovery of enhanced oil supplies in the Gulf of Guinea gave rise to the view that West Africa itself might become the 'new Middle East' for energy production (Keenan 2008). This, when combined to existing energy interests (for example, French reliance on uranium supplies from Niger for its nuclear power plants), seemingly encouraged Western actors to more actively apply a security lens in their approach to (West) African development. Despite the end of the Cold War, therefore, security-driven approaches to African affairs once more took firm hold within official imaginations. Interestingly, Abrahamsen (2005) notes that this official focus often highlighted a moral imperative to 'assist' developing countries to deal with their own security threats. A blend of realist realpolitik and liberal 'development' discourse thus came about within the securitisation of development. Notably, she identifies the then UK Prime Minister, Tony Blair, as one of the key influences upon the collective approach devised by the US and USA in the era of the George W. Bush Presidency. She also reflects that the realist security lens threatens to trump liberal norms associated with human wellbeing:

"securitisation" of the continent [is] evident not only in the British government's discourse but also more broadly in, for example, U.S. policies and in academic debates. Through this securitisation, dealings and interactions with Africa are gradually shifting from the category of "development/humanitarianism" to a category of "risk/fear/security," so that today Africa is increasingly mentioned in the context of the "war on terrorism" and the dangers it poses to Britain and the international community. (2005: 56)

Importantly, in terms of debates about African agency, there has also been analytical focus on the ways in which local elites have responded to securitisation agendas to buttress their own patronage networks (Bergamaschi 2014; Charbonneau 2014; Fisher and Anderson 2015). With relevance for Bayart's concept of extraversion, certain local elites have mirrored the security discourse of the 'West' in their own policy pronouncements. In cases such as Mali, local government officials are seen to have deliberately identified potential 'threat' groups to donors to leverage additional finance (Omeje 2010). Kennan (2004: 490) documents similar situations in the case of Algeria and Niger in relation to their own Tuareg minorities, who she deems are being deliberately provoked as part of a climate of securitisation. African governance actors are therefore not understood to be passive 'victims' of Western security agendas, but as resourceful agents able to 'work the system' to their own material advantage. Fisher and Anderson (2015: 132) remark that the securitisation of development since the early 2000s:

gives rise to crucial questions about African agency... Through their willingness to take ownership of the security agenda, African regimes have played a conscious role in securitizing their relationship with donors. Securitisation is not something that the West has done to Africa, but rather a set of policy imperatives that some African governments have actively pursued.

In this vein, parallels have also been drawn between contemporary strategies aimed at supporting trusted African regimes against perceived barbarism, and colonial-era policies of indirect rule. Duffield (2005: 144) indicates that the current securitisation agenda may find antecedents in terms of how European empires utilised local officials to pursue their own power interests. Rather than always rely upon direct military intervention, Europe's colonial regimes often relied upon their African partners on the ground to undertake security operations. This strategy is seen to be mirrored in terms how contemporary military equipment, training and capacity-building is offered to African elites deemed to be on the side of Western donors. Duffield (2005: 149) explains that the growing 'respectability of interventionary liberal imperialism' draws upon longer histories of colonial rule. Accordingly, it is illustrative to now examine these debates in more detail via a case study focus on French interventions in the 2000s. The next section examines the policies of the Sarkozy and Hollande administrations in terms of crises within the Sahel region. It provides assessment of French undertakings—and motivations—in the case of Mali, as well as Ivory Coast. This case study focus considers securitisation and current conflict zones in terms of the concept of neo-colonialism.

FRENCH PREROGATIVES IN FRANCOPHONE AFRICA: SECURITISATION AND/OR SOVEREIGNTY?

France historically has stood accused of neo-colonial interventions in Africa, particularly in the immediate period of decolonisation. President Charles De Gaulle's foreign policy privileged an imagined *Francafrique* as a vital construct able to project French grandeur onto the global stage (Chafer 2005). France—by maintaining close economic, monetary and military ties to its erstwhile African colonies—would maintain a sphere of influence as part of a so-called 'family' arrangement with Francophone African elites. France would therefore remain a truly great power, able to influence events rather than standing as a mere satellite of either superpower. Moreover, French officials—as Europeanisation began as part of the creation of the EEC—began to speak also of the need for *Eurafrica*, and of Eurafrican economic and aid arrangements. With parallels to the concept of Francafrique, the Eurafrican construct emphasised the interdependence of the two regions, based upon Europe's demand for raw materials and Africa's need for continuing aid, trade and technical support from the metropole.

During the Presidency of Jacques Chirac in the 1990s, however, there was increasing focus on how France might insulate itself from international criticism for its perceived unilateralism in African affairs. The fallout from the Rwandan genocide, perpetrated in 1994, shook Gaullist foreign policy assumptions. France stood accused in global fora, including the UN, of having first supported—and then abetted—Hutu extremists who later fled the country with the apparent assistance of France's *Operation Turquoise*. In response to this—as well as economic pressures upon the French state itself—France's policy approach towards Africa was more fully internationalised, or perhaps more properly, Europeanised (Bagoyoko and Gibert 2009: 800). French elites began more and more to look to the EU as a collective means of implementing policy preferences when dealing with crises in African governance (particularly in Francophone former colonies). Following on from reconciliation with the UK during the St Malo summit in 1998, France began to work more closely with this other former colonial power to forge ahead with joint European endeavours such as the European Security and Defence Policy (ESDP)—now known as the Common Security and Defence Policy (CSDP) (Chafer 2005: 17). French recourse to the EU for potential military interventions in Africa also found expression within the subsequent Presidencies of Nicolas Sarkozy and Francois Hollande. Both presidents—similarly to Chirac—couched France's Africa policy within the wider contours of Europe. Europeanisation, in this sense, has provided a degree of greater credibility and legitimacy to what otherwise would be perceived as French unilateralism and 'neo-colonialism' in the region.

Importantly, however, there is mounting concern that France—while embracing the opportunities for collective endeavours in Africa under the EU umbrella—has not truly dissipated its neo-colonial instincts when approaching questions of security (and regime preferences) in its former colonies. Rather France now stands accused of utilising the EU as a means of 'camouflaging' or veiling its underlying economic and security national interests in Africa via recourse to the normative discourse of Europeanisation (Bagoyoko and Gibert 2009: 800). France is seen to have worked within the EU to cultivate a normative discourse on 'fragility' and state security in Africa, emphasising European values associated with democracy, individualism and human rights. By relying on the credibility of 'normative power Europe', France has been able to continue its geopolitical pursuit of core economic and security interests while developing greater international acceptance of its actions. Indeed, the majority of European peacekeeping operations in Africa have been dominated—both in terms of military personnel and strategic planning—by French actors. For example, Operation Artemis—undertaken in the DRC in

2003—by the European Union Force (EURFOR) allowed France to reassert its leadership in the Great Lakes region, regaining a certain degree of credibility lost in the aftermath of Operation Turquoise. Bagoyoko and Gibert (2009: 800) convincingly argue that:

> Operation Artemis offered an interesting illustration of the progressive Europeanisation of France's involvement in African crises… [it was] an interesting synthesis of the interests of the EU and one of its member states, since it reconciled a young ESDP in search of credibility and a former colonial power in search of legitimacy after some deeply contested unilateral interventions. It also enabled France to re-engage in the Great Lakes region… [and] to share the costs of military and defence cooperation.

Nevertheless, France has not always restricted itself to collectivism even after the criticism it received after the Rwandan genocide. Most recently in 2013, French military forces launched Operation Serval (2013–2014) in Mali to combat what was perceived as an Islamist threat in the north of the country. The erstwhile Malian president—once championed as the 'solider of democracy'—had been overthrown in a military coup in 2012. This had opened up opportunities for a northern insurrection against the central authorities in the capital city (Bamako) in the south. The northern forces—while initially deemed to be an offshoot of Tuareg nationalism (often described as being a Sahelian equivalent of the Kurdish dilemma in the Middle East) was soon deemed to constitute Islamist forces (Boas and Torheim 2013: 1281; Olsen 2014: 291). The French presidency under Hollande therefore authorised use of military force under Operation Serval, having first obtained a UN Security Council resolution supporting French action (thus seeking to guard France against accusations of neo-colonialism and unilateralism).

Despite UN support, as well as initial popular support among southern Malians, French intervention in the conflict has been criticised on a number of grounds, not least France's desire to perpetuate economic and political influence. France's interest in the prompt resolution of the Malian crisis is seen not only in terms of attempts to deal with an Islamist insurgency, but also its desire to protect its corporations' uranium mining in neighbouring Niger (since the mining operations fall close to the Mali-Niger border). The extraction of this key commodity is essential for French energy security, given their high domestic use of nuclear power plants. The intervention, in this hue, can be seen less of a humanitarian concern than an economic concern for the French state vis-à-vis Areva (the French nuclear energy firm) and energy demands at home. Boeke and Bart (2015: 806) underscore the significance of these uranium deposits for France:

> France's primary national interests in Mali are economic and security-related. Mali's eastern neighbour Niger is the world's fourth-largest uranium exporter. The mines at Arlit and Akoka, near the border with Mali and also situated in Tuareg country, are exploited by Areva, one of the world's biggest producers of uranium and one of France's national economic champions. Niger's uranium provides 20 per cent of the fuel for France's 58 nuclear reactors, which are in turn responsible for generating nearly 75 per cent of France's electricity.

It is perhaps worth noting here that Niger itself remains one of the poorest developing countries according to the UN Human Development Index (Larsen and Mamosso 2014). Despite its raw material wealth—and its intensive uranium exports to France—the country remains in the condition of underdeveloped predicted by Nkrumah in his condemnation of neo-colonial trade and production.

Concerns have also been raised that the roots of the Malian crisis can be traced to France's influence over development policies in the country. The French government's close aid and economic ties to the regime of Amadou Toumani Touré (the erstwhile president overthrown in 2012) precipitated his eventual downfall. French budget support monies—alongside that of other Western donors—enabled the regime and its unwise decision to rely upon armed leaders in the north (who eventually proved a liability in terms of the Bamako government's domestic credibility). Moreover, France's insistence upon a series of controversial policy reforms—including proposed changes to gendered family laws and the creation of an anti-fraud officer who named and shamed key politicians—fundamentally damaged Touré's domestic base of support (Bergamaschi 2014: 349–352). More broadly, the historical foundations of Tuareg resentment towards Bamako authorities in the south of the country are seen to be rooted in the 'divide and rule' policies of French colonial administrations (Boas and Torheim 2013: 1281). The recent crisis is thus rooted in (neo)colonial relationships, particularly in terms of how the regime's popularity was undermined by policy impositions pursued by budget support donors. An official within AFD in fact remarked that they 'chewed and digested' each key policy initiative with regards to Touré's ill-fated regime (Bergamaschi 2014: 349–352). Budget support, being utilised for 'policy dialogue', in part led to the regime's downfall given donors' preference for controversial reforms, including those to domestic family law in a traditionalist Muslim society (ibid.).

It is important to note that Operation Serval was not an isolated event in the contemporary period of French relations in Africa (post-Chirac). With parallels to the intervention in Mali, French troops had also been utilised in Ivory Coast in 2010–2011 to militarily support the electoral claims of Alssane Ouattara against those of then President Laurent Gbagbo (after the vote count was contested by the sitting president). France's use of troops in Abidjan—including the seizure of the capital city's airport—played a crucial role in the eventual capture of Gbagbo in April 2011. France, moreover, had played an earlier part in the Ivorian civil war, with French units destroying the Ivorian airforce in 2004 (in retaliation for an Ivorian attack on French peacekeeping forces in the north). Again with parallels to the situation in Mali, certain analysts point to the influence of Western donors themselves (including the French) in the precipitation of instability in Ivory Coast in the first instance. Charbonneau (2014) points to policies of structural adjustment, including privatisation and trade liberalisation schemes, as having put pressures on the social fabric of the Ivorian state. He argues that 'the amalgamation of conditions of austerity and the shrinking of policy options encouraged more radical politics, exacerbated xenophobic tendencies, and led to serious sociopolitical crisis and civil war' (2014: 624). Interestingly, he also notes the role of Ouattara as the Prime Minister responsible for implementing privatisation of Ivorian assets in the 1990s, often with major gains for French companies:

> French corporations… control vital sectors of the economy: telecommunications (France Telecom), banks (Societe Generale, Credit Lyonnais, BNP-Paribas), transportation (Air France; Groupe Bollore ´ through SAGA, SDV, and Sitarail), water (Groupe Bouygues), and energy (electricity and hydrocarbons; involving Groupe Bouygues and Total). (ibid.)

Interestingly, however, Laurent Gbagbo—despite his nationalist assertions during his Presidency against French influence—is seen to have continued economic policies based upon French FDI. Despite his anti-French rhetoric, and his eventual downfall due to French support for

Ouattara, the Gbagbo regime maintained course with economic policies based upon heavy French corporate involvement (ibid.).

This pattern of French military intervention in African countries where France possesses keen economic and energy interests is repeated in the case of Chad. The Idriss Deby regime, in power since the 1990s, has utilised French aid and military assistance to maintain its elite hegemony. France has notably engaged in military operations to help the regime put down opposition-led rebellions, including episodes in 2006 and 2008 (in response to Deby's amendment of the constitution to prolong his term limit, which France supported). France also worked within the UN Security Council and the European Council of Ministers to gain consent for a multilateral peacekeeping operation in 2008, in which French troops constituted over two-thirds of EUFOR personnel (Fisher and Anderson 2015: 137). Chad's discovery of oil, meanwhile, has strongly informed the views of external actors with regards to the extent that they are willing to intervene in Chad's internal affairs (although the discovery did not in itself create the political instability which has affected the country). Not only are French energy interests at play, but also that of emerging powers such as China who—from the view of Paris—are encroaching on their traditional sphere of influence vis-à-vis 'Francafrique':

> the crisis has already developed a dangerous international dimension, setting Western interests, represented by French and American support for Déby against Sudanese and Chinese backing for the Chadian rebels... Paris maintains three military bases... [its] presence allows France to pursue its geostrategic interests in central Africa but has also been used to shield Déby who came to power with the help of France's external intelligence agency. (Massey and May 2006: 446)

The role of the Deby regime in securing foreign corporations' access to oil-rich tracts has provoked protests, including an incident in 1997 where the regime stood accused of massacring 200 citizens who protested against the construction of a new oil pipeline. In the early 2000s, the regime also utilised around $4.5 million of oil proceeds to buy armaments, helping to precipitate the conflicts seen in the mid-2000s and early 2010s (Harshe 2003: 116).

It is important to note that across these external security interventions—whether in Mali, Ivory Coast or Chad—French authorities have utilised a normative language of development, human rights, and protection to legitimise their interventions in the affairs of 'sovereign' African states. Perhaps most interestingly in the case of Mali, President Hollande presented his government's military support to the regime as a 'gift' to the Malian people which, in part, helped to rectify past injustices endured during Empire. A discourse of French obligation to Mali was also welcomed—and utilised—by Malian political elites themselves in securing—and legitimising—the role that French forces played in their survival:

> the intervention was framed by President Hollande as repayment of the country's historical debt toward Mali and this was 'a more acceptable framework of gift and counter gift between states and peoples'. In Bamako, three months after the French intervention, some individuals argued that 'France had the moral and political *obligation* to accept and honour President Traoré's request for intervention (Wing 2016: 72)

This interplay between the discourse of French patrons and that of their client regimes in countries such as Mali, Chad and Ivory Coast strikes at the heart of debates surrounding African elite agency in their dealings with external actors. It also resonates with debates surrounding Nkrumah and the concept of neo-colonialism. It is necessary to restate here that Nkrumah (1963, 1965) did not deny that African elites would play an active role in sustaining systems of neo-colonialism after formal independence had been achieved. He recognised—alongside other critics of neo-colonialism such as Frantz Fanon—that certain African leaders would wholly encourage foreign colonial powers (such as France) to maintain their economic and political dominance in African states. Neo-colonial elites (or comprador classes, to utilise the term favoured by dependency theorist, Dos Santos) would 'play the game' in order to secure their own ascendancy in their nation-state. This, moreover, again ties into the concept of 'extraversion' favoured by Bayart, albeit within his discussion of so-called neo-patrimonial regimes. African elites—such as those in Bamako welcoming French military assistance—do utilise the discourse and 'development' vocabularies of the donor community in order to lever in additional resources for their patronage networks. They also utilise strategic 'development' and 'security' discourse to justify the internal–external bond to their own citizenries. This does not nullify or contradict, however, the central tenet within Nkrumah's writings—namely, that neo-colonialism—acts as a force which effectively nullifies the genuine exercise of political and economic self-government in Africa. Predatory elites—sustained in power and enabled in their mal-governance by foreign benefactors—may utilise the state apparatus for personal gain while ignoring the long-term economic interests of their citizens, who are denied any genuine democratic recourse. Unlike the 'essentialist' views often expressed within the neo-patrimonialism literature, this scenario is not best explained in terms of the 'Big Man' caricature. Instead, it is best explained by Nkrumah in terms of a dual marriage—between the power politicking of authoritarian African elites and the geopolitical/commercial interests of foreign actors, who are prepared to sustain the divorce between predatory regimes and the interests of African citizenries. The nation in such circumstances not 'sovereign' or genuinely self-governing (in terms of setting economic and social policies attuned to its own domestic needs) but rather is penetrated by foreign elements to such an extent as to warrant classification as neo-colonial territories.

It is almost redundant to state the obvious point that not all African regimes that utilise donors' discourse of securitisation in their own interests should necessarily be deemed 'neo-colonial'. The case of Paul Kagame in Rwanda—who has sought to move away from the orbit of France in response to its earlier support and shelter of Hutu genocidaires—indicates that certain developmental regimes may bolster their power position through 'extraversion' to international security discourse. In this case, Kagame has successfully courted aid monies from the USA and the EU as part of apparent 'peacebuilding' initiatives in order to overcome state 'fragility'. His government, in this context, has sought to draw upon donors' own concerns with security and violence in Africa in order to increase aid flows (as well as to gain a degree of policy space from potential donor criticism of his anti-democratic leanings). Nevertheless, the Rwandan regime still must acquiesce to donor concerns in other spheres, notably in terms of the EU's EPAs and free trade openness (to sustain aid flows). Following on from this discussion of security and conflict in the case of French interventions in the Sahel region, it is now pertinent to examine the security and development nexus in the case of EU policies on migration from Africa. The European Commission (2016a, b) has recently enhanced its security discourse with regards to the 'migrant crisis', and has pinpointed a number of African states as potential sites of European instability (given potential high volumes of migrants from these countries). Accordingly, a number of migration partnership agreements are being concluded—with the EU utilising aid conditionalities as a form of leverage to ensure African governments' compliance with such accords. This will now be explored with a view to the potential encroachment of African sovereignties, and to the warnings of Nkrumah.

MIGRATION, SECURITY AND SOVEREIGNTY

It is important to acknowledge that security agendas within 'development' do not merely arise in terms of military interventions by former colonial powers such as France. Security concerns also find expression in a number of other ways—including, crucially, donor approaches to the question of migration from the Global South to the Global North. In the case of Africa, there is a particular movement on the part of the EU and its member states to bolster their (perceived) security interests against 'irregular' migration from the continent (Guilbert 2016; Fanjul 2016; Trocaire 2016; European Parliament 2016). In the wake of the Arab Spring and the refugee crisis in Europe, the European Commission and European Council have sought to proactively engage African countries to tackle the issue of irregular migration flows. One of the key events in this regard was the Valletta Summit held in November 2015 between the EU and African Heads of State and Government. This was held so as to devise an Action Plan on migration issues, as well as a 'political statement' on a joint EU–African understanding on the need for such policy collaboration (EU–Africa Valletta Summit Political Statement 2015).

The summit has since been followed by EU communications in June 2016 about the need for new partnership frameworks with individual African nations on migration. The European Commission (2016), in particular, has highlighted its intention to use both positive and negative instruments to ensure African countries' engagement with the EU on mitigating irregular migration, and on accepting the return of those found 'illegally' in Europe. Importantly, the European Commission (2016) has made clear here that aid monies will be given towards migration mitigation efforts within African countries—in terms of bolstering border patrols and civil service apparatus responsible for registering citizens, as well as identifying those who have already travelled into Europe. The European Commission (2016) has also firmly stated that aid monies may be withheld (a negative instrument) if African countries fail to adequately assist the EU with its attempts to deal with irregular migration.

Aid, in this fashion, is being used as a means of leverage vis-à-vis African countries' acquiescence to stricter policies to prevent their citizens from migrating to the European continent (c.f. European Parliament 2016).

This focus on enhanced collaboration between African states and the EU on migration has been presented as a humanitarian concern by the EU institutions. In their official discourse (aimed at European publics as well as African political leaders), key EU actors such as the current Foreign Policy chief, Federica Mogherini, insist that migration is a positive global phenomenon. As part of this discourse, she expresses the view that Africa–EU joint action can promote 'win-win' outcomes for all. She also stresses that irregular migration can be dangerous for participants taking the dangerous sea-routes across the Mediterranean (especially since the EU's abandonment of the Mare Nostrum programme that had rescued individuals in danger of drowning). Accordingly, irregular forms of migration must be tackled:

> Migration is a positive thing for the world, but we need to do it in a regulated way. It is a global, complex phenomenon, it concerns the EU as much as countries of transit or origin...Our approach is a new one, based on a win-win partnership. (European Commission 2016)

This positive development discourse focused on 'win-win" outcomes is also expressed within the Valletta Action Plan itself. The document makes clear that the EU will actively assist African governance capabilities with regards to the prevention of irregular migration, as well as the repatriation of citizens who successfully leave for Europe without the necessary paperwork. This is couched in the language of aid and concern for the wellbeing of African countries and their peoples. Notably, the Action Plan regularly stresses that it seeks to protect human rights at all costs, and in all circumstances. For instance, support for border management is contextualised in terms of an overarching concern for human rights:

> Support to the rule of law and law enforcement, judiciary and border management authorities in order to tackle smuggling of migrants and trafficking in human beings, including on tracing and seizing assets and criminal proceeds, as well as on crime investigation and prosecution. Support could include capacity building and provision of relevant equipment. *Human rights dimension will be fully reflected in capacity-building and training projects.* (EU-Africa Valletta Action Plan 2015; emphasis added)

EU action to help African states govern migration is therefore presented as a benevolent contribution to developing countries—preventing people smuggling and ensuring human rights throughout.

Nevertheless, despite this development discourse, there is much concern that instruments such as the Valletta Action Plan represents the securitisation of development in another form. Namely, that the EU's focus on migration mitigation—and its tying of aid monies in the process—is a regressive step towards the securitisation of the Africa–EU relationship (Wirsching and van Dillen 2016; Mohamed 2016; Trocaire 2016). There is particular concern that the tying of aid monies to African countries' migration control, and towards the building of border force capabilities, diverts money away from genuine humanitarian initiatives. This has been expressed not only by African civil society groups, but also by European Parliamentarians themselves. A briefing issued by the European Parliament (2016) on initiatives undertaken since the Valletta Summit makes this clear in stark language:

> The development-migration nexus has evolved [since Valletta and]... may lead to the 'instrumentalisation' of development aid for migration management purposes. The European Parliament has taken a clear stand on this issue, calling... for the retention of poverty alleviation as the main goal of EU development policy.

This concern is strongly reinforced by a detailed CONCORD report on the development migration nexus which laments that poverty reduction may become a subordinate issue to the security outlook of the EU vis-à-vis the need to limit irregular migration from Africa:

> CONCORD deplores that security and economic interests continue to prevail in the EU policy and institutional approach to migration and development. The emphasis on border controls and security undermines the achievement of the EU's global development objectives... [aid] continues to be instrumentalised to serve 'migration management' objectives, with readmission agreements as common precondition to aid delivery. (CONCORD 2015: 2)

This stark picture of the securitisation of EU development policy, to the detriment of poverty reduction, is corroborated by Mohamed (2016) who expresses firm opposition to the tying of aid monies to African governments' acquiescence to the EU migration agenda:

This principle of 'aid conditionality' signals the twisting of the very nature of development cooperation, in stark contradiction with the promise of the proposed new Consensus on Development that this will not see 'any diversion of effort' from the 'prime focus of poverty eradication'.

The positive 'win-win' language of the European Commission is thus challenged on the grounds that its migration agenda alters the very nature of development assistance, transforming it from one of (ostensible) humanitarian concern to one explicitly informed—and motivated—by security considerations.

The practical workings of migration partnership frameworks, moreover, do in large part substantiate these civil society concerns about the tying of aid monies to policy decisions (that is, policies to restrict migration) on the part of African governments. The EU Africa Emergency Trust Fund, for instance, pledges up to €1.8 billion to secure and implement 'compacts' with individual African nations on the Valletta Action Plan. The recipient states thus far have predominantly been those of the Sahel region, within which the EU is particularly keen to intervene. Niger has received more than €100 million for Valletta-related projects for 2016; Ethiopia has received €97 million, while Mali has received €91.5 million. Interestingly, these aid figures outstrip the assistance offered to Nigeria, another country to sign a bilateral compact, which has received only around €36 million despite its large population. Niger, Ethiopia and Mali, moreover, stand among the top five recipients of the 11th EDF (2014–2020) itself. From this ACP-EU aid instrument, Niger has been allocated €596 million; Ethiopia has been allocated €745 million, while Mali has been allocated €615 million (Toaldo and Barana 2016). In this context, commentators have drawn comparison between these EU–Africa aid linkages and the controversial 'cash for co-operation' deal signed between the EU and Turkey (Barigazzi and Palmeri 2016). Many are sceptical about the ethics of tying monies meant for poverty reduction with the de facto policy purchase of African governments' migration stance. One particularly vocal critic, Guy Verhofstadt, leader of the Liberal group in the European Parliament, has emphasised that many of these African countries (similarly to Turkey) will be home to large numbers of refugees from both internal and neighbouring conflicts (for instance, Mali in wake of Operation Serval and the northern insurrection). Verhofstadt, with reference to the potential parallels to the Turkey deal, argues that it would be wrong for the EU to say to such African countries: 'okay we give you the money, now you keep the refugees' (ibid.).

Furthermore, there is concern about the EU's intervention in individual countries that have been prioritised for joint undertakings as part of Europe's migration agenda. In Mali, for instance, the EU alongside France has undertaken deep interventions within government. Specifically, the EU 'incentivized Mali to establish a new, control-oriented dimension of its migration policy' which saw €1 million investment in a border control project created by the French International Technical Policy Cooperation Department (SCTIP) and run with the co-operation of the Malian Ministry for Internal Security and Civil Protection. This €1 million investment came directly from the EU's AENEAS programme despite the clear jeopardy that such initiatives might pose to genuine 'country-ownership' of migration policies by the recipient government (Trauner and Deimel 2013: 25). In addition, the EU announced in December 2016 that it had concluded an agreement with Mali whereby Malian civil servants would travel to Europe to help identify, and then repatriate, Malian citizens found to be present in the EU (predominantly France) without legal paperwork. Not only are French authorities (with EU monies) therefore directly operating within Mali to promote migration controls, but so too are Malian officials being apparently obligated to travel to Europe to assist with repatriation procedures there. This arrangement, however, was met with fierce condemnation from Malian civil society groups who queried whether the true allegiance of the government was to the citizenry, or to donors. As a result, the Malian foreign minister has since denied that this arrangement vis-à-vis Malian civil servants was in fact agreed upon (contrary to the announcements issued by the European Commission). The minister, Abdoulaye Diop, stated that 'at no point was there any question of signing an agreement that would allow the expulsion of countrymen [living] in Europe illegally' (Schwarz 2016). Whether this Malian position holds in wake of French pressure remains an open question.

Importantly, such evidence of popular misgivings among African citizenries and civil society has also found resonance in the context of ECOWAS. There is concern that the EU's interventions not only in Mali, but within other countries such as Niger and Mauritania, means that the stated ambitions of ECOWAS to augur free movement of peoples within the trade bloc will be wholly undermined. There is also concern that the securitisation of migration as part of the Valletta Agenda—funded by the EU through initiatives such as the Emergency Trust Fund—will have negative implications in terms of seeking asylum or work in neighbouring African countries. A joint civil society statement issued by the West African Observatory on Migrations (WAOM) and the Pan African Network for the Defense of Migrants' Rights (PANiDMR), among other organisations, expressed their anger that migrants are being 'hunted' like criminals by African governments funded by European agencies. In stark terms, these civil society actors condemned the fact that:

> The lure of European financial aid to fight against migration transforms the African political authorities into real persecutors of their brothers and sisters who are looking for work to live and feed their families... The European Union, at the expense of its humanist values... outsources its security migration policy. African civil society calls for the African Union commission, the Economic Community of West African States (ECOWAS) and all African heads of state to... engage resolutely in a real regional integration process. Only a true African integration could prevent our countries to always be the instrument of European policy. (Joint NGO Statement 2016)

To add to concerns about human rights violations, the EU has also been seen to discuss migration aid assistance with the authoritarian Eritrean government in the Horn of Africa. A European Commission official apparently remarked that the talks should 'under no circumstances' become public due to the reputational hazard it would pose to the EU project (Webber 2016).

It is in this context of expressed concerns about human rights violations, and African governments becoming mere 'instruments' of European policy, that it is useful to reflect on Nkrumah's warnings about neo-colonialism. Nkrumah warned that aid incentives from former colonial powers would mean that certain African elites would become more beholden to external agendas than to the needs of their own populations. He indicated that aid would be utilised to pursue the economic, political *and security* concerns of Western donors in the Cold War context. This would include aid conditionalities attached to policy-making processes, to ensure that government action in the erstwhile African colonies would meet with the overarching interests of the donor. Nkrumah also warned that these neo-colonial governments (under the sway of donor interests) would resort to violent means and police their own citizens in a fashion that secured donor agendas while undermining genuine forms of sovereignty and self-determination in Africa.

It would appear, therefore, that the EU's migration agenda—as pursued in the aftermath of the Valletta Summit—does bear some parallels to the form of donor intervention predicted by Nkrumah (1965) in his treatise *Neo-colonialism: The Last Stage of Imperialism*. While of course these interventions are no longer couched in the geopolitics of the Cold War, nevertheless, the European Commission and the European Council pursue deep policy changes in African state ministries. Such initiatives even involve the potential secondment of EU border officials into African territories and, vice versa, the sending of African officials to Europe to assist repatriation efforts (enabled through the strategic granting of aid). Certain African elites, such as Malian politicians based in Bamako, have acquiesced to EU policy agendas even in situations where West African civil society organisations (and individual citizens) lament how African countries are becoming mere 'instruments' for the security concerns of European donors. Moreover, certain African elites continue to accept European aid in exchange for stricter border and migration controls despite the ways in which such ventures negatively impinge on civil liberties and human rights. The joint civil society statement noted above, for instance, came after a notorious case in which a Malian citizen jumped to his death in an attempt to escape police authorities in Mauritania, where he had been working without official papers. This episode, civil society groups believe, was precipitated by Mauritania's own alignment to EU migration concerns and its use of EU aid and technical support to enhance the surveillance and prosecution of Africans deemed to be in the country illegally (since the EU is concerned that such Sahelian states are used as transit zones for migrants who eventually seek opportunities in Europe itself).

Furthermore, Nkrumah's insistence upon the need for pan-African solutions to neo-colonialism is echoed within the wording of the joint statement from civil society movements. Notably, the call for African Union action—as well as from regional organisations such as ECOWAS—broadly chimes with Nkrumah's own understanding that African countries acting alone would be vulnerable to the pressures of Western aid-giving and power politicking. Whereas the European Commission to date has sought to conclude compacts with individual African nations (notwithstanding the collective negotiations with African Heads of State and Government at Valletta), the African Union does hold the potential for a cohesive African continental response to the policies and interventions pursued by the EU institutions in their desire to tackle 'irregular' migration. As will be discussed in more detail in Chap. 8 with reference to African agency and strategies for mitigating external donor and corporate influences, pan-African solutions do hold promise for a more robust response to the pressures emanating from Brussels (and from former headquarters of European Empire in Paris, and indeed London). The current situation, therefore, in which West African unity itself is being brought into question as a result of individual compacts with the European Commission is particularly lamentable. Some caution should also be noted here in the sense that Nkrumah warned that a focus on sub-regional integration itself, if pursued at the expense of continental unity, would be a false panacea to the challenges posed by former colonial powers and channels of neo-colonial influence.

THE DEVELOPMENT-SECURITY NEXUS AND COMPETING DISCOURSES IN AFRICA-EUROPE TIES

The above discussion of the 'securitisation of development'—both in terms of recent French interventions in countries such as Niger, Mali and Ivory Coast—and EU policies on irregular migration—demonstrates a disjuncture between donor discourse and the tangible impact of donor interventions for ostensible beneficiaries in Africa. Both French military interventions, and EU interventions for migration policy reform, are explained in terms of a pro-poor development discourse that emphasises respect for human rights, country ownership and for the wellbeing of African citizens. Notably, President Hollande explained French military assistance to Mali in terms of colonial obligations inherited from Empire. He therefore justified his government's intervention as a gift to the people of Mali. Meanwhile, the European Commission—in particular the foreign policy High Representative—explains that EU interventions to bolster border controls and to facilitate repatriation of the 'sans papiers' (those without official migration papers in Europe) are undertaken in the spirit of win-win co-operation. Mogherini emphasises that migration can be a potential boon for development (for instance, via remittances) and that it is a constituent part of globalisation, but that nevertheless Europe must work with its African partners to regulate the process out of due concern for human rights.

However, when these European (French member state and supranational EU) interventions are considered in terms of their practical implications for African peoples and societies, it becomes clear that the securitisation of development is wholly problematic not only in terms of human rights, but also in terms of the self-determination of African citizenries within the nation-state. Despite the progressive imaginaries of European development discourse, the tangible impact of such policies regularly worsens conditions for ordinary African citizenries. For example, the recent intervention in Mali by French forces, while initially welcomed by southern Malian populations, was preceded by French policies which widened the chasm between northern (Tuareg) communities and the authorities in Bamako. Indeed, the Malian government has been encouraged by the securitisation agenda initiated by Western donors to portray certain segments of its own population as a security risk—leading to the alienation of the Tuareg in the lead up to the insurrection. Moreover, French economic policies of structural adjustment combined to 'good governance' initiatives led to (more) resentment against authorities in Bamako—helping to contribute to the outbreak of conflict in the first instance. The intervention under Operation Serval, meanwhile, appears to have failed to restore long-term stability within the country.

The EU's endeavours to tighten border controls and migration policies within African countries (particularly those in the Sahel region) also threaten to exacerbate conditions of ill-being in Europe's former colonies. Notably, the 'deep' intervention associated with technical and aid support to ministries responsible for domestic security has prompted certain governments to harass nationals of neighbouring African countries resident within their borders. As noted above, the Mauritanian officials and police have allegedly 'hunted' citizens from countries such as Mali, often with dire consequences for civil liberties and human rights. More broadly, the EU's migration compacts with African governments such as Mali—spurred by the Valletta Action Plan—raise real questions about African state institutions becoming mere 'instruments' for policy designed in Europe for the benefit of Europeans. As noted by the joint statement of West African civil society actors, many local citizens fear that their own governments now work more to enact European-driven migration and security agendas than to secure livelihoods and prosperity. Not only is sovereignty challenged in the case of overt external interventions (for example, in terms of French military endeavours in wake of disputed elections in countries such as Ivory Coast) but also through more subtle means (such as aid conditionality in terms of assistance to individual ministries).

Altogether, therefore, there is a real need for critical engagement with European discourse as it pertains to security and 'development' in Africa. Not only do progressive narratives of poverty reduction and win–win partnerships assist European officials in the justification of policy interventions in Africa to European electorates. But—perhaps more worryingly—such discourse is often utilised by African elites themselves (in countries such as Mali) to justify collaboration with European agendas, and to lever in addition aid resources through strategies of extraversion. African elites do exhibit agency here, seeking to rationalise their alignment (often) to European donor policies and strategies in a manner that does not alienate their own citizenries. The dilemma lies, however, in the fact that their alignment to European agendas often does more to worsen conditions for their own populations than to spur genuine forms of pro-poor development. Certain African elites (as per the above discussions) are co-opted via aid-giving and implement policies which undermine human rights in their countries. A critical engagement with discourse—aligned to Nkrumah's prescient warnings about neo-colonialism in which certain African elites forfeit their duty to further genuine forms of self-determination—can help us to critique European security agendas and their consequences for poorer citizenries in Africa.

CONCLUSION

This chapter has examined European security agendas in Africa, and the ways in which interventions are regularly portrayed as 'development' opportunities for recipients. A progressive language of the 'gift' (Hollande), of win–win co-operation, and of egalitarian partnerships is utilised by European officials to justify sustained interventions in Africa, whether in terms of military operations or in terms of migration initiatives. With certain historical parallels to 'Francafrique' and 'Eurafrican' language, contemporary European officials emphasise that Europe and Africa are destined to work together to address common problems arising from aspects of globalisation. Whether tackling Islamic extremism or working to prevent 'irregular' migration, ever closer partnership is deemed necessary between European donors and African aid recipients.

This chapter has argued, however, that there are certain parallels to be drawn between the current securitisation of development and the warnings issued by Nkrumah in terms of neo-colonialism in Africa. Nkrumah presciently warned that former colonial powers (in particular) would continue to interfere in the political, economic and military affairs of newly independent African nations. He maintained that while the flags of Empire would be replaced with the standards of newly independent African nation-states that, nevertheless, newer forms of coercion would be enacted. In particular, he warned about the strategic use of aid monies to effectively 'buy' the acquiescence of African elites to externally driven policy agendas (despite the negative impact such action might have for local populations). Moreover, he warned in the Cold War context that former colonisers would continue to safeguard their geopolitical interests, through military force if required. This, according to Nkrumah, would likely take the form of a former colonial power deciding to military support one group of African elites over another competitor group. Accordingly, Nkrumah's insights do appear relevant in the current context of French interventions in the Sahel region. Not only have French military interventions been undertaken with an eye to securing vital French interests (such as uranium), but donor policy initiatives surrounding economic reform and 'good governance' are seen to have prompted crisis in the first instance. The situation of Mali, for example, demonstrates the way in which French policies, particularly, helped to provoke civil strife, with the French benefactor then intervening to support its elite partners in the country.

The examination of EU migration policies, likewise, underscores that Nkrumah's insights remain relevant in the contemporary analysis of African countries' relations with external donors. EU interventions in Africa—following on from the Valletta Summit—demonstrate how donors continue to undermine genuine sovereignty and self-determination through strategic recourse to aid as leverage. Elite politicians in African countries have acquiesced to EU policy demands regarding irregular migration in order to sustain aid flows. This has even involved the situation where African civil servants may apparently travel to European capitals in order to assist with the repatriation of their own citizenry (although latterly denied by the minister in question given civil society uproar). It is clear in these circumstances that EU aid monies act to denude the genuine policy autonomy—and empirical sovereignty–of the African countries that acquiesce to migration partnership agreements. Certain African elites align themselves to European policies—in some cases aligning to Europe's own securitisation discourse—in order to lever in additional aid flows to sustain their own power networks (with parallels to Bayart's [2003] discussion of elite extraversion in Africa). However, rather than viewing such EU–Africa linkages through the prism of the so-called neo-patrimonial state, it is clear that EU policy interventions and aid monies are the root cause of such power scenarios. EU aid monies—such as through the Emergency Trust Fund—prolong certain elites in power and perpetuate a divorce between citizens and government. This on-going relevance of Nkrumah is now discussed in relation to the UN SDGs in the next chapter. Again, the significance of donor 'development' discourse comes to the fore in terms of the legitimation of what can accurately be defined as neo-colonial situations in Africa today.

REFERENCES

Abrahamsen, R. (2005). Blair's Africa: The politics of securitization and fear. *Alternatives: Global, Local, Political, 30*(1), 55–80.

Amosu, A. (2007). Dangerous times for Africa. *Review of African Political Economy, 34*(114), 711–713.

Bagoyoko, N., & Gibert, M. (2009). The linkage between security, governance and development: The European Union in Africa. *Journal of Development Studies, 45*(5), 789–814.

Barigazzi, J. & Palmeri, T. (2016, July 6). EU plans Africa cash-for-cooperation migration deal, *Politico*. Available at: http://www.politico.eu/article/eu-plans-africa-cash-for-cooperation-migration-deal-europe/. Accessed 25 Mar 2017.

Bergamaschi, I. (2014). The fall of a donor darling: The role of aid in mali's crisis. *Journal of Modern African Studies, 52*(3), 347–378.

Boas, M., & Torheim, L. E. (2013). The trouble in Mali—corruption, collusion and resistance. *Third World Quarterly, 34*(7), 1279–1292.

Boeke, S. & Bart, S. (2015, July 23). Operation 'Serval': A strategic analysis of the French intervention in Mali, 2013–2014. *Journal of Strategic Studies*, pp. 1–25.

Carmody, P. (2005). Transforming globalization and security: Africa and America post-9/11. *African Today, 52*(1), 97–120.

Chafer, T. (2005). Chirac and 'la Françafrique': No longer a family affair. *Modern & Contemporary France, 13*(1), 7–23.

Charbonneau, B. (2008). Dreams of empire: France, Europe, and the new interventionism in Africa. *Modern & Contemporary France, 16*(3), 279–295.

Charbonneau, B. (2014). The imperial legacy of international peacebuilding: The case of francophone Africa. *Review of International Studies, 40*(3), 607–630.

CONCORD. (2015). *The EPA between the EU and West Africa: Who really benefits? Convergence of EU policies for development.* Brussels: CONCORD. Available at: http://www.concord.se/wpcontent/uploads/Spotlight_2015-TRADE-EPA-April_2015-EN.pdf. Accessed 25 Mar 2017.

Duffield, M. (2005). Getting savages to fight barbarians: Development, security and the colonial present: Analysis. *Conflict, Security and Development, 5*(2), 141–159.

EU-Africa valletta summit. (2015). *Political statement.* Valletta: European Commission.

European Commission. (2016a). *Towards a new partnership framework with third countries under the European agenda on migration: FAQ factsheet.* Brussels: European Commission.

European Commission. (2016b). *Sustainable development: EU sets out its priorities.* Brussels: European Commission.

European Parliament. (2016). *Growing impact of EU migration policy on development cooperation, European parliamentary research service, briefing October 2016.* Brussels: European Parliament.

Fanjul, G. (2016, June 9). *Five reasons why the EU's "Marshall Plan" against migration is a bad idea.* London: Overseas Development Institute. Available at: https://www.odi.org/comment/10409-five-reasons-why-eu-s-marshall-plan-against-migration-bad-idea. Accessed 26 Mar 2017.

Ferguson, J. (2005). Seeing like an oil company: space, security and global capital in neoliberal Africa. *American Anthropologist, 107*(3), 377–382.

Fisher, J., & Anderson, M. (2015). Authoritarianism and the securitization of development in Africa. *International Affairs, 91*(1), 131–151.

Guilbert, K. (2016, December 16). Africa: Expert views—Can "Carrot-and-Stick" aid deals stem migration from Africa to Europe, *Reuters.* Available at: http://www.reuters.com/article/us-europe-africa-migrants-idUSK-BN1451KV. Accessed 25 Mar 2017.

Harshe, R. (2003). Politics of giant oil firms: Consequences for human rights in Africa. *Economic and Political Weekly, 38*(2), 113–117.

Joint NGO Statement. (2016). *Joint NGO statement ahead of the European Council of 28–29 June 2016—NGOs strongly condemn new EU policies to contain migration.* Available at: http://www.ccme.be/fileadmin/filer/ccme/20_Areas_of_Work/01_Refugee_Protection/2016-06-28-Final_joint_NGO_statement_with_signatories_124.pdf. Accessed 26 Mar 2017.

Kennan, J. (2004). Terror in the Sahara: The implications of US imperialism for North and West Africa. *Review of African Political Economy, 31*(1), 475–496.

Keenan, J. (2008). US militarization in Africa: What anthropologists should know about AFRICOM. *Anthropology Today, 24*(5), 16–20.

Keukeleire, S., & Raube, K. (2013). The security-development nexus and securitization in the EU's policies towards development countries. *Cambridge Review of International Affairs, 26*(3), 556–572.

Larsen, R. K., & Mamosso, C. A. (2014). Aid with blinkers: Environmental governance of uranium mining in Niger. *World Development, 56*, 62–76.

Massey, S., & May, R. (2006). The crisis in Chad. *African Affairs, 105*(402), 443–449.

Mohamed, M. (2016). *Migration, peace and development: When concrete action clashes with a positive vision.* Oxford: Oxfam. Available at: https://oxfameu. blogactiv.eu/2016/12/22/migration-peace-and-development-when-concrete-action-clashes-with-a-positive-vision/. Accessed 25 Mar 2017.

Nkrumah, K. (1963). *Africa must unite.* London: Heineman.

Nkrumah, K. (1965). *Neo-colonialism: The last stage of imperialism.* Sixth Printing—New York International Publishers, 1976.

Olsen, G. R. (2014). Fighting terrorism in Africa by proxy: The USA and the European Union in Somalia and Mali. *European Security, 23*(3), 1–17.

Omeje, K. (2010). Whose security? The global security debate and the African paradox. In J. Abubakar, K. Omeje, & H. Galadima (Eds.), *Conflict of Securities: Reflections on State and Human Security in Africa* (pp. 17–42). London: Adonis and Abbey.

Schwarz, T. (2016, December 19). Mali denies agreement on failed EU asylum seekers, *Modern Ghana.* Available at: https://www.modernghana.com/news/744146/mali-denies-agreement-on-failed-eu-asylum-seekers.html. Accessed 25 Mar 2017.

Toaldo, M., & Barana, L. (2016). *The EU's migration policy in Africa: five ways forward, European council on foreign relations.* London: European Council on Foreign Relations. Available at: http://www.ecfr.eu/article/commentary_the_eus_migration_policy_in_africa_five_ways_forward. Accessed 26 Mar 2017.

Traumer, F., & Deimel, S. (2013). The impact of Eu migration policies on African countries: The case of Mali. *International Migration, 51*(4), 20–32.

Trocaire. (2016). Development adrift: The EU migration partnership framework: The emerging paradigm of security and conditionality (Migration Policy Paper No. 3). Maynooth: Trocaire. Available at: https://www.trocaire.org/sites/default/files/resources/policy/eu-migration-partnership-framework.pdf.

Webber, F. (2016). *Locking down Africa.* London: Institute of Race Relations. Available at: http://www.irr.org.uk/news/locking-down-africa/. Accessed 25 Mar 2017.

Wing, S. (2016). French intervention in Mali: Strategic alliances, long-term regional presence? *Small Wars & Insurgencies, 27*(1), 59–80.

Wirsching, S., & van Dillen, B. (2016). *Migration for development and human rights: The need for EU policy coherence.* Brussels: DEVEX. Available at: https://www.devex.com/news/migration-for-development-and-human-rights-the-need-for-eu-policy-coherence-87826. Accessed 25 Mar 2017.

CHAPTER 7

The UN Sustainable Development Goals and Neo-Colonialism

INTRODUCTION

The UN Sustainable Development Goals (SDGs) have been presented by donor institutions as a progressive step forward in North–South relations. Donor discourse emphasises that the SDGs will bring about partnerships for development conducive to economic growth in Africa (UN 2015; European Commission 2016c). While the preceding Millennium Development Goals (MDGs) are seen to have focused heavily on humanitarian aspirations at the cost of economic growth, the UN SDGs by contrast are viewed to put economic development front and centre of the post-2015 agenda. Distinct from economic policies pursued by donors in the Washington Consensus, meanwhile, the SDGs are said to align to Post-Washington Consensus norms regarding the need to translate economic growth into social prosperity. As part of this approach, donor discourse presents the business community as a necessary partner for pro-poor development. Rather than be viewed as a potential source of exploitation, the private sector is fully welcomed as the engine for poverty reduction (UN 2015: 23–24).

This chapter queries whether the UN SDGs are a progressive programme for development and poverty reduction. With focus on Nkrumah's (1963, 1965) concerns about neo-colonialism in Africa, the chapter assesses whether donor and corporate interventions undertaken in the name of the SDGs do facilitate pro-poor economic growth. The chapter explicitly considers the implications of the SDGs

© The Author(s) 2018
M. Langan, *Neo-Colonialism and the Poverty of 'Development' in Africa*, Contemporary African Political Economy,
https://doi.org/10.1007/978-3-319-58571-0_7

for African development with regards to two key target Goals associated with this pro-poor economic agenda, namely, Goal 8 on *Decent Work and Economic Development* and Goal 9 on *Industry, Innovation and Infrastructure*. The first of these two goals is examined given the renewed emphasis of the UN SDGs on PSD and job creation. The goal is considered in terms of a case study focus on the palm oil sector, with particular attention to Ghana. Palm oil is illustrative to examine given its status as a priority sector in governments' own economic plans (note for instance the PSIs of the Kufuor administration). The major role of Unilever, moreover, is interesting to consider given its role as both producer and consumer (in terms of processing palm oil into other products). Unilever played one of the leading roles in the construction of the UN SDG platform as part of the business community's engagement with the post-2015 agenda. The chapter then examines Goal 9 in terms of the EU–Africa Infrastructure Trust Fund (EU-AITF). This has been hailed by the European Commission (2016c) as a significant contribution to Africa's business enabling environment—understood in terms of key infrastructure conducive to private sector operations (such as electricity pylons and roads). The EU-AITF is also interesting to examine given the role of aid blending and DFIs within its operation.

The chapter is structured as follows. The first section considers the context of the UN SDGs and their apparent volte face to economic growth as compared to the preceding UN MDGs. This highlights the centrality of PSD and the business enabling environment within current donor approaches to international development. The second section then examines Goal 8 with regards to the palm oil sector. The third section thereafter considers Goal 9 with regards to the EU-AITF. The final section then reflects on the potential relevance of Nkrumah's concept of neo-colonialism for making sense of continuing power imbalances in the post-2015 era.

THE UN SDGS AND THE PIVOT TO PSD?

The UN SDGs are the current global benchmarks for development adhered to by the UN agencies, the major donors (such as the World Bank, the EU, USAID and DFID), as well as civil society and private sector 'partners' within fora such as the UN Global Compact (Gregoratti 2010). The goals came into effect in 2015 and will be evaluated in terms of a fifteen-year timeframe which the UN has set for their implementation (thus expiring in 2030). Significantly, the UN SDGs are viewed as universal targets meaning that developed countries are also expected to align themselves to the achievement of the goals in their own national economic and social policies.

One of the most striking elements of the SDGs is their renewed focus upon economic growth and business flourishing. In the aftermath of the global financial crisis, donors appeared increasingly aware of the importance of production, manufacturing, and commodity trading in their economic strategies, to balance out the financial sector. They concluded, moreover, that the preceding UN MDGs had focused too narrowly upon humanitarian indicators (surrounding issues such as child mortality and maternal health) at the expense of economic growth (Scheyvens et al. 2016: 372). Donors argued that the post-2015 agenda would have to recognise the need for economic advancement in developing countries for them to achieve long-term social prosperity (Mawdsley 2015: 340–342). While humanitarian concerns are therefore present within the UN SDGs (note Goal 3 for instance), nevertheless, there is increased emphasis upon the need to realise pro-poor forms of economic growth and *business activity* in developing regions. This is married to donors' discursive emphasis on the need for public-private partnerships and for increased involvement of the private sector in development. In this context, the UN Global Compact—established under the MDGs to inspire business action on development—has gained increased prominence in current SDG fora (Gregoratti 2018; forthcoming). Notably, the UN Global Compact's (2015) own guide on the SDGs—created to inform businesses about ways to assist the goals' attainment—outlines the pro-business narrative of the post-2015 agenda. For instance, the document reflects the strong emphasis on public–private 'partnerships':

> The Sustainable Development Goals (SDGs) define global sustainable development priorities and aspirations for 2030 and seek to mobilize global efforts around a common set of goals and targets. The SDGs call for worldwide action among governments, business and civil society to end poverty and create a life of dignity and opportunity for all, within the boundaries of the planet. (2015: 2)

It also makes clear that the UN SDGs explicitly rectify an apparent omission within the UN MDGs with regards to the vital role of business in fostering development:

Unlike their predecessor, the Millennium Development Goals, the SDGs explicitly call on all businesses to apply their creativity and innovation to solving sustainable development challenges. The SDGs have been agreed by all governments, yet their success relies heavily on action and collaboration by all actors. (ibid.)

This strong discursive emphasis on business involvement in development is perhaps not too surprising in the context of the negotiations which led up to the formulation of these SDG benchmarks. Global business conglomerates—including major stakeholders in African economies such as Unilever—played an active role in the UN's High Level Panel (HLP) which was tasked with finding a pathway forward at the end of the Millennium Goals. Business interests were also represented, meanwhile, in other influential bodies such as the UN Open Working Group (OWG) 'alongside groups representing indigenous peoples, women, children and youth, and farmers' (Scheyvens et al. 2016: 374). Business leaders used these policy platforms to promote a free market approach to development focused upon FDI and trade liberalisation (Quintos 2015: 2; Weber 2017: 3). The role of Unilever CEO Paul Polman was especially notable. As Pingeot (2014: 11) documents:

Unilever, and... CEO Paul Polman, stand out... a member of the HLP, the SDSN Leadership Council and the board of the Global Compact.... Unilever participates in the Global Compact LEAD group... Unilever is a member of both the World Business Council on Sustainable Development (of which Paul Polman is the vice-chairman) and of the World Economic Forum, two business associations involved in the post-2015 process.

Pingeot (2014: 20) also usefully points to the fact that while recent reports issued by groups such as the UN Global Compact emphasise the pivotal role of business in development 'they almost simultaneously deny the influence and impact of the corporate sector until now'. Namely, the SDG's focus on PSD and the business enabling environment is presented as a novel turn in development policy. Business is viewed as the 'missing link' in development interventions, able to ensure that the UN SDGs will be more successful in stimulating long-term poverty reduction as compared to the UN MDGs.

As Pingeot (2014) alludes to, however, there has already been a strong focus on PSD and the role of business throughout the broader history of donor interventions in developing countries. The OECD, for example, has played a key historical role in cementing donor commitment to PSD rationales from the mid-1990s onwards. A series of OECD publications in that timeframe emphasised that the creation of a business enabling environment, and engagement of private sector actors, was an essential component of sustainable development. For instance, an OECD (1995: 3) publication, *Private Sector Development: A Guide to Donor Support*, has striking resemblance to the PSD/growth discourse of the current UN SDGs. This document stressed that:

> consensus is now emerging on a new model for sustainable development... key features of the new model are the changing roles of the state and the private sector. Increasingly, the creation of wealth and the generation of employment are seen to involve the state primarily as the architect of a positive enabling environment.

The free market and pro-business discourse of the SDGs is therefore not something novel. It is instead a regurgitation of long-standing donor norms concerning the need to align poverty reduction strategies to the interests of the private sector. While the UN MDGs marked a shift towards a human needs framework (often associated with Amartya Sen and Martha Nussbaum), the UN SDGs by contrast mark a *return* to a more solidly free market focus. This is also not to say that free market policies designed to support business were not pursued in the timeframe of the UN MDGs (2000–2015). The launch of the WTO Doha Development Agenda (DDA) in this period is but one example of donors' long-standing commitment to the promotion of business in 'development'. The DDA was pursued in the language of pro-poor PSD, emphasising that its conclusion would be conducive to both FDI and the MDGs in developing countries. The creation of the UN Global Compact during the UN MDGs also demonstrates that this earlier framework did not omit private sector concerns (Gregoratti 2010). The SDGs, in this context, are a *reification* and *extension* of existing donor norms concerning the inclusion of corporations within development strategies. Mawdsley (2015: 344) articulately makes this point:

> economic growth is being ideationally and institutionally reinstated as the central and prior condition for "development". This is not just deepening the existing poverty reduction-era focus on "bottom billion capitalism"... but extending towards new and expanding goals of large-scale

public–private partnerships, donor support for major commercial investments, private equity initiatives and deepening financialisation.

It is also important to recognise that while corporations found a special place within UN negotiating fora in the lead up to the SDGs' adoption, that developing country governments were often frustrated by developed country tactics. The tactic of 'forum-shifting' often ensured that many structural issues regarding North–South trade and aid patterns were insulated from the post-2015 negotiating agenda (Muchhala and Sengupta 2014: 30–33). Developing countries' concerns about trade liberalisation and the impact of premature tariff dismantling for nascent agro-industry, for example, were not redressed in the SDG talks. Instead, these matters were deemed to be the remit of the WTO. Muchhala and Sengupta (2014: 30) rightly observe that such tactics ensure that 'systemic issues are kept out of reach for the one global arena (the UN) that has an equitable governance structure'. Thus while business attained a privileged seat in key UN decision-making fora, developing countries often found that their priority issues were kept out from genuine deliberation. In this context, it is necessary to examine whether donors' pro-poor SDG discourse is tangibly translating into progressive outcomes in developing countries, with specific attention to Africa. The next sections therefore consider Goals 8 and 9, followed by consideration of Nkrumah's concept of neo-colonialism and its current relevance.

UN SDG Goal 8: Whither Pro-Poor Development in Africa's Palm Oil Sector?

SDG discourse concerning pro-poor business development is especially interesting to consider in the context of the palm oil sector in Africa. Unilever played a crucial role in the formulation of the current SDG framework. Its business model relies upon both the production and utilisation of palm oil as a key ingredient of consumer goods including 'packaged bread, breakfast cereals, margarine, chocolate, ice cream, biscuits, and snack food' (Amnesty International 2016: 3). Unilever—along with other major players in the industry—has routinely voiced their support for African countries to abide by sustainability norms in terms of the regulation of palm oil production. Unilever CEO Paul Polman notably welcomed the *Marrakech Declaration for the Sustainable Development of the Oil Palm Sector in Africa* agreed by the Central African Republic, Ivory

Coast, the DRC, Ghana, Liberia, Republic of the Congo, and Sierra Leone (Partnership for Forests 2016). Unilever's CEO emphasised the potential positive contribution of the sector to poverty reduction:

> Palm oil, if produced sustainably, can play a key role in poverty allevia-tion by helping farmers thrive economically while adopting sustainable agricultural and business practices. I am pleased that these countries are demonstrating their commitment to sustainable palm oil by signing the Marrakesh Declaration. (ibid.)

Unilever—along with other industry leaders such as Wilmar—has also become an important member of the Roundtable on Sustainable Palm Oil (RSPO). Established prior to the formulation of the UN SDGs them-selves, the RSPO nevertheless finds itself comfortably aligning to the post-2015 consensus. The RSPO Impact Report (2016) identifies five SDGs which it now explicitly works towards: 'zero hunger, clean water and sanitation, decent work and economic growth, responsible con-sumption and production and life on land'. Unilever, the wider RSPO membership, as well as the African state signatories of the Marrakesh Declaration particularly commit themselves to tackling deforestation. Through working with smallholders and educating them on sustainable production methods, the African palm oil industry will apparently be able to provide sustainable production to its local and international consumers.

Despite these ostensible steps towards a more responsible palm oil sector, there are a wide range of civil society groups and 'development justice' activists who remain unconvinced about the willingness of cor-porate and donor players to genuinely align their economic interests to social and environmental norms (Quintos 2015: 14). There is much notable criticism that the industry is not acting to deal with the negative social and environmental consequences of monocropping. Production in African contexts is increasingly based upon the single cultivation of palm oil as a valuable cash crop (UNEP 2011: 2). Pressure to meet both local and international demand has led to smallholders boosting palm oil yields at the expense of food crops. This not only has obvious implica-tions in terms of food security concerns in food insecure regions such as West Africa, but also has potentially severe environmental consequences. A report from the UN Environment Programme (UNEP 2011: 3) makes clear that from an 'ecological point of view, oil palm monocul-tures might form impervious barriers to species' migration and result in greater susceptibility to plant diseases'. The RSPO, meanwhile, appears unable to meaningfully discourage monocropping, or indeed to prevent deforestation (its principle aim). The Environmental Investigation Agency (EIA) and Grassroots explain that auditing practices relating to the RSPO are unable to prevent unsustainable business activity:

> Auditing firms are fundamentally failing to identify and mitigate unsustainable practices by oil palm firms. Not only are they conducting woefully substandard assessments but the evidence indicates that in some cases they are colluding with plantation companies to disguise violations of the RSPO Standard. The systems put in place to monitor these auditors have utterly failed (Grassroots and EIA 2016: 3).

In terms of the processing stage of the palm oil industry, meanwhile, there are concerns about the environmental and social consequences of palm oil mill effluent (POME). This by-product contaminates local water and soil. It is particularly known for causing extreme algae growth in water bodies, which in turn leads to diminished fish stocks for local communities (Iwuagwu and Ugwuanyi 2014). There are additional concerns that the fertilisers and pesticides which smallholders and out-growers use in the cultivation of palm oil are hazardous for their long-term health (Suarez et al. 2013: 3; Humanity United 2015: 6). Plantations—despite RSPO and donor sustainability pledges—continue to practice intensive agri-business, which demands that plantation workers or out-growers (labouring on land contracted out to them by large companies) must use hazardous inputs to boost production (Krinninger 2017). Current global demand for palm oil is outstripping supply in African contexts, with many processors utilising imported palm oil to supplement the locally sourced variety. In these circumstances, the RSPO does not fully challenge industry expansion, which itself largely overrides sustainability norms (with consequent problems associated with monocropping, POME and hazardous fertiliser/pesticide use) (Pye et al. 2016: 2). It should also be noted here that the fertilisers and pesticides—with parallels to POME—pose a significant threat to local water bodies and fish stocks. This again has deleterious consequences for fishermen and for local communities (in terms of both access to fish and clean drinking water (Ogada et al. 2014).

Furthermore, the failure of the UN SDGs to meaningfully tackle, and redress, systemic issues surrounding trade, corporate power, and donor aid relations with African countries negatively impacts upon 'pro-poor' strategies aimed at making palm oil sustainable. For example, the

Ghanaian government under President Kufuor sought to support the creation of smallholder associations in the palm oil sector as part of a developmental state economic strategy. Under the PSIs (discussed earlier in relation to EU budget support in Chap. 3), the Kufuor government proposed to establish Corporate Village Enterprises (COVEs) which would unite palm oil smallholders in collective business entities. Not only would COVEs give these smallholders better bargaining power vis-à-vis palm oil processors, but they would encourage them to 'adopt improved planting materials, husbandry technologies and commercial orientation so as to immediately increase their holdings and output' (Government of Ghana cited in Asante 2012: 16). The Kufuor government also explained that such policies would feed into wider import substitution strategies, with higher yields of local palm oil leading to falling import bills (ibid.).

The PSI ambitions for palm oil and the establishment of COVEs, however, were successfully frustrated by the opposition of both foreign investors and budget support donors in the Ghanaian context. The major corporate players in the sector had given their initial support to the Kufuor government's PSI. Unilever chairman, Ishmeal Yamson, had apparently even accompanied the Ghanaian president on a high-level delegation to Malaysia to better understand industry practices in that country (ibid.). Corporate leaders soon made their disquiet known, however, with regards to COVEs. Namely, the establishment of smallholder business associations would disrupt the existing sector model where out-growers are contracted on an individual business to large-scale plantations (and therefore obliged to sell their produce solely to their agribusiness partner). The COVEs would disrupt this existing status quo and provide a challenge to the market dominance of the big corporate actors. The PSI for palm oil, given its developmental focus on improving the position of poorer farmers within the industry, would represent a material threat to foreign investors' business interests and profit margins. Asante (2012: 23–24) in her extensive report on the PSI in the palm sector provides interview evidence with corporate stakeholders to corroborate this stark picture of corporate opposition to the Ghanaian government's policy agenda:

> Interviews … revealed massive disagreements between these oil-palm business elites and the NPP government's decision to employ the COVE model… These disagreements were apparently so serious that…

participants such as the Twifo Oil Palm Plantation (TOPP) actually walked out of the meeting, refusing to participate further in the PSI-Oil Palm programme.

This corporate intransigence with regards to the developmental state policies of the Kufuor government was bolstered by donors' own opposition to the PSIs. As discussed in Chap. 3, the donor community under the MDBS group threatened to curtail financial support for the government unless it conformed with free market policies and did away with developmental state strategies (Gerster n.d.). Intervention in the economy—for example, with the creation of COVEs in palm oil production—was deemed unacceptable by the major donors, including 'development' partners such as the European Commission and the World Bank (ibid.). The PSIs were therefore stifled by a combination of corporate and donor pressures upon the Kufuor government. The Ghanaian political class soon acquiesced to external demands, and the PSIs consequently resulted in only modest changes within the nation's priority economic sectors.[1]

Smallholders in the Ghanaian palm oil sector have, meanwhile, lamented the government's apparent inaction with regards to import flooding of cheaper produce from countries such as Malaysia, a key competitor in the industry (although COVEs would have arguably gone a long way to redress this issue by bolstering local production in Ghana). Due to the current Ghanaian sector's insufficient production capacity, imports have been used to support domestic processing activities, as well as to partially supply Ghanaian households' demand for palm oil as a daily cooking oil (Asante 2012: 16). Ghanaian smallholders have repeatedly requested that the government should utilise tariff measures to discourage the importation of foreign palm oil and to protect local production. They argue that a combination of import tariffs and government aid to producers would protect (and expand) livelihoods in this strategic economic area. Charles Twumasi-Ankrah, an executive member of Oil Palm Smallholder/Outgrowers (a sectoral body in Ghana) explains that farmers expect the Ghanaian government and foreign investors to prioritise local production:

> Any decision to not protect the palm sector will eventually affect the local farmers and indigenous companies. Protection of duty is needed ... There are some companies with open commitment to source 300,000 tonnes of

palm products from Africa; this will be possible only by framing polices to favour growth of the palm sector and not favour the importers. (cited in Ekow Essabra-Mensah 2015)

The government—despite such calls—has, however, been reticent to increase import tariffs for fear of further donor fallout (Gerster n.d.). As discussed in Chap. 3, Western donors already successfully challenged local initiatives to raise import tariffs upon frozen poultry produce entering into Ghana. The IMF particularly made its objections known to the Kufuor government despite the initial votes of the Ghanaian parliament that legislation was wholly necessary in this area. Calls for higher import duties on palm oil, in this context, have met with government inaction (ibid.).

Perhaps most worryingly, systemic issues surrounding worker rights abuses and low pay remain endemic within the African palm oil sector despite the UN SDG pledges made by the leading industry players. A recent report by Amnesty International (2016) criticises the RSPO for failing to adequately ensure that its corporate members genuinely abide by decent work norms. Amnesty International (2016: 10–11) particularly name Wilmar, its subsidiary companies, and some of its suppliers, as having allegedly exploited workers even within our current post-2015 setting:

> Wilmar, its subsidiaries... and its suppliers... have abused workers' rights to just and favourable conditions of work, health, and social security. Wilmar, and those companies that buy from it, do not have an adequate due diligence process in place to identify, prevent, mitigate and account for how they address adverse human rights impacts linked to their business operations.

Worryingly, Wilmar—one of the leading palm oil operators in Africa—is also condemned for apparently continuing 'land-grabbing' exercises to bolster production capacities (with parallels to the NAFSN discussed in Chap. 2). In Uganda, for example, Friends of the Earth International have partnered with local groups such as the National Association of Professional Environmentalists (NAPE) to draw attention to Wilmar's practices that allegedly contravene SDG norms. Frank Muramui, the director of NAPE, argues that the company has sold false promises to local people in exchange for valuable land tracts:

> This project was sold to the residents of Kalangala [in Uganda] with promises of employment and a brighter future. But they were not fairly

compensated for the loss of their livelihoods, and now without access to land face a daily struggle to get by. (cited in Friends of the Earth International 2015)

In this context, therefore, there are grave concerns that both companies' and donors' discursive alignment to the UN SDGs does not represent a genuine opportunity for pro-poor growth in the African palm oil sector. While pledges have been made to prevent deforestation, for example, there nevertheless remain real problems concerning social and environmental justice. Due to market pressures and questionable auditing practices, there remain many instances of worker exploitation, land grabbing and environmental contamination. These problems remain endemic within the industry despite ostensible corporate and donor support for the social and environmental norms expressed within the UN SDGs. The failure of the UN SDGs to meaningfully address systemic issues associated with trade liberalisation and donor imposition of free market policies on developing countries also means that policy space for genuine pro-poor policies is closed down. The status quo characterised by the dominance of foreign investors in African palm oil remains unchallenged to the detriment of genuinely pro-poor alternatives (such as the COVEs once favoured by the Kufuor government as part of a developmental state strategy).

Many civil society groups and activists therefore remain unconvinced about the positive contribution of the UN SDGs to decent work and pro-poor growth in priority economic sectors such as palm oil. Many fear that the UN SDGs merely supply companies and donors with a new discourse with which to legitimise continuing practices of social and environmental exploitation within free market systems. Pye et al. (2016: 2), in a comprehensive report for Stiftung Asienhaus, remark that initiatives such as the RSPO merely utilise 'sustainability' discourse as a branding exercise without challenging inequalities that persist throughout the sector (whether in Africa or in Asia):

"sustainable palm oil".... [is] a branding exercise that offers to assuage the moral conscience of the consumer... but the scope for sustainable practices at the plantation level is limited (monocrop production is not questioned)... RSPO certification responds to consumer concerns without seriously addressing the... problems caused by the industry.

The language of decent work and of equitable economic growth found within the SDGs, and propounded by palm oil conglomerates, plays a double role. It acts to salve consumer concerns surrounding environmental and social exploitation, while at the same time apparently veiling injustices in terms of labour rights, land-grabbing and environmental contamination. In the words of Sekou Touré, Africans labourers remain 'hewers of wood and drawers of water' within cash crop economies without benefiting in terms of genuine poverty alleviation or national economic prosperity. The chapter now considers the situation of UN SDG Goal 9 on infrastructural development, with particular focus on EU–Africa relations and the EU-AITF. This again raises concerns about potential disjuncture between pro-poor development narratives espoused under the UN SDGs and the material consequences of donor and corporate interventions for poorer African citizens.

UN SDG Goal 9: Building African Infrastructure for Pro-Poor Development?

Goal 9 of the UN SDGs complements the framework's wider focus on PSD and economic growth. It calls for the enhancement of infrastructure and industry in order to stimulate socially progressive forms of business expansion. Improvements to infrastructural assets in developing countries, in particular, will create the economic conditions for social development and poverty reduction. In the moralised discourse of the UN (2015: 24–25), the post-2015 development partners under goal 9 will:

> Develop quality, reliable, sustainable and resilient infrastructure, including regional and transborder infrastructure, to support economic development and human well-being, with a focus on affordable and equitable access for all.

Interestingly, in terms of this pro-poor donor discourse, the European Commission has been a firm advocate of the moralised tone of the UN SDGs, and of Goal 9. European officials have made clear that the SDGs do provide a genuine opportunity for poverty elimination in the Global South. They insist, moreover, that the goals' current emphasis on PSD and economic growth chimes with existing EU policies in its relations with developing countries. In fact, the concept of sustainability itself is viewed as a European contribution to international development debates. Hence, the creation of the SDGs is viewed as evidence of Europe's normative power in the global arena:

> Sustainability is a European brand. The EU has a strong starting position and track record, with a high level of economic development, social cohesion, democratic societies and a commitment to sustainable development which is firmly anchored in the European Treaties. (European Commission 2016c)

The EU institutions have also been clear that Europe's relationship with the ACP countries will continue to be governed by core moral norms associated with sustainable development. The European Commission has particularly committed itself to the continuation of development ties beyond the Cotonou Agreement, which expires in 2020. It makes clear that the post-Cotonou framework will enshrine sustainable development norms, with a view to the conclusion of the UN SDGs in 2030. One striking element of EU discourse here is the inclusion of non-state 'partners' within development co-operation. With clear echoes of the UN SDGs' discussion of public-private partnerships and of the need for business to ally with traditional donors for poverty reduction, the European Commission (2016d: 6) emphasises the need for private sector engagement:

> The development landscape is expanding... The private sector is increasingly a key partner in fostering more sustainable models of development. Combining public and private resources to leverage more investments is allowing to step up engagement, also in challenging environments. A realignment of global resources and investment is needed to achieve sustainable development.

Again, however, it is important to note that donor discourse concerning the 'increasing' role of the private sector downplays the way in which PSD has been front and centre of donor policy even prior to the current UN SDGs. The European Commission has historically been a firm advocate of the private sector's inclusion within 'development'. Even during the early years of the ACP-EU Lomé Conventions (1975–2000), European officials made clear the need for the involvement of the business community in poverty reduction drives. For instance, the European Council President, Peter Barry, at the signing of Lomé III in 1985 spoke of the need to 'bring into play private operators on both sides'. The Danish Development Minister, meanwhile, explained to the Joint ACP-EEC Council of Ministers in 1987 that 'the increasing role of private investment and the private sector in the development process' had to be recognised (*The Courier* 1985: 7; ACP-EEC Joint Council of Ministers 1987: 18). ACP representatives themselves, meanwhile, identified a need for assistance to the private sector during this earlier Association framework. For example, F.N. Macharia, the then chairman of the ACP Conference of National Chambers of Commerce, remarked at the ACP-EEC trade operators' conference in 1987 that ACP countries' prosperity could 'only be realised if the governments and the private sector of the ACP work with the international community to pool their knowledge and aspirations' (IPS 1987). Soon thereafter, the text of Lomé IV itself identified the need to make the ACP private sector 'more dynamic and [to] play a greater role' in development. Consequently—according to the treaty—Europe should support 'a healthy, prosperous, and dynamic ACP private sector' (ACP-EEC Lomé Convention IV 1989: 30–31; 55). The EEC subsequently began to direct structural adjustment support to newly created ACP private sectors. This initially began with modest EEC assistance to SMEs in the ACP countries (*The Courier* 1994).

What is perhaps 'new', however, is the European Commission's enhanced focus on so-called aid blending initiatives, as previously highlighted in Chap. 3. In the context of the UN SDGs, European officials are lauding the contributions of the recently established EU-AITF as a means of meeting Goal 9 via aid blending initiatives. According to the EU-AITF's (2015: 4) report, the trust 'aims to increase investment in infrastructure in sub-Saharan Africa by blending long-term loans and risk capital with grant resources' from the EU institutions and European member states. The report makes clear, moreover, that the 'technical and lending capacities are provided by EU development finance institutions, as well as the African Development Bank' (ibid.). The EU-AITF chairman, in a joint preamble with Directorate-General Development of the European Commission, also articulated a firm 'pro-poor' development discourse which invokes the UN SDGs as a legitimating component:

> Investment in infrastructure is crucial to foster sustainable and inclusive growth and to achieve the Sustainable Development Goals (SDGs) agreed at the United Nations in September 2015. In a period of limited economic growth, public finances are constrained. As such, the most effective use of public funding is to catalyse private finance through multilateral development banks (MDBs). (EU-AITF 2015)

Contributions by institutions such as the EIB are thereby presented as benevolent contributions to African development, as well as to EU aid financing objectives.

There are significant grounds, however, upon which to contest this pro-poor discourse of sustainable development under UN SDG Goal 9 as espoused by the EU-AITF and the European Commission. The EU-AITF (2015) report highlights a number of infrastructure projects in African countries that are said to bode well for both economic growth and social prosperity. The report notably highlights assistance to capacity in a port in Congo-Brazzaville, thus helping the facility to accept larger vessels and thereby handle higher volumes of traffic. This is financed by the EIB alongside the French ADF, as well as the Development Bank of Central African States. Similarly, the EU-AITF (2015) points to a ports development project in Comoros, an island state off East Africa, which will apparently lower import costs for the nation by improving its off-loading facilities. The EU-AITF report additionally points to a number of other infrastructure schemes, including highway construction and energy projects, which will ostensibly enhance African countries' business enabling environment.

It is important to understand, however, that these EU-AITF initiatives are not necessarily conducive to genuine forms of pro-poor economic growth. Following Nkrumah (1965), there are in fact grounds to contest their 'development' credentials on the basis that they merely subsidise (neo)colonial patterns of production and trade. The construction of such 'enabling' infrastructure projects, financed by European banks, is conducive to the continued outflow of African raw material exports and the inflow of cheap manufactured commodities from the EU member states. Rather than constituting a genuine boon to sustainable development, therefore, there is scope to view such initiatives as mere arteries for the continued exploitation of the African continent. Eurodad (2015: 17) convincingly make this point in explicit language. Eurodad query who are the genuine beneficiaries of these aid blending infrastructure schemes:

> [a] key question to ask… is: who is the final beneficiary of the road, railway, port or even airport? Are there local communities behind the call for this infrastructure project? All too often communities tend to require different kinds of infrastructure projects than private sector companies operating in the extractive sector, whose infrastructure needs relate to their ability to increase their production capacity and to reach (external) markets.

Table 7.1   EU-AITF and priority sectors (2015 report)

Sector	Grant amount (EUR)	Percentage of total funds	Number of projects
Multisector	1,300,000	0.2	2
Information & Communication Technology (ICT)	18,347,737	2.8	6
Water	47,100,000	7.2	7
Transport	202,455,042	30.9	29
Energy	385, 663,496	58.9	60
Total	654,866,275	100.0	104

Source EU-AITF (2015)

In the words of Nkrumah (1965), the contribution of the contemporary EU-AITF appears as 'revolving credit'. Namely, that the EU-AITF provides a de facto subsidy to European foreign investors operating in Africa and (in the case of Comoros' import handling facilities) to European exporters selling their goods to African consumers.

Substantiating these concerns, the EU-AITF (2015) report demonstrates that the majority of its financing does go towards major transport and large-scale energy projects conducive to the business enabling environment of major foreign investors operating within African recipient states. Projects more attuned to the needs of the local population, such as water, or to SME firms, such as Information and Communication Technology (ICT), appear as Cinderella sectors in comparison. Table 7.1 demonstrates this skewed nature of the EU-AITF's prioritised funding.

Since the implementation of these projects is largely undertaken by European construction and energy companies, moreover, the EU-AITF acts as a form of 'boomerang aid' (c.f. Langan 2012). Namely, EU project monies provide de facto subsidies for commercial contractors from the European member states. This has regularly been the case with, for instance, the construction of roads and highway projects in Africa. In one notorious example—the construction of the Kampala Northern Bypass in Uganda—an Italian firm received large quantities of EU aid despite missing key deadlines and (allegedly) using sub-standard materials. President Museveni himself condemned what he deemed the construction of 'third world roads' by European companies funded by the European Commission. With parallels to the EU-AITF, there were also concerns that the road itself (funded by the 10th EDF) did more to serve the business needs of large foreign commercial operators than the needs of ordinary citizens or local SME entrepreneurs (Langan 2011).

Interestingly, the European Commission has become increasingly sensitive to such criticisms of its infrastructure spending in Africa. Its report on the Africa Investment Facility (AIF)—a scheme which will complement the separate EU-AITF—makes clear that monies will go towards transport corridors to support agri-business operations. The European Commission (2015) report also makes clear, however, that poorer households will benefit from road construction in the timeframe of the UN SDGs. The document explicitly notes that transport needs are estimated at US$36 billion in sub-Saharan Africa each year. It explains that it is necessary to 'create a transport network that provides adequate regional, national, rural and urban road connectivity completed by adequate rail, port and airport infrastructure' (2015: 5). It states in explicit terms, moreover, that 'transport is an integral part of daily subsistence *for the poor*... to get to markets, jobs, health care and education services' (ibid.; emphasis added). Nevertheless, the granting of the lion-share of EU infrastructure funds to projects associated with the business enabling environment (and not to health and education services) does leave the distinct impression that aid monies are guided by European commercial interests rather than by genuine norms of sustainable development. Akopari (2017), meanwhile, notes that civil society campaigners condemn the EU for financing 'main structuring roads rather than roads in and leading to rural areas'.

Despite these concerns, however, the EU makes very clear that it will continue to subsidise extractive and other developmentally dubious commercial operations in Africa via transport infrastructure. The European Commission's (2016c, d, e, f) statements on post-Cotonou co-operation demonstrates that the EU will continue to prioritise the business enabling environment, even where road-building and other large-scale infrastructure initiatives do more to assist European enterprise than local entrepreneurs or poorer communities. For instance, the European Commission's final joint communique to the European Parliament and European Council on the post-Cotonou relationship clearly demonstrates its intention to focus on PSD activities and the business enabling environment (in conjunction with ideological support for free market EPAs). The document states that:

The new partnership should... promote a stronger role for the private sector in creating inclusive sustainable growth and jobs. This requires stronger action to improve the policy and regulatory framework, as well as the business climate. Particular attention should be given to the investment climate and addressing the need for increased investment. (2016d: 10)

Again there is discursive emphasis that there is currently *insufficient* private sector involvement in development and that this must be somehow rectified. Civil society critics of European corporate behaviour in Africa counter that there is already too much foreign business involvement in African 'development'. The European Commission's (2016b) document also outlines the need for greater infrastructure spending. The post-Cotonou framework therefore will continue patterns of aid blending already seen under the EU-AITF and the AIF. The communique states here that:

The development of infrastructure, including sustainable transport and energy networks, is a key driver for inclusive sustainable growth, in particular of those infrastructure necessary to boost the regional economic integration, to access the world market, to unlock critically isolated areas and to facilitate mobility in dense urban areas. (ibid.)

This will of course raise further concerns for civil society entities such as Eurodad (2015) which are already worried about the impact of transport corridors that entrench extractive activities and perpetuate (neo) colonial patterns of trade and production. Nevertheless, the European Commission justifies its post-Cotonou plans on the basis of the UN SDGs. Such PSD and infrastructure initiatives, it is claimed, will continue to support the SDGs from 2020 up to 2030:

The partnership should work towards increased prosperity of its people by fulfilling the SDGs... to meet the needs of all, in particular among the poorest and most vulnerable, ensuring that all human beings can fulfil their potential in dignity. (2016b: 12)

The use of SDG discourse to legitimise developmentally dubious commercial and donor activities in Africa underscores the fact that the UN platform may not necessarily result in benevolent outcomes for poorer peoples. The SDGs may do more to veil, or justify, existing patterns of (neo)colonial trade and production, focused on free markets and FDI despite regressive outcomes for 'the poor'. More broadly, it raises questions about ideational power in terms of donor and corporate relations with African countries. African states appear bound within inequitable trade and aid arrangements. And yet these are perpetuated (and reinforced) by moralised development narratives. This ties into the work of Nkrumah, particularly his scepticism surrounding the benevolent development language utilised by former colonial powers as they sought to continue their influence in the African continent. However, it should be noted that Nkrumah did not sufficiently consider ideational power as a feature of neo-colonialism. This is discussed in the next section with specific focus on the language of the UN SDGs.

The UN SDGs and Development Discourse: Entrenching Neo-Colonial Relations?

Nkrumah usefully predicted that donors would utilise 'development' interventions as a means of maintaining political and economic influence over newly independent African countries. His predictions about the use of aid as a 'revolving credit', the vested interests of major corporations, and the ability of corporate-donor coalitions to overcome the sovereign will of African governments (such as that of President Kufuor and his ill-fated PSIs) bear out during the examination of Goal 8 and Goal 9 of the UN SDGs. In the case of palm oil, for instance, his remarks about African agricultural production appear pertinent:

> Africa is a paradox which illustrates and highlights neo-colonialism. Her earth is rich, yet the products that come from above and below her soil continues to enrich, not Africans predominantly, but groups and individuals who operate to Africa's impoverishment. (1965: 1)

Nkrumah's concerns that these development interventions would ultimately perpetuate colonial patterns of North–South trade, and that African governments would thus rely more upon aid than their own taxpayers, appear prescient in light of the UN SDG's failure to tackle systemic inequalities. In fact, civil society groups such as Eurodad rightly point to how interventions justified via SDG development discourse perpetuate and entrench conditions of ill-being and poverty in Africa.

Nkrumah also usefully alluded to the power of ideas in cementing donor agendas and corporate interests in the neo-colonial situation in Africa. Specifically, he pointed to neo-colonial influence within the cultural and education spheres. Nevertheless, he subordinated this influence to the material weight of financial centres and corporations:

> Though the aim of neo-colonialism is economic domination, they do not confine their operations to the economic sphere. They use the old colonialist methods of religious, educational and cultural filtration... but all of this indirect subversion is as nothing compared with the brazen onslaught of international capitalists. (1965: 35)

This statement underscores the (neo)Marxist influences behind Nkrumah's analysis of Africa's relationship with former colonial powers from the 1950s into the era of independence. While acknowledging the role of ideas (rather implicitly through reference to religious and cultural indoctrination) he places much more emphasis on the material power of foreign capitalist entities.

Having considered the current UN SDGs, however, as well as donor discourse throughout the previous chapters, it must be said that ideational forces should not be underestimated, or omitted from critical analysis. The continuing influence of donors such as the European Commission, and corporations such as Unilever, owes a significant part to ideational elements. Namely, these external players are able to rationalise—and moralise—their continuing 'development' interventions. Through discursive overture to popular development discourse, as currently embodied within the sustainability agenda, these external actors are able to present their policies and practices as being beneficial for 'the poor' within African countries. Rather than represent a threat in terms of (neo)colonial patterns of trade, or in terms of the frustration of African governance initiatives such as the ambitious PSIs in Ghana, external actors, via SDG discourse, are portrayed as vital 'partners' for social and economic progress. Again it is useful here to reflect on the sweeping moral statements issued by the European Commission (2016a) as but one example of the resonance of the UN SDGs in justifying continued policy interventions in Africa:

> Europe and the ACP countries share principles which should remain the foundations of our societies… our common objectives should be to foster sustainable growth and decent jobs for all, ensure human development, tackling climate change, turn migration and mobility into opportunities… On top of that, a renewed partnership would strengthen the political dialogue and consolidate our trade agreements

In this one illustration of donor discourse, the European Commission seamlessly joins moral narratives pertaining to the SDGs and poverty reduction with 'political dialogue' and the consolidation of free trade agreements (the controversial EPAs in African regions). This is not mere rhetoric to be easily dismissed, but lays the foundations for the construction of a 'common sense' acceptance of the need for EU free trade policies and political dialogue (on issues such as the PSIs) in African countries. UN SDG discourse, in this circumstance, helps insulate the European Commission from potential criticism of premature tariff liberalisation and of its use of budget support/policy dialogue as leverage to frustrate developmental state agendas in 'sovereign' states such as Ghana.

Additionally, the SDG discourse surrounding PSD initiatives and public-private partnerships for development plays an important role in cementing free market approaches to 'development'. As already noted, SDG discourse implies that the private sector is the missing link, in terms of its alleged omission from previous development agendas such as the UN MDGs. The explicit inclusion of Goal 8 and Goal 9—combined to the reinvigoration of the UN Global Compact—is thereby seen as a vital step forward in achieving the economic basis of poverty reduction in Africa. Again, however, it would be misleading to present the private sector as having been absent from donor development strategies in the years leading up to the current post-2015 consensus. Instead, it would appear that the UN is anchoring itself to free market rationales to bolster its own credibility vis-à-vis influential donors such as the World Bank, USAID, and the European Commission. The UN's embrace of PSD discourse within the formulation of the SDGs also satisfies influential corporate actors such as the Unilever CEO who played such an active role within various UN negotiating fora in the lead up to 2015. Pingeot (2016: 189) convincingly argues in this context that:

> Within the sustainable development agenda, the UN is using its links to business—through partnerships and multi-stakeholder initiatives—to align

itself with the hegemonic discourse and gain legitimacy and authority in a neoliberal world.

Rather than present solutions to systemic inequalities (pertaining to trade liberalisation), the UN SDGs appear to offer a business-as-usual formula for poverty reduction in African countries. Namely, African states should partner with foreign investors and donors to construct 'socially responsible' production patterns in key sectors such as palm oil. As civil society actors attest to, however, the material realities of production on the ground do not align to sustainability norms, whether in terms of social justice or in terms of ecological integrity. The forms of PSD promoted in the name of the SDGs—for instance in the important case of palm oil—recalls Fanon's (1961: 141) concerns about foreign investments that merely perpetuate the economic patterns of colonial times:

> [neo-colonialism] does not even succeed in extracting spectacular concessions from the West, such as investments which would be of value for the country's economy or the setting up of certain industries. On the contrary, assembly plants [or in the case of palm oil, plantations and processing factories] spring up and consecrate the type of neo-colonialist industrialisation in which the country's economy flounders.

Nkrumah's (1965) analysis of—and warnings about—neo-colonialism do therefore appear justified even in the contemporary setting of the UN SDGs. Donors continue to utilise aid to subsidise developmentally dubious forms of extractive processes and agri-business along (neo)colonial patterns of production and trade. Donors also continue to utilise aid to subvert empirical sovereignty and nationally oriented decision making within African governance systems. Corporations themselves, meanwhile, seek out influential positions within global governance institutions, and partner with donors to achieve a desirable 'enabling environment' in African countries. However, Nkrumah's relative lack of analysis of the ideational aspects of development does require some redress in a modern application of the concept of neo-colonialism. From a critical constructivist standpoint, there is need to more fully recognise—and deconstruct—donor language and its role within North–South aid and trade networks (c.f. Fairclough 2001; Van Djik 1993). The example of the UN SDGs and their pro-business narratives provides a useful illustration of how 'development' discourse plays an important role in bolstering both corporate and donor power within Africa. To paraphrase Cox (1981), language is always for someone and for some purpose. In the case of the SDGs, the language of PSD, the enabling environment, business partnerships/engagement and pro-poor economic growth provide a useful veneer for donors' and corporations' perpetuation of economic asymmetries between the developed regions (such as the EU) and developing states in Africa.

This is not to say, however, that civil society groups or even African governments themselves are powerless to confront systems of neo-colonialism as practiced in the era of the UN SDGs. Increasing awareness of the need for 'development justice' and to hold donors and foreign investors accountable in terms of their moralised statements on poverty reduction indicate that there is potential for progressive coalitions to challenge neo-colonialism in Africa. Civil society campaigns against the operations of palm oil conglomerates combined to innovative strategies (such as the Kufuor government's ill-fated PSIs) indicate that there is scope for progressive forms of agency to be displayed. African actors are not condemned to forms of regressive extraversion in which external resources are continuously sought within relations of neo-colonialism. Instead, there are potential avenues through which donor interventions and corporate exploitations can be meaningfully confronted. However, such civil society and state strategies are likely to fall short in the absence of African Union and pan-African solutions. Nkrumah (1965) regularly—and correctly—expressed the view that pan-Africanism would provide the only genuine form of resistance to external interference in Africa's economic and social affairs. These issues are explored in the next chapter with reference to African civil society, governments and pan-African institutions.

CONCLUSION

This chapter has considered the UN SDGs with particular emphasis on their pivot to PSD and economic growth. While the preceding UN MDGs are often viewed as having focused on humanitarian indicators, the current SDG benchmarks are seen as embracing an economic hardheadedness focused on business activities and growth strategies. In this way, the private sector is viewed as the missing link in development policies—that is, as a partner that heretofore has been insufficiently integrated within donor and developing country development strategies. UN SDG Goals 8 and 9, in particular, emphasise the need to stimulate business in developing contexts and to ensure that public–private part-nerships are created to facilitate poverty reduction. By focussing on businesses' creation of decent jobs and the enabling environment, devel-opment partners will ostensibly achieve the economic basis of widespread social prosperity and human wellbeing.

The chapter's focus on palm oil and the EU-AITF, however, indi-cates how the operation of the UN SDGs in terms of both corporate and donor interventions may not lead to progressive outcomes for 'the poor' in Africa. On the contrary, the language of sustainable develop-ment may provide donor and corporate players with a rejuvenated 'development' discourse with which to justify, and moralise, their con-tinued regressive operation within African countries. By propound-ing a pro-poor SDG agenda in business communications and donor platforms, foreign actors can legitimise free market activities in Africa on the basis of job creation and growth. However, when their inter-ventions are considered more closely—as with palm oil investments and the EU-AITF—there are serious grounds upon which to contest whether sustainability norms are genuinely being upheld. For example, the RSPO that sets out to monitor company compliance with social and ecological sustainability pledges is found seriously wanting in a series of civil society reports, particularly on the grounds of auditing processes. The EU-AITF, meanwhile, channels the lion-share of its funding to large-scale infrastructure projects more attuned to foreign investors' commercial interests than to the needs of SME enterprises or local com-munities. It would appear therefore that European construction firms and European investors chiefly benefit from aid blending monies, build-ing and utilising infrastructure that lubricates (neo)colonial patterns of trade and production in Africa.

Finally, the chapter has considered the on-going relevance of Nkrumah's (1965) analysis for making sense of donor and corporate behaviour in Africa in the era of the UN SDGs. His scepticism sur-rounding donor aid initiatives and certain forms of predatory business investment appears well founded even in the contemporary post-2015 setting (more than five decades since the initial publication of *Neo-colonialism: The Last Stage of Imperialism*). However, it is important to take seriously the role of discourse and ideas in perpetuating forms of neo-colonial intervention in Africa. Nkrumah's analysis, focused more chiefly upon economic power and aid flows, did not sufficiently elabo-rate upon ideational factors associated with 'development'. Perhaps, this is unsurprisingly given the early stage of development endeavours in which he wrote—namely in the immediate years after de jure independence had been obtained. Nevertheless, any modern engagement with the concept of neo-colonialism does need to consider how development discourse often supports donor and corporate agendas, helping to present their interventions as morally necessary for poverty eradication, economic growth and social progress. Similarly, any emancipatory strategy must consider how counter-narratives and alternative discourse might be constructed in a fashion that seeks to promote more genuine forms of African sovereignty as part of economic and social planning. The next chapter examines the agency of African civil society, governments and pan-African institutions, with attention to the significance of discourse therein.

Note

1. The Kufuor government should nevertheless be credited with the ambitious scope of the PSIs, notwithstanding allegations of their links to oil conglomerates (via the E.O. Group discussed in Chap. 2).

References

ACP-EEC Joint Council of Ministers. (1987). *Annual report of the ACP-EEC Joint Council of Ministers*. Luxembourg: European Commission. Available at: http://aei.pitt.edu/6002/01/003236_1.pdf. Accessed 8 Oct 2009.

ACP-EEC Lomé Convention IV. (1989). *Fourth ACP-EEC Lomé Convention signed at Lomé on 15 December 1989*. Available at: http://database.balcanicooperazione.it/content/download/2408/16192/file/IV+Lom%E8+convention.pdf. Accessed 8 Oct 2009.

Amnesty International. (2016). *The great palm oil scandal: Labour abuses behind big brand names: Executive summary 2016*. London: Amnesty International.

Asante, E. (2012). *The case of Ghana's President's special initiative on oil palm (PSI-Oil palm)* (DIIS Working Paper, 2012: 11).

Cox, R. (1981). Social forces, states and world orders: Beyond International Relations theory. *Millennium Journal of International Studies, 10*(2), 126–155.

Essabra-Mensah, E. (2015). *Local oil palm growers cry for protection*. Accra: B&FT Online.

EU-AITF, (2015). *Annual report*. Brussels: European Union Africa Infrastructure Trust Fund.

Eurodad, (2015). *A dangerous blend? The EU's agenda to 'Blend' public development finance with private finance.* Brussels: Eurodad.

European Commission. (2015). *Action document for the creation of the Africa infrastructure fund.* Brussels: European Commission.

European Commission. (2016a). *Towards a new partnership framework with third countries under the European agenda on migration: FAQ factsheet.* Brussels: European Commission.

European Commission. (2016b). *Sustainable development: EU sets out its priorities.* Brussels: European Commission.

European Commission. (2016c). *Fact sheet: Towards a renewed partnership with African, Caribbean and Pacific countries after 2020.* Brussels: European Commission.

European Commission. (2016d). *Final joint communication to the European parliament and the council: A renewed partnership with the countries of Africa, the Caribbean and the Pacific.* Brussels: European Commission.

European Commission. (2016e). *Final communication from the commission to the European parliament, the council, the European economic and social committee, and the committee of the regions: Proposal for a new European consensus on development: Our world, our dignity, our future.* Brussels: European Commission.

European Commission. (2016f). *Commission staff working document: Assessing the 2005 European consensus on development and accompanying the initiative "Proposal for a new European consensus on development" accompanying the document "Communication from the commission to the European parliament, the council, the European economic and social committee and committee of the regions proposal for a new European consensus on development our world, our dignity our future.* Brussels: European Commission.

Fairclough, N. (2001). *Language and power.* London: Longman.

Fanon, F. (1961). *The wretched of the earth.* Reprint—London: Penguin Classics, 2001.

Friends of the Earth International. (2015). Ugandan oil palm project taken to court over land grab claims. *Friends of the Earth International,* 19 Feb 2015. Available at: http://www.foeeurope.org/uganda-palm-oil-court-land-grab-190215. Accessed 25 July 2017.

Grassroots, & EIA. (2016). *Who watches the watchmen? Auditors and the breakdown of oversight in the RSPO.* London: EIA.

Gregoratti, C. (2010). Growing sustainable business in Eastern Africa: The potential and limits of partnerships for development. In P. Utting & J. Marques (Eds.), *Corporate social responsibility and regulatory governance* (pp. 203–254). London: Palgrave.

Gregoratti, C. (2018). *The UN Global Compact.* London: Routledge. Forthcoming.

Humanity United. (2015). *Free and fair labor in palm oil production: Principles and implementation.*

IPS. (1987, November 12). Hurdles to ACP/EEC trade identified. IPS. Available at: http://www.sunsonline.org/trade/process/during/uruguay/regional/11140087.htm. Accessed 25 Mar 2017.

Iwuagwu, J., & Ugwuanyi, J. (2014). Treatment and valorization of palm oil mill effluent through production of food grade yeast biomass. *Journal of Waste Management.* Online version available at: https://www.hindawi.com/archive/2014/439071/. Accessed 25 July 2017.

Krinninger, T. (2017). *Big palm oil is making the rules.*

Langan, M. (2011). Private sector development as poverty and strategic discourse: PSD in the political economy of EU-Africa trade relations. *Journal of Modern African Studies, 49*(1), 83–113.

Langan, M. (2012). Normative power europe and the moral economy of Africa-EU ties: A conceptual reorientation of normative power. *New Political Economy, 17*(3), 243–270.

Mawdsley, E. (2015). DFID, the private sector and the re-centring of an economic growth agenda in international development. *Global Society, 29*(3), 1–20.

Muchhala, B., & Sengupta, M. (2014). A Déjà vu agenda or a development agenda? A critique of the post-2015 development agenda from the perspective of developing countries. *Economic and Political Weekly, XLIX*(46), 28–30.

Nkrumah, K. (1963). *Africa must unite.* London: Heineman.

Nkrumah, K. (1965). *Neo-colonialism: The last stage of imperialism.* Sixth Printing—New York International Publishers, 1976.

OECD (1995). *Private sector development: A guide to donor support.* Paris: OECD.

Ogada, M., Mwabu, G., & Muchai, D. (2014). Farm technology adoption in Kenya: A simultaneous estimation of inorganic fertilizer and improved maize variety adoption decisions. *Agricultural and Food Economics, 2*(12). Open access available at: https://agrifoodecon.springeropen.com/articles/10.1186/s40100-014-0012-3. Accessed 25 July 2017.

Partnerships for Forests. (2016). *Seven African governments sign the TFA 2020 marrakesh declaration for the sustainable development of the oil palm sector in Africa.* (Partnership for Forests).

Pingeot, L. (2014). *Corporate influence in the post-2015 process.* Aachen: Bischöfliches Hilfswerk.

Pingeot, L. (2016). In whose interest? The UN's strategic rapprochement with business in the sustainable development agenda. *Globalizations, 13*(2), 118–202.

Pye, O., Daud, R., Manurung, K., & Siagan, S. (2016). *Workers in the palm oil industry: Exploitation, resistance and transnational solidarity.* Koln: Stiftung Asienhaus.

Quintos, P. (2015). *The post-2015 corporate development agenda: Expanding corporate power in the name of sustainable development.* Quezon City: IBON.

RSPO. (2016). *Impact report.* Kuala Lumpur: RSPO.

Scheyvens, R., Banks, G., & Hughes, E. (2016). The private sector and the SDGs: The need to move 'beyond business as usual'. *Sustainable Development, 24*(6), 371–382.

Suarez, A., Kim, H., Kim, H., & Madhavan, M. (2013). *Measuring environmental externalities to agriculture in Africa.*

The Courier. (1985). ACP–EEC Convention Lome III, *The Courier*, Special issue No. 89 January–February. Brussels: European Commission. Available at: http://aei.pitt.edu/1778/01/Lome_III_dossier.pdf. Accessed 8 Oct 2009.

The Courier. (1994). *Dossier: The private sector—country reports: Eritrea, Chad.* Brussels: European Commission.

UN. (2015). *Transforming our world the 2030 agenda for sustainable development.* New York: United Nations.

UN Global Compact. (2015). *SDG compass: UN executive summary.* New York: United Nations Global Compact.

UNEP. (2011). *Global environmental alert service (GEAS): Taking the pulse of the planet: Connecting science with policy.*

Van Djik, T. A. (1993). Principles of discourse analysis. *Discourse and Society, 4*(2), 249–283.

Weber, H. (2017). Politics of leaving no one behind: Contesting the 2030 sustainable development goals agenda. *Globalizations*, pp. 1–16; early view edition.

CHAPTER 8

Agency, Sovereignty, and Neo-Colonialism

Introduction

Having assessed the contemporary relevance of Nkrumah's work for making sense of, and critiquing, neo-colonial relations between African actors and external donors/corporations, it is important to consider African agency for progressive change. In particular, it is relevant to explore Nkrumah's own understanding of the means for Africans to oppose, and defeat, relations of neo-colonialism. His major treatise, *Neo-colonialism: the Last Stage of Imperialism* (as well as his earlier book, *Africa Must Unite*) develops a convincing line of argument regarding a need for pan-African solutions to the crisis of 'development' after formal liberation. Nkrumah argued that a Union of African States would be necessary to give African peoples the economic and political clout to guard against external influence and to ensure that African resources benefited African citizenries. He argued that regional formations such as ECOWAS might prove a stumbling block to continental African unity and was dismayed by the gradualist stance of other African leaders, including Julius Nyerere (Nkrumah 1963: 178).

This chapter examines avenues for African agency for achieving genuine development free from neo-colonial intervention, particularly in terms of pan-African solutions in the context of the African Union. This discussion is foregrounded by consideration of agency in terms of the concept of state sovereignty. A number of notable interventions by Brown (2012, 2013) have challenged the idea that African state sovereignty

© The Author(s) 2018
M. Langan, *Neo-Colonialism and the Poverty of 'Development'*
in Africa, Contemporary African Political Economy,
https://doi.org/10.1007/978-3-319-58571-0_8

is threatened by external donors. Instead, Brown argues that African states' possession of legal, juridical sovereignty enables African politicians to realise some meaningful political agency in their diplomatic dealings with foreign partners. The chapter critiques Brown's claims in the context of Nkrumah and his concept of neo-colonialism. Thereafter, the chapter considers the role of African civil society organisations (including trade justice movements and trade unions), as well as individual African states to challenge neo-colonialism in current North–South relations. It then examines the African Union, with discussion of NEPAD and its regrettable neo-liberal contours. This assessment of African agency—in terms of civil society, states, and the African Union—is discussed with particular reference to the EU and its negotiations for EPAs. Not only does the EU's contemporary pursuit of 'reciprocal' free trade in Africa mirror the concerns Nkrumah held about the then EEC's pursuit of Association in the 1960s, but it also draws wider attention to concerns about interventions in African economies, and 'ladder kicking' (c.f. Chang 2003).

The discussion is structured as follows. The chapter first explores African agency in terms of the concept of state sovereignty with regards to recent interventions from Brown (2012, 2013). This foreground issues surrounding African state actors' ability to enact change in their relations with powerful donors and corporations from Europe, and beyond. The chapter then examines the progressive opportunities offered by civil society activism for bringing about positive change in Africa through challenges to donor and corporate agendas, notably the EU's EPAs. Thereafter, it considers the potential of individual African countries to challenge neo-colonial relations, with discussion of the democratic developmental state. The chapter then examines pan-African solutions to neo-colonialism with attention to the work of Nkrumah (1963, 1965). It considers whether the contemporary African Union might provide a forum for genuine challenges to external donor and corporate influence where they are deemed harmful for development (such as the EPAs). Finally, the chapter concludes with a recap of the on-going relevance of Nkrumah and his critique of neo-colonialism in Africa.

State Sovereignty and African Agency

Before considering African agency in relation to civil society, the democratic developmental state, and the African Union, it is relevant to first reflect on interventions by Brown (2012, 2013) on the relationship between agency and state sovereignty. Brown has challenged critical scholars of African affairs by reminding them that African elite actors do preside over nation-states that are legally recognised within the international system as sovereign entities. That is, the international Westphalian system of nation-states legally recognises the sovereignty of countries such as Ghana. Ultimate authority over the territory of the African state therefore falls to its recognised government (Brown 2013: 262, 268). On this basis, Brown (2013: 273) contends against the views of scholars such as Gruffydd-Jones who argue that external donors diminish African state sovereignty through aid conditionalities and other forms of policy leverage:

> While African policy autonomy may indeed be severely compromised by the aid relationship, the recognition of the right of African states to govern their own societies is not seriously questioned by donors through the aid relationship.

Brown (2013: 271) reminds us that African states retain legal sovereignty and will continue to do so, barring some form of military occupation or foreign seizure of territory. With certain parallels to Bayart's concept of extraversion, Brown (2012, 13) contends that African elites can use the legal sovereignty (or juridical sovereignty) of their states to enhance their own agency (or scope for independent action) when dealing with external partners. African elites possess an ultimate authority over conduct within the legally defined territory of the nation-state in question. They can use this authority as a bargaining chip, or leveraging device, when conducting diplomacy with external elements, for instance over aid matters:

> The need for [aid] negotiation in the first place comes about precisely because any aid programme requires the agreement of the recipient, because that recipient possess sovereign independence and with it the right to agree or refuse aid programmes. (2013: 281)

For Brown, critical scholars' claims that donors and foreign governments are denuding African sovereignty are misleading.

Brown's (2012, 2013) statement that African countries possess legal or juridical sovereignty is of course true. Ghana, for instance, gained legal independence in 1957 and has very recently celebrated the sixtieth anniversary of this feat—with due recognition being given to the leading role of its first President, Kwame Nkrumah. The argument being advanced by critical scholars such as Gruffydd-Jones, and within the preceding chapters, is not that legal sovereignty is absent. Ghana's presence within the UN General Assembly is testament to its legal status as an 'independent' nation-state. Critical scholars argue that external elements are denuding genuine, empirical or de facto sovereignty. While legal sovereignty is certainly present, African elites regularly find themselves in a 'catch twenty-two' where they are often compelled to capitulate genuine decision-making to foreign benefactors, or else to repudiate foreign aid and impose austerity on already impoverished peoples. This double-bind is captured by luminaries such as Nkrumah and Fanon. The former, in *Africa Must Unite,* explained that:

> many of the leaders of the new African find themselves in a perplexing position… They are strongly dependent on foreign contributions simply to maintain the machinery of their governments. Many of them have deliberately been made so weak economically, by being carved up into many separate countries, that they are not able to sustain out of their own resources the machinery of independent government. (1963: 184)

In this context, he stated that he understood why certain elites had sought an accommodation with foreign powers and had submitted to conditions of neo-colonialism, rather than enact austerity on their already deprived fellow citizens:

> I recognise the impossible position in which they were placed when the transfer of power took place. Their frontiers were not of their own choosing, and they were left with an economic, administrative, and educational system which, each in its own way, was designed to perpetuate the colonial relationship. (ibid.)

This point was also forcefully made by Fanon (1961: 97) in *The Wretched of the Earth* when he declared that colonial powers told their aspiring colonies, 'since you want independence, take it and starve'.

> the apotheosis of independence is transformed into the curse of independence… the colonial power says: "Since you want independence, take it and starve."… A regime of austerity is imposed on these starving men… An

autarkic regime... with the miserable resources it has in hand, tries to find an answer to the nation's great hunger and poverty.

Thus, the agency to which Brown (2012, 2013) alludes vis-à-vis aid negotiations is the agency of the less developed African state to temporarily spurn foreign donors with the outcome of austerity (and their likely ousting at the hands of a destitute section of the citizenry, or at the hand of foreign powers, as with Nkrumah himself). Or the agency to accept relations of neo-colonialism owing to a need for foreign aid to sustain basic services in the here and now.

To take a recent example discussed in Chap. 2, the Ghanaian government appeared to have the sovereign state authority to say 'no' to the buy-out of Kosmos' existing oil stake by ExxonMobil, utilising its juridical legal power. Even in this instance, however, meaningful Ghanaian elite agency was severely constrained by the realities of a neo-colonial situation in which the legally independent state was 'free' merely to replace a US oil investor with a Chinese substitute. Owing to the depressed economic situation based on a (neo)colonial pattern of trade and production, the immediate demands of an impoverished citizenry for basic services that oil revenues sustain, and a lack of necessary technical and human resources to devise a fully nationalised oil industry, Ghana's leaders faced an impossible double bind. Either they could reject foreign involvement altogether and impose austerity as oil revenues stalled (and donor budget support most likely withdrawn) or they could select which foreign corporation (American or Chinese) would profit from Ghana's natural resources and use the oil concession as a lifeline to sustain basic services. As Nkrumah (1963: 174) explained for countries that accommodate themselves to such neo-colonial quandaries: 'the independence of those states is in name only, for their liberty of action is gone.'

Brown (2012: 13) is correct to the extent that African elites in states such as Ghana can lean on juridical state sovereignty to (at times) choose their foreign patron. In Ghana's case, however, they are still not able to obtain the fruits of a genuine, empirical sovereignty. This is especially true when donors combine to thwart the will of presidents and ministers. Note for example, President Kufuor's ill-fated PSIs which sought to enact a developmental state strategy. In this instance the MDBS group successfully manoeuvred to stall and defeat a developmental state approach, since it fell outside their free market strictures. Kufuor—in the words of Fanon (1961)—had the rather illusionary 'choice' of whether to plough ahead with the PSIs without donor financial support (an impossibility given the colonial pattern of economic production he had inherited) or to bow to donor demands, accept the demise of the PSIs, and ensure the short-term provision of basic services (while not seriously dealing with the structural conditions of poverty in his country). In these circumstances, it does seem churlish and inaccurate for scholars to insist that such African elites—owing to the legal sovereignty of the state—may enjoy a good or even acceptable degree of agency in their dealings with donors/corporations. It is in rare historical conditions—such as in Rwanda in relation to donors' 'genocide guilt'—that African elites are able to temporarily carve out sufficient policy space so as to approach the substance of empirical state sovereignty (Reyntjens 2004).[1] For countries such as Ghana, not to mention so-called 'fragile states', elites' autonomy is regularly thwarted, and genuine, empirical sovereignty denied within the contours of neo-colonial economic and political relations.

To claim that African state sovereignty is regularly denuded by relations of neo-colonialism is not to claim that African groups are bereft of any type of agency whatsoever. Of course, this would be an absurd position, one which is often (wrongly) equated with the concept of neo-colonialism. A regressive form of agency is regularly exercised by certain state elites in the form of 'extraversion'—leveraging in additional aid flows through flattery of foreign donors and their aid agendas (for instance, on securitisation and terrorism). However, the fact that African states have obtained legal sovereignty, does not guarantee, or meaningfully bestow, progressive agency in a situation of neo-colonialism. Progressive agency, in the neo-colonial situation, must be rethought in terms of strategies for equipping Africa's nation-states with a real, empirical sovereign power. Perhaps paradoxically, the best—and likely only—avenue for this is via the strengthening of pan-African institutions where sovereignty is pooled among the individual African countries.[2] A pan-African approach is explored in more detail in the penultimate section of the chapter. First, however, the possibilities for progressive agency on the part of African civil society movements and democratic developmental states to resist relations of neo-colonialism are considered in more detail. As discussed below, the agency of civil society and nation-states can only be partial and incomplete in the absence of a federal Union of African States as envisaged by Nkrumah (1963, 1965).

Civil Society Organisations and African Agency

Much scholarly attention has been given to the role of civil society bodies in realising a progressive form of African agency for social development and poverty reduction. At the beginning of the 1990s, a growth of 'liberal pluralist' literature welcomed the proliferation of African non-governmental organisations (NGOs) (Hearn 2007). NGOs and their leaders were viewed as a means of achieving pro-poor outcomes through action for rural development, environmental sustainability, gender justice, and fair trade. This would offset—or perhaps even replace—the role of national governments which had apparently failed in their duties to adequately provide for the basic needs of their citizenries (ibid.). NGOs dedicated to progressive values and to meaningful partnership with foreign donors (and corporations) would help to bypass some of the worst forms of neo-patrimonial rule in Africa to deliver goods and services directly to vulnerable populations.

This zeitgeist for NGOs remains somewhat present in the era of the Post-Washington Consensus, albeit the early enthusiasm expressed by liberal scholars is now more fully tempered by a critical literature that points to the neo-liberal logic of NGO service provision (Hearn 2007; Powell and Seddon 1997; Shivji 2006; Wright 2012; Mohan 2002; Mitlin et al. 2006). For these critical scholars, the turn to NGOs in the 1990s is contextualised in terms of the Washington Consensus that then prevailed. Donor SAPs successfully roll-backed the contours of state provision. States in Africa were deemed to be clientelistic, neo-patrimonial and broadly corrupt. SAPs therefore enacted a neo-liberal vision of the small nightwatchman state that would not stifle free market activity or economic entrepreneurship. A proliferation of African NGOs, financed with foreign aid money, is seen as a natural outgrowth of this paradigmatic preference. Since the government had already been constrained by SAP austerity—and in many cases, its civil service capacity reduced in scope—NGOs would stand as a substitute organ for the provision of essential services (ibid.). Moreover, critical scholars point to the potential co-optation of NGO personnel by foreign governments and business elites. Certain NGOs may not be a progressive instrument for poverty reduction and 'development' but, conversely, might be used to frustrate the empirical sovereignty of Africa's governments. In this vein, others point to the way in which NGO recruitment in Africa might potentially sap domestic political will to challenge foreign pressures (Mitlin et al.

2006). Namely, that highly educated African individuals might choose to enter the financially secure realm of international NGO employment than to labour within ill-paid social movements or, progressive political parties. Co-opted NGOs, from a Gramscian framework, might help to both maintain a neo-liberal hegemony while frustrating the emergence of a counter-hegemonic bloc (ibid.).

It is important to state, however, that there are a myriad of NGO exemplars in which progressive policy change has been advocated, often in spite of donor and foreign investor preferences. The case of ACP–EU relations and the European Commission's pursuit of EPAs provides an illustrative snapshot. An array of trade justice groups and NGOs in African countries has pointed to the inherent dangers of signing FTAs/EPAs with industrialised European member states. Groups such as the National Association of Nigerian Traders (NANTS 2010) and SEATINI Uganda (2013, 2017) have expressed their concern that enhanced inflows of cheap European commodities (upon EPA tariff dismantling) will leave little room for domestic industry to grow in African states. Vital sectors such as textiles and tomato agro-processing will likely retract, or disband altogether, upon the import flooding of cheap European goods. They have demanded that their respective governments thus withhold their signatures from the EPAs being negotiated in sub-regions (including West Africa as Trommer [2011, 2014] convincingly documents).[3] Other groups, meanwhile, have called upon the EU to enhance its promised 'Aid for Trade' provision in the event of EPA implementation. These African NGOS, often in alliance with progressive European counterparts, point to the need for additional funding towards Africa's productive business capacity if the EPA is to be genuinely 'pro-poor'.

Of course, there is much doubt as to whether Aid for Trade could (in any format) meaningfully translate a FTA/EPA into a genuine development opportunity for African countries. Ladder-kicking, when combined to short-term aid, is ladder-kicking nonetheless (c.f. Chang 2003). Civil society campaigns aimed at enhancing Aid for Trade flows—while acquiescing to the general principle of free trade as embodied by the EPAs—run the risk of accommodating European commercial instincts at the expense of developmental strategies. Moreover, as Orbie et al. (2017) point out, certain NGOs have been incorporated by the European Commission into 'participatory' events aimed at enhancing the legitimacy of the EPA process itself. There is a danger therefore that such

groups might be essentially co-opted by the EU as a means for supporting the roll-out of trade deals that do not align to the economic needs of
African countries. With parallels to the critical literature that has pushed
back against the assumption that NGOs always and necessarily represent
a progressive voice for African development, there exists the danger that
certain African NGOs—when invited to official participatory EPA meetings—might lend credence to EU free trade agendas (while ultimately
failing to mitigate the negative implications of such agreements for nascent agro-processing and manufacturing sectors in the ACP group).

It should also be noted that trade union movements have played a
progressive role in voicing concerns about EPA implementation. Hurt
(2017) provides an extensive and convincing overview of the ways in
which Southern African trade unions have influenced the national/
regional discourse with regards to the SADC region's EPA with the
European Commission. Southern African trade unionists have played
an important role in combining with their European trade union counterparts to pressurise the EU member states to reconsider the 'development' potential of free trade. Importantly, Hurt (2017) remains sceptical
of the ability of trade unions to play a wholly transformative role, and to
usher in an alternative policy agenda that would replace the EPAs altogether. In this sense, he is cognisant of the limitations of trade union
movements to realise a progressive agency to fundamentally oppose, and
derail, disadvantageous trade agreements with former colonial powers.
This is a key point to stress with regards to both NGOs and trade unions
in Africa. Namely, that they may be able to voice dissent and to provide
a basis for counter-hegemonic discourse. This, in some circumstances,
might open up greater avenues for African governments themselves to
query, critique and postpone regressive donor agendas such as the EPAs.
Rarely, however, does their action result in the profound transformation
of what might accurately (in the context of EPAs) be deemed as neo-
colonial trade and production ties between African countries and foreign
donors. Even where there has appeared to be ground breaking success
via NGO agitation—such as the creation of the EITI—these initiatives
regularly fall well short of their promised pro-poor objectives. As the
next section discusses, the agency of African democratic developmental
states is also restricted in the face of (neo)colonial relations.

The Democratic Developmental State and African Agency

The agency of the African state has also been the subject of much debate in terms of development and North-South ties. In addition to the interventions of Brown (2012, 2013) on the concept of sovereignty, there has also been much focus upon the concept of the democratic developmental state. Critical scholars such as Mkandawire (2002, 2010) indicate that African states might usefully adopt a developmental strategy aimed at industrialisation and value addition. This would involve a greater degree of state involvement and planning in the economic life of the nation than possible within the (Post-)Washington Consensus. The developmental state model would also necessitate the construction of an insulated and competent administrative service that would be able to resist the lure of sectoral interests and corruption. Moreover, political elites themselves would have to find an attractive nationalist discourse with which to imbue the developmental state project with widespread public and private sector legitimacy. In some ways, meanwhile, an African developmental state would have to 'learn' from the experiences of East Asian countries such as Japan, Malaysia and Singapore that successfully achieved a mixed-market model of economic diversification and upgrading. Mkandawire (2002, 2010) warns, however, that there is no single blueprint for African countries to follow and that these historical developmental states achieved their success as much by 'trial-by-error' as much as through competent economic choices.

This discussion surrounding the democratic developmental state in Africa touches upon two controversies. First, it brings to the fore questions about the linkages (if any) between authoritarian government and poverty reduction (c.f. Mkandawire 2002, 2010; Edigheji 2010; Kieh 2015; Kim 2010; Henderson 1999). Specifically, the East Asia developmental states were not paragons of democratic rule, quite the contrary. Elites, such as South Korea's President Park, actively suppressed dissent—including from trade unions—as they sought to enact often disruptive economic changes as part of an industrialisation and value addition strategy (Henderson 1999; Kim 2010). The aim of a *democratic* developmental state in Africa seeks to combine the economic 'take-off' enjoyed by the historical East Asian regimes with respect for democratic standards. The proponents of the democratic developmental state deny that there is any solid correlation between authoritarianism and growth (Mkandawire 2002, 2010). Additionally, they insist that democratic norms are essential to ensure that any economic gain translates into widespread social prosperity. Interestingly, in terms of the contributions of Kwame Nkrumah, these debates echo critiques of his government in Ghana prior to the coup d'etat which removed him from power. Nkrumah became increasingly intolerant of political and social dissent as Ghana became a de facto one-party state. He justified this authoritarian turn in passages of *Africa Must Unite*, arguing that it was necessary to prevent factionalism and ethnic tensions conjured up by a mischievous opposition party (Nkrumah 1963: 78).[4] Of course, Nkrumah (1963: 180–181) also advocated for what today would be termed the 'developmental state' where government plays an important role in achieving a mixed-market economy geared towards rapid industrialisation and diversification. The potential results of his efforts—if not for the coup d'etat—remain an interesting point for counterfactual historical surmise. Nevertheless, his reputation (both political and intellectual) remains somewhat damaged as a result of his apparent authoritarianism. Whether his authoritarianism—if it had then translated into economic success— would have seen as a legitimate and/or necessary price for prosperity is again open for counterfactual history.

The debate surrounding the democratic developmental state in Africa also touches upon a second controversy regarding foreign influence (akin to the earlier discussion of Brown [2012, 2013] and African state sovereignty). The successful implementation of a developmental state model presupposes that an African nation-state would be able to achieve necessary policy space, and prerequisite capital, to launch a mixed-market industrialisation programme. The case of Nkrumah's government in Ghana again raises an interesting case in point since his government's developmental discourse arose the suspicion and hostility of foreign donors (who supported the coup d'etat in 1966). Nevertheless, during the height of the Cold War in the 1970s, certain Western-leaning African countries were able to implement a degree of developmentalist policies. The Kenyan government, for instance, was able to implement a mixed-market model with some successes in the construction of a viable cotton-textiles value chain (Kenyan Association of Manufacturers 2006). However, the debt crisis and the launch of the Washington Consensus into the 1980s soon undermined the economic, and political, foundations of the Kenyan developmental state. In return for longer periods for debt repayments, Kenya agreed to implement SAPs, including state divestment from textiles parastatals, and the opening up of the domestic market to foreign clothing imports (including cheap second hand branded goods from the EEC/EU member states) (ibid.).

More recently, Botswana has been hailed as a success story of a developmental state in Africa. Many attribute its success to the diamond industry where industrial-scale deep underground mining has bolstered government coffers. Nevertheless, critics such as Hilborn (2012) are sceptical as to whether Botswana does constitute a developmental state per se. Its relative dependency on natural resources—and capital investment from foreign investors into this lucrative sector—queries whether Bostwana's political elite have genuinely departed from a colonial pattern of extraction. Moreover, the recent experience of Ghana's Kufuor government and its PSIs queries whether—even in the Post-Washington Consensus—foreign donors can tolerate developmental models in countries that are currently reliant on budget support for vital welfare services. Outside of Africa, meanwhile, the experiences of the East Asian financial crisis of 1996/1997 have brought into question whether the historical developmental states were themselves able to sustain a mixed-market approach in the face of foreign pressures. Henderson (1999) details how international financial institutions pressured East Asian countries into unwise liberalisation agendas. This, he convincingly argues, created the conditions for the crisis and ultimately for the collapse of a developmental state approach. This is combined to discussion that the success of the East Asian countries in the Cold War period owed to the Western institutions' (unusual) tolerance of mixed-market approaches within developing countries. Western governments effectively acquiesced to policy innovation on the part of their East Asian clients to ensure a degree of social cohesion and economic growth, useful for staving off the threat of Communism.

Altogether, therefore, there is much interesting debate about the ability of the African state—in a developmental guise—to exhibit progressive agency to rework (neo)colonial patterns of economic growth, trade and exchange. Certain commentators are optimistic that individual African nations would be able to, and perhaps are today (such as Ethiopia and Rwanda) achieving something akin to the East Asian experience. Ultimately, however, the question of empirical sovereignty arises and whether an individual African nation would be able to gather the prerequisite capital to fund an ambitious mixed-market economic plan. Or whether aid-dependent states, such as Ghana, would be frustrated by foreign donors as they attempted to undertake policy innovations that depart from donors' preferred free market prescriptions. This is a problem of which Nkrumah was highly cognisant, even as he attempted to mobilise the Ghanaian economy away from colonial patterns and onto the heights of industrialisation. It raises the broader question, therefore, of viable strategies for supporting African developmental states to (i) raise sufficient capital, and (ii) to resist potential external pressures to default to the colonial pattern of trade.[5] Nkrumah forcefully argued here for the construction of a Union of African States that would provide newly 'sovereign' countries with the collective economic and political clout to achieve genuine poverty reduction for their peoples. Nkrumah's insights about pan-African initiatives are considered in the section below, with reference to the contemporary era of African development.

PAN-AFRICANISM AND AFRICAN AGENCY

Nkrumah anticipated that individual African states—and civil society movements—would not ultimately have the capacity to transform (neo)colonial pattern of economics and trade. Nation-states would fall foul of the dangers of neo-colonial trade and aid agendas, or else attempt an independent path bereft of the necessary capital and economies of scale to successfully achieve 'development'. The legacy of colonialism in terms of weak economic capacity would necessitate African elites to sooner or later accommodate themselves within neo-colonial relations, or else to forfeit FDI and aid with the onset of what Fanon called 'austerity' regimes. Nkrumah, in the Ghanaian situation, sought in the short-term to balance his developmental approach with certain assistance from foreign donors and investors. He justified this on the basis that his government would ensure that this was a temporary measure and that the forms of foreign investment into Ghana would be subordinated to the domestic needs of economic planning and the wellbeing of the citizenry. Nkrumah, as well as his detractors, were well aware of the potential paradox that this posed—namely that this liberation figure at once condemned neo-colonialism while accepting the immediate need for aid and investment to sustain the Ghanaian state.

Crucially, however, Nkrumah insisted that such accommodation would only be a short-term measure given his longer-term ambitions to realise a pan-African solution to the dangers of foreign donor and corporate pressure. African countries, he argued, could overcome colonial economics and guard against neo-colonial influences if they united as part of a Union of African States. A federal union, involving the political and economic coming together of newly 'sovereign' states, would be the best means of ensuring economies of scale necessary for industrialisation and economic take-off. Moreover, the political cohesion of African states within a federal union (including a continental government and federal parliamentary assembly) would ensure that foreign entities such as the USA and Britain/France would no longer be able to play 'divide-and-rule' strategies within relations of neo-colonialism. The Union of African States—through collective self-reliance—would eventually be able to wean its members from foreign aid and to help them achieve the economic prosperity necessary for the alleviation of poverty and ill-being. Interestingly, Nkrumah envisaged that this union would extend to north Africa regardless of religious and ethnic divergences (of course, this is now highly complicated by the Arab Spring and the pitiful situation of the Egyptian military dictatorship, as well as the de facto collapse of Libya, in wake of foreign interventions).

With relevance for contemporary debates about the EU's pursuit of EPAs with sub-regions such as ECOWAS and SADC, Nkrumah also warned that sub-regionalism would prove a stumbling block to greater African unity. Departing from the preferences of his presidential counterpart, Julius Nyerere of Tanzania, he insisted that African countries must immediately unite and eschew the gradualist position of the Monrovia Group (especially associated with Tanzania and Liberia). Nkrumah's Casablanca Group of states, including Guinea, sought to pave the way forward for the federal unity of Africa. Guinea and Ghana went as far as to announce their unity as a stepping stone towards the Union of African States. Additionally, Nkrumah warned about the dangers of the newly formed European Economic Community (EEC) as it sought to achieve 'Eurafrican' association between its members and African countries. Nkrumah predicted that any such trade and aid association (notwithstanding the EEC's initial concession to African countries in terms of their right to impose tariffs on European goods) would be the association of the 'rider and the horse'. Unconditional and unilateral association between African countries and the EEC would ensure that a (neo)colonial pattern of trade would continue. European member states would seek out African markets as a dumping ground for their manufactured and processed goods. African countries, for their part, would remain a source of agricultural commodities and minerals necessary for the functioning of European industry. On this basis, Nkrumah (1963: 182) queried whether the EEC's offer of market access for African exporters was truly a benevolent act, since European industrialists had little choice but to import African commodities due to the relative lack of such primary goods in Europe itself. Nkrumah also (rightly) predicted that the EEC's use of aid monies would be combined to its trade interests to perpetuate the colonial pattern of exchange. Again, he identified the dangers of the EEC's neo-colonial prerogatives should the newly 'independent' countries fail to join together within his envisaged Union of African States.

In the context of contemporary relations of neo-colonialism— explored in the preceding chapters—Nkrumah's call for African unity appears as both a relevant strategy for emancipatory change, and a sad indictment of how African states failed to unite in the immediate period of decolonisation. Most interestingly, his erstwhile intellectual rival— Julius Nyerere—left office at the height of the Washington Consensus lambasting neo-colonialism in Africa, as well as his own failure to adequately anticipate its dangers (Nyerere 1978). Nyerere admitted in 1997 that, with hindsight, the federalist strategy of Nkrumah's Casablanca Group would have provided African countries with the clout to have improved upon the colonial pattern of imbalanced trade (Ndlovu-Gatsheni 2013: 69–70). He explained that African dignitaries' suspicions as to Nkrumah's motives, as well as their personal desire to hold onto as much individual authority as possible, undermined the political will for federalism in the 1960s:

> Kwame Nkrumah was the state crusader for African unity. He wanted the Accra summit of 1965 to establish Union Government for the whole of independent Africa. But we failed. The one minor reason is that Kwame, like all great believers, underestimated the degree of suspicion and animosity, which his crusading passion had created among a substantial number of his fellow Heads of State. The major reason was linked to the first: already too many of us had a vested interest in keeping Africa divided. (ibid.)

Current influential scholars such as Mkandawire (2010, 2011) concur that pan-African solutions to problems of African development ought to be more seriously considered. Mkandawire (2010) laments that the African Union has thus far failed to provide a transformative vehicle in terms of Africa's economic and political relations with external elements. He points to the failings of the New Economic Partnership for African Development (NEPAD) launched in the 2000s as part of an 'African Renaissance' driven by leaders such as President Mbeki of South Africa. Mkandawire (2010) remarks that the free market focus of NEPAD, and its encouragement of even greater flows of foreign capital into Africa, was enthusiastically welcomed by donors and the international financial institutions. He pertinently remarks that this fact alone should give pause to African leaders about the benefits of NEPAD for genuine poverty reduction. Related to his support for pan-Africanism, Mkandawire (2010) convincingly states that any prospect for developmental states in Africa is not only bound up in competent bureaucracies. But equally importantly, it is dependent upon African elites being able to construct a legitimating discourse that binds civil society and the indigenous business community to a project of economic (and political) nationalism. It is useful to reflect here that a pan-African discourse, and pan-African institutions, could play a vital role in successfully realising developmental state strategies. With overtures to the discourse of Nkrumah himself—as articulately expressed in both *Africa Must Unite* (1963), and *Neo-Colonialism: The Last Stage of Imperialism* (1965)—African leaders would likely find the language with which to justify mixed-market solutions in contrast to the economic malaise encompassed by free market strictures under the (Post-) Washington Consensus.

A strengthening of the African Union by developmentalist elites would, in the current context of neo-colonial relations, also help to improve individual nations' prospects for genuine development and poverty reduction. Noting Nkrumah's concerns about the EEC, it stands to reason that African countries' ambivalence regarding the current EU EPAs would have been augmented by a greater commitment to pan-African institutions. As Nkrumah predicted, a proliferation of Regional Economic Communities (RECs) such as ECOWAS and SADC provided the opportunity for the 'divide and rule' approach adopted by the European Commission in the EPA negotiations (Babarinde and Wright 2013). Not only have individual African nations been pitted against one another in terms of EU pressure to comply with the terms of regional EPAs (for instance, Nigeria being pressured to sign to ensure EU market access for exporters in less developed neighbours such as Ghana) but the regional formations themselves have been pitted against one another as part of a hubs-and-spokes arrangement (ibid.). The sub-regional logic of the EPA negotiations has broken down the erstwhile unity of the ACP bloc which had successfully—and collectively—negotiated for developmental concessions in the preceding Lomé Conventions (founded in 1975 amidst UN calls for a New International Economic Order).

African countries in the lead up to a post-Cotonou pact with the EU from 2020 onwards would do well to consider the potential of pan-African co-operation for achieving more equitable trade arrangements. Solidarity within the corridors of the African Union might empower African sub-regions to renegotiate the terms of EPAs as their material impact—import flooding and deindustrialisation—become clear as the agreements come onstream. The EPAs, despite what the European Commission might wish, are not set in stone and can be challenged given the 'safeguard' and 'competitiveness' clauses contained within their wording (for instance, the West African arrangement which concedes that a Competitiveness Observatory will be established to ostensibly guard against import flooding, as well as a safeguard clause which, in theory, would allow West African tariff hikes against excessive influx of European commodities). Whether West African countries will be able to capitalise on these openings for contestation of free trade within the EPA will depend not only upon unity within each sub-region, but also upon the role of the African Union in cementing opposition to the travails of premature liberalisation across the continent.

More broadly, pan-Africanism would augment the agency of African civil society and individual states to offer transformative alternatives to (neo)colonial patterns of economic and political relations. In each of the previous chapters considered—whether on corporate power; Western donors; 'new' donors; trade policy; securitisation, conflict and migration; or the UN SDGs—pan-African unity is an essential component of pro-poor responses. The EITI, for instance, might be transformed into a genuinely emancipatory structure if the African Union—as a federal union envisaged by Nkrumah—took meaningful action to mobilise oil producing states to hold foreign companies and their government sponsors to account. And in the longer-term, the African Union could mobilise sufficient resources to encourage full nationalisation of oil resources, following a Norwegian model of oil prospecting. Governments such as in Ghana would no longer be apparently beholden to the interests of Tullow Oil or Kosmos. Ghana's people, with the support of a federal

African Union, could realise a genuinely transformative model of oil exploration (with echoes of the Latin American situation; Nkrumah himself was a keen proponent of 'Bolivarian' solutions even prior to the rise of Hugo Chavez). Pan-Africanism, in the face of a myriad of neo-colonial quandaries currently facing African governments, could offer a real path to emancipatory agency in the continent.

Neo-Colonialism as Critique

The above discussion has focused upon the concept of neo-colonialism as advanced by Nkrumah, as well as other African socialists such as Fanon and Nyerere. Rather than standing as an antiquated rhetorical device, the concept does help us to make sense of the current predicament of certain African states such as Ghana. Moreover, it helps us to understand the potential dangers facing countries such as Rwanda that have (currently) managed to carve out greater policy space (in this case, on the basis of genocide guilt from foreign donors). Nkrumah was correct to indicate that genuine, empirical sovereignty would be illusory while African countries remained 'balkanized'. His calls for the Union of African States—following a federal model akin to the USA—remain convincing in light of the 60 years of 'development' states such as Ghana have experienced with the assistance of foreign donors and corporations. Despite the altruistic intentions which may exist among certain personnel within donor bodies (such as the European Commission), the free market prescriptions which they advance, and which their corporations enjoy, lock-in African countries into poverty and maldevelopment. In this context, Falola convincingly challenges the idea that the concept of neo-colonialism should be discarded within modern academic discussion:

> how can one theory replace another so fast, how can scholarship resemble fashion and weather, changing so rapidly? Why should scholars of Africa follow and accept all fast-changing academic trends, if their conditions are either constant or changing for worse? Why should they keep replacing one mode of analysis with another if they are yet to overcome their own limitations, both practical and intellectual? They can do so in order to participate in the debate in a 'global academy,' but they must consider the consequences for Africa. (cited in Ndlovu-Gatsheni 2013: 13)

While the concept of neo-colonialism may no longer enjoy academic currency in polite conference circles and journals, Nkrumah's work does deserve much more thorough engagement in contemporary debates surrounding African 'development'.

The relevance of Nkrumah's thesis is clear in the context of corporate involvement in African countries as examined in Chap. 2 in relation to oil extraction and agri-business. Western oil firms, and their Chinese counterparts, have played a highly visible role since the discovery of oil in the mid-2000s. However, social gains for the Ghanaian citizenry have been diluted by the non-signing of a standard PSA. Critics fear that such opaque arrangements have been made possible by intermediaries such as the E.O. Group, who seem to have achieved remarkably generous terms for Kosmos, a US oil entity (The Enquirer 2010). The alleged personal ties between the E.O. Group and the administration of President Kufuor raise concerns that personal networks have been indirectly utilised by foreign companies as a means of securing lucrative oil concessions in African developing countries (ibid.). Moreover, the apparent insinuations of bribery made against Tullow Oil in Uganda—by a rival company, Heritage Oil—underscore Nkrumah's fears about foreign corporate manipulations (The Telegraph 2013). Agri-business mobilisation for the NAFSN, moreover, raises questions about the 'pro-poor' credentials of corporate-led food security initiatives. The creation of land corridors has led to violation of subsistence farmers' human rights. NAFSN corporate partners' emphasis on cash crop production as part of intensive agri-business also queries whether the needs of Ghana's poorer citizenry are truly front and centre of this initiative (Pan Africanist Briefs 2014). African government's signing of CFAs as part of the NAFSN framework also points to the use of such policy agendas to 'lock-in' states to further rounds of free market liberalisation, irrespective of the historical social consequences of such measures (Oakland Institute 2016).

Relations of neo-colonialism again come to the fore when considering Western donor aid – in the form of project aid, budget support and aid 'blending'. As Chap. 3 illustrated, UK DFID, the European Commission and the World Bank support PSD aid initiatives in the name of poverty reduction and development. They support the aforementioned NAFSN despite its regressive consequences for food security and subsistence farming in Africa. The European Commission, moreover, embraces a discourse of Aid for Trade in the era of the Cotonou Agreement. Its Aid for Trade monies, however, often go towards subsidisation of European corporate interests, for instance a Madagascan EPZ dominated by French investment (despite low pay for local workers and a lack of taxation revenue for the domestic government). Budget support, meanwhile, advances opaque forms of donor 'policy dialogue', for instance, in the case of the Kufuor government's erstwhile PSIs. The MDBS group, in this instance, effectively overrode the developmental state strategy of the Ghanaian government, while successfully blocking rise on poultry tariffs, and ending kerosene subsidies. Aid blending, meanwhile, has been embraced by EU institutions as an innovative tool for boosting aid spending in a time of European austerity. However, the mix of public aid monies with DFI private capital is dubious in terms of its development outcomes. As Counter Balance, Eurodad, and the European Parliament itself explain, DFI monies regularly support extractive industries and intensive agri-business, exacerbating regressive (neo)colonial patterns of trade and production. Despite the language of sustainable development, aid blending does more to 'lock-in' poorer African states into a neo-colonial pattern of economic and political relations with the European metropole.

The role of 'new' donors such as China and Turkey in Africa further cements a view of the on-going relevance of the concept of neo-colonialism and Nkrumah's writings. The role of Chinese firms, supported by authorities in Beijing, demonstrates that Africa's natural resource wealth is not merely attractive to Western enterprise but stands at the centre of this emerging superpower's energy security. Chinese corporations have emphasised, alongside the Chinese government, that they are providing 'win-win' opportunities for their African partners. Infrastructural development is lauded as a benevolent token of Sino-African co-operation. The Chinese authorities also emphasise that they strictly respect the sovereignty of recipient states, and that their aid-giving and investment is not attached to the liberal conditionalities imposed by Western counterparts. However, when examining the impact of Chinese investments and largesse in both the Zambian and Angolan cases there is significant ground upon which to call into question this Chinese donor discourse. The situation of the Michael Sata government, for instance, demonstrates that even on the question of higher taxes upon Chinese investors (as opposed to more radical strategies for wholescale nationalisation), that African elites find that they operate 'agency in tight corners' (Lonsdale 2000). The linkages between Angola's Dos Santos regime and Chinese actors, meanwhile, demonstrates that the features of the so-called neo-patrimonial state in Africa are intimately linked to the enabling role played by foreign benefactors. Mal-governance is made possible, and sustained, via the strategic interventions of the Chinese government and its corporate entities. Furthermore, in the case of Turkey's neo-Ottoman pretensions in Africa, the 'virtuous power' of Erdogan and Davutoglu comes into critical light. While assisting Somalia in a time of famine, nevertheless, Turkish oil prospectors have a keen eye on the oil reserves of its Puntland province. Turkish arm industries, meanwhile, seek to continue profitable dealings with African elites (while the Turkish government itself is accused of having materially abetted armed Islamist groups). Turkey's pursuit of FTAs akin to the EU's EPAs (owing to its status within the Customs Union) also challenges the notion that Turkish development co-operation offers a progressive alternative to 'traditional' Western actors. Despite the emphasis of Turkish discourse on the neo-colonialism of the West, Turkish involvement can equally be seen to fall within the contours predicted by Nkrumah.

The pursuit of 'reciprocal' free trade ties between donors and African countries (as highlighted by the EU's EPAs in Chap. 5) also underscores contemporary concerns about (neo)colonial patterns of production and trade. The European Commission has vigorously pursued what it presents as a pro-poor and development-friendly trade vehicle with African sub-regions, including West Africa in which a regional EPA is now in partial application. Officials such as Peter Mandelson have loudly voiced their perspective that the EPA will assist African countries' to successfully integrate into the global economy, with positive impacts for export-oriented sectors and for individual citizens (through jobs and infrastructural development). Civil society groups, both in Africa and the EU member states, however, convincingly point to the way in which the EPAs will result in import-flooding of cheaper European commodities into sensitive markets in developing countries. Nation-states such as Ghana will find that fledgling agro-processing and manufacturing sectors retract, or else disband, upon implementation of EPA tariff dismantling. While the European Commission insists that Aid for Trade combined to a 'sensitive goods basket' will mitigate any adverse effects of liberalisation, critical commentators insist that the EU is 'kicking away the ladder' of development by insisting upon premature free market conditions. African countries, they fear, are being locked into (neo)colonial patterns of trade and production, remaining as exporters of raw commodities and minerals, while relying upon European imports for value-added processed/manufactured goods. The direction of EU Aid for Trade, moreover, highlights that the use of aid monies regularly subsidises European corporate investment in developmentally dubious sectors, including textiles EPZs. Whether this device will be able to translate the EPAs into a development-friendly trade deal is therefore in serious doubt. Nkrumah's predictions about the use of trade—and aid—agreements to keep African countries as economic subordinates to the European metropole appears prescient in the context of the ACP-EU Cotonou Partnership Agreement and the imminent implementation of the EPAs.

The securitisation of development also poses serious concerns about the neo-colonial present in Africa. The involvement of France in the affairs of Sahelian nations such as Mali raises important questions about 'sovereignty' in the period since legal decolonisation. Not only have French donor preferences concerning economic adjustment helped to spur crisis, but their military involvement has undermined empirical sovereignty while further alienating groups (such as the Tuareg) from central government. Language of the Western security 'gift' as utilised by Hollande, or else of Franafrique, provides a legitimating discourse. However, the material consequences of European policy impositions and military involvement do not necessarily correlate to pro-poor development objectives. On the contrary, France undermines sovereignty and longer-term conditions for social stability given its preference for economic liberalisation, amidst other controversial reforms. The EU's migration policy approach, as cemented by the Valletta Summit, is also highly problematic in terms of sovereignty and policy space in African countries. Governments, such as that of Mauritania, have accepted EU donor aid on the condition that they enhance the policing of their own population, as well as that of citizens from neighbouring states within their territory (to combat irregular migration). The EU has gone so far as to mandate that African civil servants travel to Europe to assist with the repatriation of their co-nationals (although latterly denied by the government minister in question). Altogether EU migration interventions in Africa, while justified in terms of a pro-poor development discourse, fall well short of normative drivers concerning poverty reduction and human rights. EU migration policy impositions construct security states in Africa that police their own populations on behalf of a European benefactor with little tangible improvement to the general condition of the citizenry. Again,

Nkrumah's insights about the potential co-option of African elites (as well as Bayart's concept of extraversion in terms of local overtures to security discourse) appear highly fruitful in making sense of, and critiquing, European interventions in the affairs of 'sovereign' African states.

Nkrumah's concerns are amplified when considered in the context of the UN SDGs and their pro-business 'development' discourse. Examining Goals 8 and 9 as exemplars of the UN SDG's pivot to PSD, it becomes apparent that donor and corporate interventions in the name of sustainable growth do not necessarily correlate to poverty reduction. The palm oil sector in Ghana demonstrates how leading corporations contribute to initiatives such as the RSPO and yet object to structural changes (such as Kufuor's PSIs) that might disrupt existing patterns of production. Despite initially supporting the PSIs, corporations soon opposed the creation of 'COVES' that might enhance out-growers' negotiating potential vis-à-vis agri-business plantations. Corporate and donor pressure combined to close down policy space and to undermine the PSI in palm oil, with the result that out-growers continue to suffer hardship despite the lucrative potential of this sector. The RSPO, meanwhile, falls well short of its monitoring objectives, not least in terms of its auditing processes. While the language of sustainability is regularly invoked to legitimise investment in the palm oil sector, the industry operates in a manner that does not redress the needs of poorer producers. The 'development' potential of production is thereby diminished. EU interventions for infrastructural development in Africa, meanwhile, further illustrate how UN SDG discourse is invoked to moralise dubious interventions. In this context, the EU lauds its contributions to the business enabling environment through construction of ports, roads and other infrastructure. Nevertheless, there is a distinct impression that such large-scale infrastructure projects—as predicted by Nkrumah—do more to serve the commercial needs of European investors and exporters than to bolster the position of local SMEs or communities. The creation of ports and roads, for instance, provide vital arteries within (neo)colonial systems of trade and production, as anticipated by Nkrumah in his writings in the immediate period of legal decolonisation. Altogether, sustainability discourse—when married to donor and corporate economic interests in African production—does not necessary correlate to genuinely pro-poor outcomes.

Nkrumah's insights regarding neo-colonialism—whether in the context of corporate interventions in oil and agri-business; Western donor aid modalities; 'new' donor interventions in relation to China and Turkey; trade agreements between the EU and ACP countries; the securitisation of development with particular reference to France; or the UN SDGs—appear highly relevant to contemporary African affairs. It is important to recognise, however, that in all of these instances, the construction of legitimating development discourse is a crucial part of neo-colonial relations. Namely, external actors continue to utilise pro-poor development language to moralise their interventions in the affairs of African countries as progressive action aimed at assisting the less fortunate. Moreover, in certain cases individuals involved with the roll-out of such initiatives will fully concur with such rationales, having internalised the discourse to such a degree that alternatives are foreclosed. The vigorous statements of Peter Mandelson—as EU Trade Commissioner—give one illustration of the way in which Western actors (in particular) may internalise the belief that their interventions bear fruit for poverty reduction and social prosperity in African former colonies. It is important to underscore, however, that when such development discourse is juxtaposed with the material consequences of donor/corporate agendas there is regularly a chasm between stated objectives and tangible outcomes for 'the poor'. The EPAs, to name one but initiative, are convincingly opposed by African civil society (and certain European bodies, including some MEPs) on the basis that they augur deindustrialisation amidst the import-flooding of subsidised European commodities. A modern application of the concept of neo-colonialism must—from a critical constructivist standpoint—therefore engage with both ideational and material factors in the analysis of external interventions in Africa. A critical engagement with questions of African sovereignty, moreover, must pay attention to the empirical sovereignty that African countries aspire to within Westphalian norms. It must also understand the ways in which pan-African institutions can play a vital role for the achievement of empirical and genuine forms of sovereignty, as argued by Nkrumah (1963, 1965).

CONCLUSION: NKRUMAH AND NEO-COLONIALISM IN THE CONTEMPORARY ERA OF 'DEVELOPMENT'

Sixty years since Ghana's independence in 1957, the writings of its first president on neo-colonialism unfortunately resonate in the current era of African relations with external donors and corporations. While not deemed relevant in polite academic conferences and debates, the concept of neo-colonialism does much more to help us unpack contemporary 'development' quandaries in Africa than, for instance, the popular neo-patrimonialism school. Rather than focus upon 'Big Men' personalities and supposed African culture/corruption, the concept of neo-colonialism instead pinpoints how donors and foreign investors continue to enable forms of mal-governance and deprivation in many African situations. While graft does of course exist, it is often brought about, and sustained, by donor aid flows and foreign corporations. African elites often have an impossible decision to make of whether to spurn donor aid—and budget support—and lose foreign largesse and (likely) FDI revenues. Or whether to attempt to pursue a genuine form of empirical sovereignty that entails policy space to enact developmental state policies, albeit with insufficient capital and insufficient economies of scale. This is the current challenge faced by the new Ghanaian government, for instance, despite the recent celebrations of the sixtieth year of independence.

Accordingly, those engaging with Development Studies and International Relations—either as scholars, practitioners, or indeed politicians—would do well to reflect upon Nkrumah's warnings in *Neo-colonialism: The Last Stage of Imperialism* and *Africa Must Unite*. His concerns resonate in the current timeframe of the much lauded UN SDGs. His writings accurately describe, and critique, on-going forms of donor and corporate interventions as discussed throughout the previous chapters. Moreover, his solution to the problems of neo-colonial trade and aid relations remains as a relevant and emancipatory call for a Union of African States. In the current context it points to the need to rejuvenate the African Union as a genuine forum for developmental state strategies and for unity in negotiations with foreign donors and multi-national corporations. There is no reason, for instance, that the African Union could not play an important role in co-ordinating African trade deals with the UK in the aftermath of its Brexit decision to leave the EU. Additionally, the Brexit decision could open up policy space for the African Union to work with the RECs to renegotiate the terms of the European Commission's own 'win-win' EPAs. This is but one example of where a genuinely collaborative pan-African approach within the corridors of the African Union would likely yield progressive trade results for individual

African nations, and their vulnerable economic sectors (such as poultry and tomato in wake of import-flooding).

Overall, critical scholars must engage Nkrumah's writings to critique mal-development and must insist upon his relevance within current academic debates on Africa's development situation. As Biney (2012: 139) remarks, he 'has left a valuable intellectual legacy comprising an essential analytical framework in which to comprehend our present reality'. His concept of neo-colonialism, and his discourse of pan-Africanism, are progressive tools for the genuine liberation of African countries from regressive neo-colonial trade and aid relations. Recovering the concept, and discourse, of neo-colonialism (and pan-Africanism) is a necessary step towards a more authentic study of the predicament of many African countries as they engage 'old' and 'new' donors, as well as foreign investors. Critical scholars must also not shy away from necessary discussions about the diminution of genuine, empirical forms of sovereignty in Africa. Polite engagement with donor institutions and corporations may bode well for individual academics (for instance, in terms of grants and policy 'impact' as part of a scholarly forms of extraversion), but it does not bode well in terms of emancipatory forms of critique. An honest appraisal of the neo-colonial present is the least that the academic community may offer to African countries currently experiencing the conditions that Nkrumah accurately predicted in his treatises.

Notes

1. We might also acknowledge the case of Ethiopia here which (currently) has resisted donor pressure for full liberalisation across its vital economic sectors, including telecommunications. Whitfield and Jones (2009) usefully explain that donor co-ordination has not been achieved to the same extent in Ethiopia as in other country contexts. Moreover, the elite have been imbued with a developmental state ethic, installed by their late president. As a cautionary note, however, we must remember Kenya's erstwhile developmental state successes in the 1970s (with a growing textiles sector) prior to the onsets of SAPs and the Washington Consensus. We must also note Henderson's (1999) warning with regards to the delegitimization of the developmental model in East Asia in wake of an IMF-stoked financial crash. Robert Mugabe's Zimbabwe, meanwhile, demonstrates the fate of austerity which regularly be falls African governments which seek a radical departure from donor aid regimes (Shaw 2003).

2. Interestingly, Brown and Harman do note a convincing case of progressive agency in the case of collective (pan-)African action within UN environmental summits.
3. APRODEV et al. (2016) also usefully note the strategies of poultry farmers to point to the health dangers of imported European poultry as an illustration of progressive agency (in this instance, the agency of smallholders in alignment with civil society concerns).
4. Nkrumah's former ally, and political rival, J.B. Danquah notably died of a heart attack while under 'preventive detention' in prison in 1965. The Nkrumah government suspected Danquah of possible links with the CIA, which latterly succeeded in ousting Ghana's first president in 1966, 4 months after the publication of his treatise *Neo-colonialism: The Last Stage of Imperialism*. Nkrumah's apparent turn to authoritarianism and his concerns about regional separatism must be contextualised in terms of the Congo Crisis which led to the murder of President Patrice Lumumba by Katanga rebels supported by Western governments. Biney (2012: 137–138) provides an in-depth discussion of his apparent 'decline into authoritarianism' and its causes.
5. Again, this second issue—of foreign pressures to default to a (neo)colonial pattern of trade and production—should be a current concern of developmental elites in Ethiopia and Rwanda. Henderson's (1999) warnings about the experiences of the East Asian developmental states themselves might also be usefully heeded.

References

APRODEV, & Church Development Service and Citizens Association for the Defence of Collective Interests and Interchurch Organisation for Development Co-operation. (2016). *No more chicken please: How a strong grassroots movement in Cameroon is successfully resisting damaging chicken imports from Europe, which are ruining small farmers all over West Africa.* APRODEV: Brussels. Available at: http://aprodev.eu/files/Trade/071203_chicken_e_final.pdf. Accessed 25 Mar 2017.

Babarinde, O., & Wright, S. (2013). Africa-EU partnership on trade and regional integration. In J. Mangala (Ed.), *Africa and the European Union: A strategic partnership* (pp. 123–148). London: Palgrave.

Biney, A. (2012). The intellectual and political legacies of Kwame Nkrumah. *The Journal of Pan African Studies, 4*(10), 127–142.

Brown, W. (2012). A question of agency: Africa in international politics. *Third World Quarterly, 33*(10), 1889–1908.

Brown, W. (2013). Sovereignty matters: Africa, donors and the aid relationship. *African Affairs, 112*(447), 262–282.

Chang, H. J. (2003). *Kicking away the ladder*. London: Anthem Press.

Edigheji, O. (2010). Constructing a democratic developmental state in South Africa: Potential and challenges. In O. Edigheji (Ed.), *Constructing a democratic developmental state in South Africa: Potential and challenges*. Cape Town: HSRC Press.

The Enquirer. (2010, January 20). The E.O. group's darkest secrets. *The Enquirer.* Available online at: http://www.ghanaweb.com/GhanaHomePage/NewsArchive/artikel.php?ID=175414. Accessed 9 Feb 2017.

Fanon, F. (1961). *The wretched of the earth*. Reprint—London: Penguin Classics, 2001.

Hearn, J. (2007). African NGOs: The new compradors? *Development and Change, 38,* 1095–1110.

Henderson, J. (1999). Uneven crises: Institutional foundations of East Asian economic turmoil. *Economy and Society, 28*(3), 327–369.

Hilborn, E. (2012). Botswana: A development-oriented gate-keeping state. *African Affairs, 111*(442), 67–89.

Hurt, S. (2017, March). The EU's economic partnership agreements with Africa: 'Decent Work' and the challenge of trade union solidarity. *Third World Thematics*, 1–16.

Kenyan Association of Manufacturers. (2006). *Manufacturing in Kenya: A survey of manufacturing sector*. Nairobi: KAM.

Kieh, G. (2015). Constructing the social democratic developmental state in Africa: Lessons from the global south. *Bandung: Journal of the Global South 2*(1), 1–14.

Kim, E. M. (2010). Limits of the authoritarian developmental state in South Korea. In O. Edigheji (Ed.), *Constructing a democratic developmental state in South Africa: Potential and challenges*. Cape Town: HSRC Press.

Mkandawire, T. (2002). Thinking about developmental states in Africa. *Cambridge Journal of Economics, 25*(3), 289–313.

Mkandawire, T. (2010). From maladjusted states to democratic developmental states in Africa. In O. Edigheji (Ed.), *Constructing a democratic developmental state in South Africa: Potential and challenges*. Cape Town: HSRC Press.

Mkandawire, T. (2011). Rethinking Pan-Africanism: National and the new regionalism. In S. Moyo & P. Yeros (Eds.), *Reclaiming the nation: The return of the national question in Africa, Asia and Latin America*. London: Pluto Press.

Mitlin, D., Bebbington, A., & Hickey, S. (2006). Reclaiming development? NGOs and the challenge of alternatives. *World Development, 35*(10), 1699–1720.

Mohan, G. (2002). The disappointments of civil society: The politics of NGO intervention in Ghana. *Political Geography, 21*(1), 125–152.

NANTS. (2010). *The EU-West Africa economic partnership agreement (EPA) negotiations*. Abuja: NANTS.

Ndlovu-Gatsheni, S. J. (2013). *Coloniality of power in post-colonial Africa: Myths of decolonization*. Dakar: CODESRIA.

Nkrumah, K. (1963). *Africa must unite*. London: Heineman.
Nkrumah, K. (1965). *Neo-colonialism: The last stage of imperialism*. Sixth Printing—New York International Publishers, 1976.
Nyerere, J. (1978). Foreign troops in Africa. *Africa Report, 23*(4), 10–14.
Oakland Institute. (2016). *The unholy alliance: Five western donors shape a pro-corporate agenda for African agriculture*. Oakland: Oakland Institute.
Orbie, J., Martens, D., Oehri, M., & Van den Putte, L. (2017, March). Promoting sustainable development or legitimising free trade? Civil society mechanisms in EU trade agreements. *Third World Thematics*, 1–21.
Pan Africanist Briefs. (2014, April 4). Unilever, Monsanto take over African land and agriculture. *Pan Africanist Briefs*. Available at: https://www.newsghana.com.gh/unilevermonsanto-take-african-land-agriculture/. Accessed 9 Feb 2017.
Powell, M., & Seddon, D. (1997). NGOs and the development industry. *Review of African Political Economy, 71*, 3–10.
Reyntjens, F. (2004). Rwanda ten years on: From genocide to dictatorship. *African Affairs, 103*(411), 177–210.
SEATINI Uganda. (2013, March 7). *MUDESA with support from and in conjunction with SEATINI-U is organising a students' dialogue at Makerere University*. Kampala: SEATINI Uganda.
SEATINI Uganda. (2017). *SEATINI statement on the EPA's inherent dangers and the way forward*. Kampala: SEATINI Uganda. Available at: http://www.seatiniuganda.org/publications/downloads/121-seatini-statement-on-epas-inherent-dangers-and-way-forward/file.html. Accessed 25 Mar 2017.
Shaw, W. (2003). 'They stole our land': Debating the expropriation of white farms in Zimbabwe. *Journal of Modern African Studies, 41*(1), 75–89.
Shivji, I. (2006). The silences in the NGO discourse: The role and the future of NGOs in Africa. *Africa Development, 31*(4).
The Telegraph. (2013, March 22). Tullow oil apologies to Ugandan government over bribery allegations. *The Telegraph*. Available at: http://www.telegraph.co.uk/finance/newsbysector/energy/oilandgas/9949319/Tullow-Oil-apologises-to-Ugandan-government-over-bribery-allegations.html. Accessed 9 Feb 2017.
Trommer, S. (2011). Activists beyond Brussels: Transnational NGO strategies on EU-West Africa trade negotiations. *Globalizations, 8*(1), 113–126.
Trommer, S. (2014). *Transformations in trade politics. Participatory trade politics in West Africa*. London: Routledge.
Whitfield, L., & Jones, E. (2009). Ghana: Breaking out of aid dependence? Economic and political barriers to ownership. In L. Whitfield (Ed.), *The politics of aid: Strategies for dealing with donors* (pp. 185–216). Oxford: Oxford University Press.
Wright, G. (2012). NGOs and western hegemony: Causes for concern and ideas for change. *Development in Practice, 22*(1), 123–134.

Index

Made in the USA
Columbia, SC
04 April 2021